Praise for *More Fearless Change*

"The hard part of change is enlisting the support of other people. Whether a top manager interested in improving your organization's results or a lone developer promoting a better way of working, this book will give you tools and ideas to help accomplish your goal. Best of all, they're presented in small, digestible bits."

—George Dinwiddie, independent coach and consultant, iDIA Computing, LLC

"*More Fearless Change* is a great book. Through real experiences and concise analysis, Linda and Mary Lynn identify patterns that will help change leaders quantify the situations they often face. From there, they provide practical advice for dealing with and overcoming them. I found every pattern in *More Fearless Change* took me back to a specific place and time where I struggled to find the right approach to articulate my 'great' new idea and connect with the people around me. I went from conference talks and challenging questions from skeptics to meetings with colleagues where I failed to convey practical new solutions, or to quiet times on my own where I was downright frustrated with my progress. Linda and Mary Lynn have patterns for each that helped me think through to practical, positive solutions and prepare for the future. For a topic as challenging as organization change, it's rare to find a collection of patterns that are as powerful as those you'll find in *More Fearless Change*."

—Neil Johnson, principal hardware consultant, XtremeEDA

"More secret sauce for positive organizational change! Mary Lynn and Linda make it sound so easy, but using their building blocks, it actually is. With books like these, change agents won't run out of steam while resistors will run out of excuses."

—*Jochen (Joe) Krebs, author of* Going Lean, *Agile coach, trainer, speaker, and incrementor*

"Keep the patterns in this book and *Fearless Change* handy. Whenever you are frustrated by an intractable problem, choose a pattern to try. If you still don't get the desired results, try another. Others will join in your efforts, and you'll feel the satisfaction as small successes start to add up. These patterns transformed me from an ineffective 'voice in the wilderness' to a valued collaborator."

—*Lisa Crispin, co-author (with Janet Gregory) of* Agile Testing: A Practical Guide for Testers and Agile Teams *(Addison-Wesley, 2009) and* More Agile Testing *(Addison-Wesley, 2015)*

"*Fearless Change* and now *More Fearless Change* are required reading for my doctoral students. As they explore emerging issues and are learning new concepts and ideas, my students have been able to make significant changes to their professional workplace using these patterns for introducing new ideas. We look forward to *Even More Fearless Change*."

—*Fred Grossman, professor and director of doctoral study in computing, Pace University, New York*

"This book, *More Fearless Change*, is creative work. I use these patterns with my students to take innovation into practice, and also with my collaborators working in industries to promote organizational change. This book is a significant read for people in academia and in the workplace."

—*Takashi Iba, associate professor, Faculty of Policy Management, Keio University, Japan*

More Fearless Change

More Fearless Change

Strategies for Making Your Ideas Happen

Mary Lynn Manns

Linda Rising

❦

✦✦Addison-Wesley

Upper Saddle River, NJ • Boston • Indianapolis • San Francisco
New York • Toronto • Montreal • London • Munich • Paris • Madrid
Capetown • Sydney • Tokyo • Singapore • Mexico City

Library of Congress Cataloging-in-Publication Data
Manns, Mary Lynn, 1955–
  More fearless change : strategies for making your ideas happen / Mary Lynn Manns, Linda Rising.
    pages   cm
  Includes bibliographical references and index.
  ISBN 978-0-13-396644-2 (pbk. : alk. paper)—ISBN 0-13-396644-5 (pbk. : alk. paper)
  1. Organizational change. 2. Technological innovations. 3. Industrial management. I. Rising, Linda. II. Title.
  HD58.8.M2624 2015
  658.4'06—dc23

                                                                        2014048042

Illustrator: Payton E. James

ISBN-13: 978-0-13-396644-2
ISBN-10: 0-13-396644-5

Mary Lynn:
To my daughter Alison—because a mother's love never changes.

Linda:
For Karl; everything I do is better because of you.

Contents

PART TWO

Stories in Leading Change

PART THREE

The Patterns

Foreword

On first noting this book's title, you might mistake *More Fearless Change* as a follow-on to *Fearless Change*, Linda Rising and Mary Lynn Manns' previous collaboration—but if you have not already read *Fearless Change*, don't put this book down to hunt for it first. *More Fearless Change* is written to stand alone as a collection of tactics and strategies for you to employ to increase your odds that the change you want can make it all the way from bright idea, through fruition, to "the way it is."

More Fearless Change is not a recipe book for change. Rising and Manns are far too experienced in these matters to oversimplify the situation. It is a book of patterns—nuggets you pick up and inspect—and it is up to you to decide if one or another nugget would be helpful in communicating your particular idea campaign within your organization. The tactics and strategies are not specific to any organization type. If you see a need or an opportunity to improve the long-term health of your organization, and you want to see your idea through, and you are willing to work at it, I believe that *More Fearless Change*, as a coaching guide, can provide the key.

Actually, I would suggest that you read *More Fearless Change* twice, each time from a different perspective. First, try reading the book from the relatively safe perspective of you as *change agent*: You see a need for change, and you have an idea that will facilitate that change. You need to convince those around you to join in, to invest in your idea, and to nurture it to full benefit.

Now from the scary view: After your first read, don't pick up *More Fearless Change* for at least a week. When you start rereading, imagine yourself not as the change agent, but as a *change recipient*. If you have been in this business a while, you can probably choose a real occurrence from your own experience; if not, go ahead and invent one.

Imagine, for example, that your job is being outsourced, and your company would like to outplace you as an employee of the outsourcee, which is located in <pick a distant place that does not thrill you>. You see that these requests are basically reasonable. You understand the business case the company is making. You see that this is absolutely not a case of Bad People Behaving Outrageously. You get that. So, how do you want to be treated? Which information do you expect, and from whom? Which promises would you ask for? Which time frame do you want to decide your path?

In the context of the real world, *More Fearless Change* reveals itself like a 3D stereogram. First you see it as a book to help you advance your ideas, then as a book to help you understand the complexities of how people react to proposed change.

Rising and Manns are the voices of honesty and fairness as they treat what is usually called change management, but it is not change "management" they are talking about. Theirs is a *campaign for change*, and their book is about changing the minds and behaviors of smart, emotional, real people, each of whom carries personal and career experiences from his or her past. What they address is not management, and therefore it is most worthwhile for all of us to look for help. Now turn the page. You can always read *Fearless Change* later.

Tim Lister
The Atlantic Systems Guild
New York, August 2014

Acknowledgments

Thanks to our shepherd, Joe Bergin, and to our PLoP '08 writers workshop members: Takashi Abi, Miguel Carvalhais, Christian Crumlish, Dick Gabriel, Josh Kerievsky, Christian Kohls, Ricardo Lopez, Pam Rostal, Lubor Sesera, and Steve Wingo.

Thanks to our shepherd, Klaus Marquardt, and the members of the "People" writers workshop at PLoP '09: Takashi Abi, Marco Hernandez, Jeff Hutchinson, Lise Hvatum, Christian Kohls, Jake Miller, Karl Rehmer, and Robert Zack.

Thanks to the members of the MiniPLoP '09 writers workshop: Ademar Aguiar, Brian Foote, Dick Gabriel, Ralph Johnson, Rick Mercer, and Joe Yoder.

Thanks to our shepherd Christian Kohls and the members of the PLoP '10 writers workshop: Paul M. Chalekian, Lise Hvatum, Kevin Kautz, Joshua Kerievsky, Bill Opdyke, Karl Rehmer, Rebecca Rikner, David West, and Raul Zevallos.

Thanks to our shepherd Eugene Wallingford and the members of the SugarLoaf PLoP '12 writers workshop, including Joe Yoder, Christina von Flach, Sérgio Soares, Marília Freire, Daniel Alencar, and others.

Thanks to Michael Neelon, Associate Professor of Psychology at University of North Carolina–Asheville, for his invaluable assistance with the Emotional Connection pattern.

Thanks to the MLA 540 students at UNC Asheville who helped draft the Sunset Lake story.

Thanks to Alan Dayley for his great story, "Losing My 'Champion Skeptic.'"

Thanks to Jutta Eckstein for being a good friend and long-time supporter of our work and for sharing her research with us for this book.

Thanks to our long-time friends and supporters Joe Bergin and Fred Grossman at Pace University and their team of students: Stephanie Feddock, Michele Kirchhoff, Nader Nassar, and James Sicuranza.

About the Authors

Mary Lynn Manns is a management professor at University of North Carolina–Asheville, where she was recently awarded Distinguished Professor of Social Relations for her work in change leadership. She has a Ph.D. from De Montfort University in Leicester, United Kingdom, where her thesis focused on the introduction of patterns into organizations. She has continued her work with numerous presentations at a variety of conferences and in organizations that include Microsoft, amazon.com, Avon, and Proctor & Gamble. Her publications include *Fearless Change: Patterns for Introducing New Ideas*, co-authored with Linda Rising. At her university, she guides students of all ages in learning the tools (patterns) for leading change and competing as social entrepreneurs. In 2013, Mary Lynn was the commencement speaker who transformed the typical model of speeches by encouraging the graduates to take the first steps toward changing the world as they got off their seats to dance. In her spare time, Mary Lynn helps individuals make personal change by leading "Zumba for People with Two Left Feet" workouts.

Linda Rising is an independent consultant based in Mt. Juliet, Tennessee (just east of Nashville). She has a Ph.D. from Arizona State University in the field of object-based design metrics and a background that includes university teaching and industry work in telecommunications, avionics, and tactical weapons systems. An internationally known presenter on topics related to patterns, retrospectives, the change process, and how your brain works, Linda is the author of a number of publications and four books: *Design Patterns in Communications*; *The Pattern Almanac 2000*; *A Patterns Handbook*; and, co-authored with Mary Lynn Manns, *Fearless Change: Patterns for Introducing New Ideas*. Linda has been an amateur recorder player for more than 50 years. She and her husband, Karl Rehmer, are part of three performing groups. They also enjoy bike riding, even when the hills in Tennessee are pretty steep. They also serve as board members for Habitat for Humanity of Wilson County. Find more information about Linda at lindarising.org.

Overview

Welcome, dear reader! You have picked up this book because you are someone with a great idea. Perhaps you are trying to make it happen in your organization, or in your community, or in yourself. Since writing our original book *Fearless Change*, we've been thinking about you and your struggles. Our readers have been thinking about this as well. That connection has led us to write this new book with 15 new change leadership strategies (patterns), along with insights on the original patterns to make them even better. We welcome the readers of our first book, as well as our new readers who are using the strategies for the first time, to continue the ongoing dialogue that all leaders of change need. Making a new idea happen can be difficult, but we invite you to take the journey with us!

CHAPTER ONE

Introduction

Our first book, *Fearless Change*, is 10 years old. Since it appeared, both of us have continued to study the patterns and regularly hear from others who have used them for organizational, community, or personal change. As a result, we have become even more convinced that the patterns are valuable tools for leading change, and that they are still relevant and useful today.

Ten years later, our book is still selling. It has been published in Chinese and Japanese, and partially translated into French. We continue to receive email and verbal testimonials from satisfied users, such as the following:

> *Fearless Change is a catalogue of patterns for introducing change in a company. Personally I've been in the role of change agent for years and this book provided me many "ah-hah's" which you get from reading good patterns. Most of the patterns I've applied in the past. Now I realized it and I got a name for them, which makes me more able to reuse the patterns. Some of the patterns were new to me and I've applied them immediately in my work.*

> *I had found myself moderately successful at introducing new ideas and influencing change in my organizations, but never knew why, or how to improve my ability to influence and sustain the change effort. The light bulb was illuminated immediately upon getting a few patterns into this book—I had been, in one way*

or another, using some of these patterns without realizing it. Opportunities I had failed to take advantage of in the past became obvious as well in many patterns that were new to me, and in the past went unrecognized (next time, they will either be easy to spot or part of the plan in the first place!).

The patterns are used by people leading change around the world and are also part of a game created by Deborah Preuss (http://fearlessjourney. info/). In addition, Joseph Pelrine uses the patterns in an exercise in his training, and Julia Dellnitz from Learnical uses the patterns with the LEGO Serious Play materials and methodology to plan change initiatives.[1] Some patterns were also chosen for illustration in Preston Smith's book *Flexible Development*.[2] Among other tributes, *Fearless Change* received the "best book of the year" award by Charles Ashbacher soon after its publication in 2004 and was included in David Bock's list of "books that changed my career" on amazon.com.

We know that the work is never finished. Patterns are living things. We continue to look for new ones and uncover insights on the existing ones. We definitely agree with what the prominent architect and creator of the notion of patterns, Christopher Alexander, has noted:

> *As people exchange ideas about the environment, and exchange patterns, the overall inventory of patterns in the pattern pool keeps changing. … Of course, this evolution will never end.*[3]

We have kept the target user for the change leadership patterns: You are a powerless leader. We call you the Evangelist. You sincerely believe in the new idea, but may or may not have the authority to "make it happen." Even if you have power, an enlightened evangelist will realize that when others see the value in the change, rather than having it forced upon them, they will be more satisfied and more likely to allow change to happen. The patterns help you encourage people to become so interested and involved in the initiative that they *want* to change.

In our presentations, attendees often tell us about their frustrations in persuading others to change. We hear questions about handling irrational reactions, dealing with the skeptics, or convincing a manager who won't budge. The short answer to dealing with these dilemmas is that it requires patience. Each person responds to new ideas in different ways. No one strategy works for everyone. And no approach works in every situation—each pattern must be matched to the context and problem the evangelist is facing.

In recent years, we've looked at how the change strategies appeal to each individual's logic (head), feelings (heart), and desire to contribute to the change (hands).[4] This is not a novel concept: to involve others in a new idea, help them see the logic in it, feel that it is valuable, and play a role in it. However, many leaders of change stop with a logical argument—simply providing a description of the new idea and what it can do. While this is an excellent first step, you must engage the heart and hands, too. The *Fearless Change* patterns help the evangelist do all three. Some, like Study Group and Elevator Pitch, have a rational appeal, while others, such as Emotional Connection and Shoulder to Cry On, touch the heart. Still others, such as Ask for Help and Trial Run, help others get their hands into the game. As you begin to use the collection, you will discover ways to engage the heads, hearts, and hands of those you are trying to convince.

Throughout the years, we have occasionally been asked about creating a categorization scheme or a flowchart for using the patterns. However, applying patterns cannot be done following a recipe, such as 2 "head" + 1 "heart" + 3 "hands" = mission accomplished. Change never happens in a "clean" fashion. Usually you are applying more than one pattern at a time because you are dealing with more than one problem. You are working with humans, often in complex organizations, so results are rarely straightforward and the emergent behavior might be totally unexpected. Therefore, upfront detailed planning is rarely effective. Instead, take one small step toward your goal and see what happens. You will inevitably encounter missteps and failures along the way. In most cases, your process will be one step forward followed by two steps backward. This uneven progress can be discouraging but may also teach you about the idea, about the organization, and, most of all, about yourself.

You will find that a change effort progresses as a series of experiments. When you decide to just do it, begin with baby steps, followed by time for reflection, building on small successes. Sustain momentum by repeating these patterns, learning along the way. Others have described this iterative process in various ways. Psychologist David Kolb believes all learning takes place in this kind of feedback cycle.[5] Just as children begin to understand the world around them by testing it and adjusting to it, you will do the same as you continue through the long journey of leading a change.

Every now and then, a participant in a training class will ask whether a given solution is "underhanded." This can certainly be an important issue. All influence strategies can be used for both good and bad intentions. Similarly, any tool—whether a hammer in a worker's toolkit or a pattern in a leader's change kit—can be wielded for multiple purposes. It's easy to find examples in history where these approaches have been used for both "good" ideas and ideas that were, well, not so good. We encourage our readers to continue to use the patterns to create constructive and valued changes in the world.

When some people are first exposed to the change leadership patterns, they sometimes comment, "Aren't these strategies just common sense?" This always makes us smile. It's a human tendency to confuse simple with easy! We remember a story about Dale Carnegie, who received a similar comment on the recommendations in his training based on his book *How to Win Friends and Influence People*.[6] He replied with an example. Everyone knows it's rude to talk when others are talking, but we all do it anyway. Carnegie also noted that his concepts might well be "common sense," but that they were certainly not "common practice." We agree that the *Fearless Change* patterns may seem obvious to an "expert" in change leadership, but not all of us are experts. Even experts couldn't possibly know all the possible strategies. As one reader observed, "The patterns may seem like little things, but each of them makes a bigger difference than you may think."

Some Insights since Our First Book

Insights we've acquired about many of the patterns in our first book appear in Part III, in the section "The Original Patterns with Insights." We didn't just write the first book and then stop learning. Instead, we talked with people who use our patterns and continued to study what it takes to be an effective leader of change. To reflect what we've learned, we've updated many of the pattern abstracts from our first book—these new summaries appear in the quick guide in the Appendix.

In addition, we share in the following sections our own personal insights about all the patterns and some general things we've observed about the joys and challenges in leading change.

Mary Lynn's Insights

Most of my insights on the patterns come from leading a significant 2½-year change effort in my organization. I used the patterns consistently throughout the initiative. The project was an eventual success, and it is still going strong today, but there were significant struggles in the journey to make it happen. As I faced each challenge throughout the years, I reflected on which pattern to use. In this process, I discovered implementation details and consequences we didn't include in our first book—these are added to the "lessons learned" in this book. Yes, it is certainly true what Christopher Alexander, the first promoter of the patterns concept, said—"Patterns must not be etched in stone; rather, they must grow as the users gain new experiences."[7]

During the years since the publication of the first book, I have become even more convinced of the value in making an emotional connection. Despite my expertise in putting together a good PowerPoint presentation and elevator pitch, I recognize that these types of techniques are only the first step. Other strategies must also be used, especially if listeners are emotionally tied to the old ways of doing things and are not connecting with the new ways. Before I learned this, I would often respond to skeptics with what I considered to be a stronger and more "logical" argument. I have seen other evangelists do the same, spilling out more facts about the innovation with a variety of phrases. I think this tendency may reflect the fact that it is rather easy to develop another set of bullet points in our head or simply recite something in a different way. It takes much more time to spark and nurture an emotional connection with someone whom you are hoping to persuade—to truly get to know that person so he or she trusts you and you understand the individual's needs. We are not taught how to do this in business schools. Nevertheless, many of the patterns in our first and second books will help with just these challenges—for example, Emotional Connection, Personal Touch, Ask for Help, Shoulder to Cry On, Hometown Story, Imagine That, Fear Less, and Group Identity.

I have also learned the importance of a strong marketing "campaign" for a new idea. Evangelists often stop after making a one-time hit, such as an announcement at a meeting, a presentation, or an email. But, because people aren't necessarily persuaded by simple information and because they are busy and likely to forget what they heard or saw, you need to be persistent about keeping the new idea in people's spaces. This requires the use of many different kinds of techniques with eye-catching and lively messages—what appeals to one person may not appeal to another, so you must create many different mediums. Since I didn't have the artistic expertise to make some of the items we needed, I asked for help from people who had those talents. They enjoyed designing fliers, simple brochures, bookmarks, T-shirts, and, yes, even sandwich boards! We made sure these items were released at different times throughout the change initiative and distributed as tokens at every opportunity. To be sure, some items will cost money, but you can mold your plans to match your budget. Much less expensive strategies such as the Personal Touch and Tailor Made patterns should continue throughout. In addition to regular presentations at department meetings (using the Piggyback pattern) and organization-wide listening sessions (using the Town Hall Meeting pattern), I took some time out of almost every day to knock on one or two office doors to have a short chat about the new idea. Persistent PR can be tedious, but it can also be a lot of fun to brainstorm and develop creative products that will spark the imaginations of the people you are trying to reach. The lesson learned is that you must be intentional about creating some kind of "campaign" or you may end up focusing your efforts on the development of the idea and forget to keep people informed about it.

I have also seen how the *Fearless Change* patterns, which were originally published to help with organizational change, can be useful for personal change. During our presentations on the topic of organizational change, participants often report that they can imagine how the patterns could be used to help with their personal struggles. In addition, the students in my change leadership course use the patterns to make a change that will help them improve their personal leadership skills. For example, if they believe it is the right time to make the change, they just do it, beginning with an elevator pitch that describes their personal goal. They often do some research (by enacting the External Validation pattern), attempt a trial run, or move forward with a mentor to help. Following each baby step, they take time for reflection to evaluate their next steps and determine whether they need to revise their evolving vision. They may even build a group identity with people who have a similar goal so that they can have a shoulder to cry on when things get tough and some friends to celebrate their small successes. Yes, the patterns can certainly be used to make a fearless change in yourself!

Linda's Insights

Most of my insights around the patterns have come from research in cognitive neuroscience. As some of our readers have observed, the reason why these patterns work is because many of them are based on influence strategies. I knew what influence was but I didn't know about social psychology, the study of group behavior. So I have studied influence and examined how it fits with encouraging people to change. In addition to tutorials on *Fearless Change*, I now offer training on influence strategies and better ways to think, solve problems, and make decisions. These workshops present many of the same ideas that are captured in the *Fearless Change* patterns but from a different perspective—how our brains work.

One of the many benefits of this connection with social science is that the researchers in this field do experiments. It's long been a contentious point of discussion in the patterns community that we have no proof, no data, that support our intuition that patterns are effective. Now we can point to the scientific studies of experimenters who look at the underlying principles of the organizational change patterns and verify for us that they really do work!

Cognitive scientists say our brains look for patterns even in random events—a warning to all of us who love patterns. It's so easy to pounce on what we believe are significant repeated events and infer causation. It seems naïve but I have had to realize over and over that these and other patterns are not magic. Rather, it's about the power of one person who can make a difference by taking a strong stand. For example, when I recently read the story behind the action of Rosa Parks, who started the civil rights movement by refusing to give up her seat on a bus in Montgomery, Alabama,[8] the pattern that came to my mind was Evangelist, a believer in an idea who acts on that belief.

In fact, many others before Rosa Parks had also refused to give up their seats. They were all arrested, as was Rosa Parks. The difference was that Rosa Parks was a connector (Connector is another pattern from *Fearless Change*). She knew a lot of people in Montgomery and—what's important for the outcome of the story—they knew her. When word of her arrest spread, some of her connections posted bail and took her home. Others held meetings and planned a boycott of the city's buses. These things did not happen for the other evangelists who were just as revolutionary, just as committed, just as passionate about trying to make a difference. It was the combination of the Evangelist and Connector patterns that made it work. Or was it? It seems like these two patterns were involved, but were they really necessary? I think we can say with certainty, yes. Were they sufficient? We can't be sure. We should exercise caution about describing any human setting with just a pattern name or two. Human behavior is often much more complicated.

Neuroscientists also tell us that patterns get our attention from earliest childhood. That is how we learn. This approach is sometimes called statistical learning. Babies notice that sounds are broken into parts and that the parts do not appear randomly. Statistical learning is related to our belief in causality. If a baby pushes a bottle and it always moves, the baby believes that pushing causes movement.[9] This approach to learning continues throughout our lives.

The penalty for this brain behavior is that we have a tendency to detect patterns where none exists. Since we suffer from the confirmation bias (the tendency to select information that confirms our beliefs) and tend to see what we are already convinced is true, testing ideas against what others believe will help ensure that our ideas are widely applicable. Now I see a compelling reason for including actual "known uses" from a variety of settings and users. This approach helps ensure that it's not just the good idea of the author or a brain construct that won't apply elsewhere.

A final significant learning for me came the first time I played the Fearless Journey Game.[10] I saw that when players would choose a pattern and apply it to solve a problem, they would explain why they were using it. Often the explanation of the pattern was not quite "right" and my first response was to correct them. After a few of these experiences, I finally got it. I realized it doesn't matter whether they had the same idea I did about the pattern, because they had found something that worked for them based on the name and short description of the pattern. As a result, they were able to make progress—an outcome much more important than correctness. No one owns an interpretation of a pattern.

This happens in the *Fearless Change* training classes all the time. I have the same response then—to jump in and explain the patterns—as though it were possible for all of us to have the same sense of what those patterns are all about. Mary Lynn and I have both recognized that our interpretation evolves based on our experience and the different insights we have acquired as we use the patterns. It seems each of us now has a very different definition of many of these patterns—different from 10 years ago and different from each other. I think this is a natural and good thing. We are not all the same people living within the same environment and sharing the same view of the world. There is not always an agreed-upon meaning for anything. What's important is that the patterns be useful. As both Mary Lynn and I have seen, even without a controlled experiment, the patterns work for different users in different contexts with different understandings of what the pattern will bring. Yes, the patterns work!

The New Patterns

The 15 new patterns that appear in this book are Accentuate the Positive, Concrete Action Plan, Easier Path, Elevator Pitch, Emotional Connection, Evolving Vision, Future Commitment, Go-To Person, Imagine That, Know Yourself, Low-Hanging Fruit, Myth Buster, Pick Your Battles, Town Hall Meeting, and Wake-up Call.

All the patterns have been reviewed at least once at a Pattern Languages of Programming (PLoP) conference. This means they have been shepherded by other writers, presented in a writers workshop, revised based on feedback, and then published in a conference paper.[11-13] To add further validation, each pattern includes known uses from a variety of people (to protect the identities of these people, we have changed the names of individuals and organizations, but all the stories are real accounts from leaders of change).

When the name of a pattern is used in the text to refer to the pattern as a pattern, it appears capitalized (e.g., the Evangelist pattern). If we use the pattern as ordinary language, as just a regular noun, verb, subject, or object, it won't be capitalized (e.g., "He serves as the evangelist for the team").

CHAPTER TWO

Strategize

You, as a budding evangelist, would probably agree that some time should be allotted for upfront planning before you jump feet first into a change effort. There's the usual task of creating a mission and vision, but you should also take some time for self-reflection to determine whether your values are aligned with those of the initiative. In this chapter, we introduce the new patterns Know Yourself, Evolving Vision, Concrete Action Plan, and Low-Hanging Fruit to support you in these exercises.

Know Yourself

If there is a "first pattern" in our collection of patterns for introducing new ideas, it's likely to be Know Yourself. It might seem strange that it's appearing only now, in *More Fearless Change*, but we assumed that it was part of the Evangelist pattern. Over the past 10 years, we've come to realize that this pattern is important enough to document separately. We have heard from many enthusiastic supporters of a new idea who started with high hopes but eventually burned out or simply gave up the fight because they became too discouraged with the way things were going. Leading a change initiative is hard work and takes not just a belief in the new idea but also the fortitude to face the never-ending challenges that inevitably arise along the journey that is always longer than anticipated. Without sufficient internal reserves, this journey is doomed to failure.

While the cognitive scientists tell us that we can't really understand ourselves completely,[1] some kind of objective evaluation is necessary before investing the time and energy to bring new ideas to your environment. Engage a collaborator—a fellow evangelist who is a good listener—and work together to help each other learn about your capabilities and shortcomings, your passions and phobias. Pairing in this way is a powerful way to move forward.

You should also consider how your attitudes contribute to any difficulties you might encounter.

As Craig Freshley suggests in one of his Good Group Tips,[2] in every setting there are two sides to the change problem. You might see the situation as a collection of "others" who you want to change, but the reality is that you will be required to change as well. Your tolerance for learning and agility will be tested. It's not about your list of requirements that others will meet, but rather about moving together in a direction that will also change over time.

When we assume the problem is caused by others, we are overlooking our part. We can spend a lot of time and energy wishing "they" were different, but Craig's Practical Tip is to ask, "What's my part?" If you want the problem solved, you might have to change your own behavior rather than talk about how others should change. As Gandhi noted, "Be the change that you wish to see in the world."

Evolving Vision

Bringing clarity to this important initial step of knowing yourself will then be useful to determine the goal or vision for your enterprise. We have learned in the past decade since our first book was published that this vision is not static, but rather will evolve as you and your organization begin to experiment with the new idea—it's an evolving vision.

We have also learned that in most cases, starting with a small, manageable, reasonable goal, and then taking baby steps toward that goal is more likely to lead to success than setting a world-changing, enormous, overwhelming, impossible, pie-in-the-sky goal. As one of our change leaders told us, "You need a broad strategy, but your goals should not be so rigid and narrow that they don't allow for changing situational realities."[3] While this may be inspiring at the outset, seeing little progress over time can become discouraging. But, consider what Karl Weick says about the theory of small wins—baby steps—toward attainable goals:

> *Once a small win has been accomplished, forces are set in motion that favor another small win. When a solution is put in place, the next solvable problem often becomes more visible. This occurs because new allies bring new solutions with them and old opponents change their habits. Additional resources also flow toward winners, which means that slightly larger wins can be attempted.*[4]

This fits well with Agile, the current popular approach to software development. Viewing projects as a series of small experiments that include close interaction with all stakeholders means that the product is grown slowly with input from customers, users, and the business side. The whole process consists of a series of small wins. Even failure is a "win," because it offers a chance to learn more about what customers want and what the team can do.

Concrete Action Plan

In the small wins approach of using an evolving vision, the baby steps can be defined in a concrete action plan. Research shows that one of the more effective ways to move forward is to create a specific plan for where, when, and how you will go about accomplishing your goal.[5] Here are some examples:

- *If I am bored and I feel like having a snack, then I will eat an apple.*
- *I will set an alarm to remind me to take a short break every 50 minutes.*
- *The team will meet every Friday morning at 10:00 a.m. for 30 minutes to review the goals for that week and make new goals for the following week.*

By the way, one research study shows that this approach is not effective for multiple goals.[6] This finding adds more weight to the better approach of focusing on one small win at a time.

Low-Hanging Fruit

You may want to use another new pattern, Low-Hanging Fruit, to get the most benefit from your investment of time and energy. We often assume that a complicated problem must have a complicated solution. What we usually forget is that we are always dealing with a complex adaptive system and that any change, even a small one, can have an enormous impact. Focusing on something small and easily accomplished is a very effective way to move your environment in the desired direction.

In a recent article on Forbes.com, a discussion of health care illustrates the use of this pattern:

> There are many proposals for improving cost and effectiveness of U.S. medicine, including: personalized medicine, big-data technology to find patterns and coordinate care, tightly-managed accountable healthcare systems, and marketplace incentives. These proposals tend to be complex and sophisticated, and need years to develop. We often forget that there is a simple, low-tech innovation that already holds great promise and offers a fast pay-back: re-investment in primary care providers (PCP), giving them the right role in the healthcare system and incentives.[7]

This example illustrates that a simpler approach may be possible, if you take a bit of time to analyze alternatives. One advantage that emerges from use of the Low-Hanging Fruit pattern is that it gives you something to talk about much more quickly than other more complicated courses of action.

Where to Go Next

Once you begin using the patterns in this chapter, you will want to start telling others about your new idea and encouraging them to be involved. The new patterns in the next chapter will help you with that aim.

Share Information and Seek Help

When you have a good idea, you are anxious to share it. You want to investigate what others may think about it, identify some supporters and potential resistors, gather some hints for moving forward, and get some help. Unfortunately, this is not always easy. The patterns in this chapter will help you achieve these goals—Elevator Pitch, Town Hall Meeting, Go-To Person, and Future Commitment.

Our first book introduced the In Your Space pattern and pointed out some ways to keep your idea where others can see it and hear it frequently. We have since changed the name of this pattern to Persistent PR because this name does a better job of capturing what you are doing throughout the change initiative. Spread the word, even though this takes time and effort. Despite your persistence, however, people might not take the time to listen or might misunderstand your message. Even if you believe "there is no such thing as too much communication" during times of change, you might still struggle with how to do this effectively.

Mary Lynn encountered many of the challenges in creating and communicating consistent messages while leading the development of a new idea on her campus. The answer was to use many different methods, with the hope that one or more would catch the attention of each person she was trying to reach.

Elevator Pitch

When you begin, and throughout your journey, you need to understand what your message should be. You can't, and probably don't want to, share all the details of the idea with everyone you meet. Instead, you and your team need a concise pitch that opens the conversation—an elevator pitch. This summation is by definition brief, but it can spark curiosity and invite questions. Fewer words, with a conversational style and a good opening line, will capture attention better than long prose.[1] As Anthony K. Tjan recommends, you don't want to over-sell to the point of diminishing returns.[2] An elevator pitch helps you and your listeners focus on what truly matters at that time. As the idea develops, the team can, and should, update the pitch so that it always provides an accurate summary of what's going on.

Town Hall Meeting

When you feel prepared to share your message with a larger group, it might be time to hold a town hall meeting. Try to invite as many voices as possible—involve everyone. This can be an efficient way to provide an update on the idea, gather ideas, identify supporters, and ask for their help. If you are successful at attracting a large, diverse group, this can be an exciting sign that people are interested, but it can also create bedlam as all of their voices struggle to be heard. Be prepared to provide strong leadership during the meeting so that the message is clear and all speakers make their points.

Go-To Person

The town hall meeting and your team's continuing use of your elevator pitch will likely attract some innovators and early adopters. Keep a list of these people. They are potential go-to people who can help with tasks that crop up as you and your team develop the initiative. This list may contain the names of people you can "go to" for any number of special skills you will need along the way.

Future Commitment

If you are able to anticipate some of your needs, you can ask for a future commitment from busy people. If given some lead time, they may be more willing to help. This allows everyone to plan ahead.

Mary Lynn recently asked a colleague to help with a project that was due to begin in four months. The colleague agreed more quickly than expected, so there was a bit of surprise in Mary Lynn's voice when she conveyed her thanks. "No need to be surprised," her colleague replied, "the main thing that persuaded me is that I don't have to do it now."

Where to Go Next

The patterns in this chapter will help you keep others informed about the idea and request help, but won't necessarily persuade them to jump on board. Building persistent PR with a solid elevator pitch and town hall meetings at strategic times is only a start. Your go-to people, and others whom you are trying to convince, need to be emotionally tied to the idea before they will accept it. The next chapter has some patterns to help you achieve this end.

CHAPTER FOUR

Inspire Others

Of course, you want to be inspirational! You know that others will not accept your idea if you just present a collection of facts. You must get their hearts in it, too. This chapter presents some new patterns to help with this: Emotional Connection, Accentuate the Positive, and Imagine That.

Our first book described patterns that will help you, as evangelist, communicate information about the new idea—these included Brown Bag, Study Group, External Validation, and In Your Space.[1] In the previous chapter, we introduced more information-sharing strategy patterns, Elevator Pitch and Town Hall Meeting.

It is vital to consistently publicize and provide updates throughout the change initiative; however, that effort is not enough. People are not logical beings. They can be irrational, emotional, and uncooperative for reasons that might not even make sense to you. So, in addition to listening to the facts about your idea, the people you are trying to convince must *believe* these facts are true and *feel* your idea is a good one.

You and your team will need to take time to build relationships with the people in your organization so you can understand and deal with the often strong emotions that are likely to surface during times of change. As social intelligence author Daniel Goleman tells us, "Leadership is the art of accomplishing goals through other people."[2]

We once met a CEO who didn't understand this concept. While he was busy with the implementation details during a change initiative, he hired a consultant to "deal with the people stuff." This is in stark contrast to a manager in another organization who told us, "I'm about to ask people to accept something that is going to be difficult. I better know them and appreciate their needs and concerns before I ask them to make these changes." This manager recognized what all evangelists need to understand: The people we are trying to persuade need to trust us, believe the information we are sharing is true, have confidence the change will be valuable for the organization, and, most importantly, be eager to learn more because they have faith that the idea will be beneficial for them.

Emotional Connection

Trust, belief, confidence, and eagerness are feelings. To stir these feelings, your message must have an emotional component that will inspire as well as inform. The pattern Emotional Connection describes some ways to do this. You can begin with a wake-up call to build some urgency around the problem your idea is likely to solve.

Accentuate the Positive

The Accentuate the Positive pattern encourages individuals to believe they have the ability to help with the solution. Even during the toughest stages of a change initiative, a positive attitude and message can be a powerful influence in keeping people from becoming paralyzed by the challenges; it can remind them of what is going well and the better days to come.

Imagine That

The Imagine That pattern provides an opportunity to visualize, and even feel, the problem and the ways your idea can create a solution. Rather than talking only about a list of features when describing your idea, you can include a story that begins with something like, "Imagine if you could..." As you do this, encourage your listeners to chime in with ways they can imagine using the new idea, too.

The Imagine That and Accentuate the Positive patterns can work well together. For example, when your team begins a new phase in the change initiative, you can lead them in reflection (Time for Reflection is a pattern from our first collection) that will guide everyone to imagine the best-case scenario for reaching their goals. Then, the team is primed for planning the process and the tasks that will allow them to reach their positive scenario.

More Patterns to Inspire

In addition, you can use the patterns from the first book to inspire your colleagues. Sharing a Hometown Story has a better chance of stirring emotion than presenting a series of bullet points. A Personal Touch will help individuals care about the idea when you take the time to care about them by aligning the idea with their needs. Providing a Shoulder to Cry On can ease the feelings of loss that are likely to be stronger than what may or may not be gained. Every time you Ask for Help and follow it with Sincere Appreciation,[3] you are helping people feel they are valuable additions to the initiative. Even patterns such as Fear Less and Champion Skeptic encourage resistors to feel they are respected members of the Group Identity. Most importantly, Evangelists must have the ability to build relationships and enlist others such as Bridge Builders and Guru on Your Side to assist with the difficult task of understanding and addressing the many and varied attitudes throughout the organization.

Where to Go Next

The strong emotions that are sparked by the change initiative can make or break your efforts, so the task of contending with them should not be ignored or outsourced. The new patterns introduced in this chapter—Emotional Connection, Accentuate the Positive, and Imagine That—will help you. But what can be done when the emotions appear to be highly resistant and potentially destructive? The next chapter will answer this question.

CHAPTER FIVE

Target Resistance

No matter how great your new idea is and how well prepared you are, you are bound to meet some level of resistance. This is not necessarily a bad thing. If your attitude is one of openness and learning, you can use many of the contributions from those who are less enthusiastic about your new idea to make it better. In this chapter, we introduce Pick Your Battles, Wake-up Call, Myth Buster, and Easier Path to help you make the most of any resistance you meet.

Pick Your Battles

Our first book was titled *Fearless Change*, reflecting the name of one of our favorite patterns, Fear Less. In this pattern we outlined a powerful solution: Use resistance to your advantage by learning from skeptics. Your best active listening techniques can summon up all the empathy you can muster, treat the other person's ideas with respect, and use another pattern from our first book, Involve Everyone, to try to bring everyone's contribution to your change effort.

We realize now that we needed to include some discussion on focusing your limited resources. You can't use Fear Less or Champion Skeptic (another pattern for resistors) on everyone you meet. In fact, you may be able to make use of these and other patterns on only a small subset of those who are not supporters. You will have to pick your battles.

A recent article on the Harvard Business Blog illustrates the use of this pattern:

> Dr. Laura Esserman is a breast cancer surgeon at the University of California, San Francisco, and a change agent in breast cancer research. She was sponsoring a digital mammography van to serve poor women in San Francisco. The sponsorship was taking a lot of time and effort. Her department chair was worried about the department budget and why surgeons were running a radiology service. The hospital CFO was not interested in funding a mammography service that would generate unreimbursed care. Even Esserman did not believe that mammography was the way forward for improving breast cancer outcomes. She finally saw that sponsoring the van was taking too much effort and creating unnecessary conflict with important people. When Esserman offloaded the van, it smoothed relationships with others and allowed her to focus on higher-leverage activities.[1]

Just as in this story, you will find that you can't do it all and you can't bring every resistor on board. Some people are merely pressed for time. They're not fighting your idea—they're just worried about fitting it into their already packed schedules. When you pick your battles, try to identify those people who will be the easiest to work with and focus your limited resources on them.

Wake-up Call

One way to get the attention of those who aren't sure about your proposals is to have a wake-up call. Busy people may not even be aware that your organization has problems, so you may need to point out these issues before you talk about a new way of doing things. Not everyone is sensitive to warning calls, so realize this is merely one approach to reaching potential supporters.

Myth Buster

Another technique to try is the Myth Buster pattern. This pattern describes how you can address the rumors and half-truths that will inevitably pop up in any change effort. It will not work for everyone, especially those who are vehemently tied to the myths. Facts are not always convincing. It's unfortunately the case that we are all illogical thinkers[2] and, therefore, tend to select data that match our beliefs as worthy of attention. Even so, the Myth Buster pattern can be an effective way to clarify some of the information you're trying to get out there.

Easier Path

It takes a bit of creativity to use the last pattern in this chapter, Easier Path. Research has shown that most of us make decisions based on what is easiest for us in our environment.[3] As an evangelist, you will have to be highly observant, a good listener, and a clever innovator to make appropriate adjustments in your organization that will enhance the experiences of users and make it easier for them to accept the new idea. Periodically take some time for reflection by asking, "Which barriers are presently standing in the way of this change?" and "Which barrier do I need to tackle now?" For example, if people are mired down with worry over the difficulties surrounding the idea, you might want to create an enjoyable way for them to learn with others—you can do this with another pattern, Study Group. The notion of creating an easier path is also illustrated in the following example, showing how Google makes it easier for people to have a small dessert and move on:

> We know that waistlines around the world are increasing in size and that some companies are trying to encourage employees to adopt healthier eating habits, but it's difficult to simply argue for skipping dessert. In its cafeterias, Google encourages employees to eat healthier by changing the way dessert is presented to employees. Instead of letting Googlers transfer dessert from the serving platter to a plate on their own, Google prepares plates with three-bite desserts. Those who want more dessert have to return to the line for a second plate, which makes people think twice before over-indulging.

Easier Path is one of the most powerful patterns we have in our collection, but its effectiveness depends on your insight. All the innovation you have expressed for your new idea must be matched by your enthusiasm to make it the easiest path for people to use.

More Patterns and Some Final Thoughts

These new strategies for addressing skeptics can be combined with those in our first book: Fear Less, Champion Skeptic, Bridge Builder, Corridor Politics, and Whisper in the General's Ear. The most important new pattern is Pick Your Battles, because you don't want to let resistance wear you down.

Now that you've met all the new patterns, we hope you enjoy applying them in your own environment. We are always happy to hear from our readers, so please consider sharing your experiences with us.

PART TWO

Stories in Leading Change

There is no one way to use the *Fearless Change* patterns. Just like a home builder uses a whole collection of tools when building a structure, you can think of each individual pattern as a "tool" that the evangelist and her or his team can use to address a problem in the journey of leading a change. Therefore, the specific pattern(s) you choose at any time will depend on the problem(s) and the context you are facing at any particular time along your journey of building a change.

We present two stories to give you some ideas for using the patterns: one when building an organizational change and the other when building a community change.

Enterprise Architecture

The first story is from one evangelist using the Fearless Change patterns to build an enterprise architecture program (EAP) in her organization.

My department was created a little over a year ago with no staff. We came in with vague job descriptions and no plan to identify drivers, establish principles and values, or define a mission, vision, and strategy. I am an enterprise architect and, together with a senior enterprise architect, my job was to educate the organization on enterprise architecture (EA) and define a plan to implement it over the next fiscal year. I have always considered myself the go-to person on this topic; in addition, I have experience in getting people on board with the new concepts. I believed the organization needed an enterprise architecture program (EAP) and I had the time and passion to proceed [Know Yourself], so I decided to champion this cause [Evangelist].

I started with town hall meetings but noticed that when weekly meetings were scheduled, some people felt as if it didn't matter if they missed one because they could simply go to the next. Since I needed the participants at every meeting, I used the Do Food pattern to improve attendance.

The purpose of each meeting was to discuss just enough so that attendees could analyze the concepts and think about the purpose and value of enterprise architecture [Imagine That]. Participants comprised a subset of the organization, along with the executive leadership (vice presidents, directors, and program directors). However, the entire organization received the notifications and was able to review the EAP website as plans developed [Involve Everyone].

Since our chief information officer (CIO) viewed this EAP project as a major initiative with high visibility, we needed a roadmap, using the Baby Steps[1] pattern, with milestones to successfully reach our evolving vision. As the initiative became a priority for the EA team and the executive management grew increasingly interested in its success, I asked to become the official point person. Leadership of this initiative's rollout was eventually added to my official duties [Dedicated Champion].

We anticipated that the first iteration of the rollout would take about five weeks. To begin, I created a high-level proposal, with flexible dates. Dates changed based on responses and feedback [Time for Reflection].

During the first week, I worked with the senior enterprise architect to finalize the EA mission, vision, strategy, and 100-day roadmap. We developed an elevator pitch and rehearsed responding to questions like "Who is the EA team and what do they do?"

Our persistent PR started with a repository for collaboration to help people learn the new concepts. The EAP website allowed everyone to review information, provide feedback, and share their ideas. The site also hosted discussions, a calendar of events, tools, artifacts, meeting minutes, status, and links to other important enterprise architecture sites and references. Invitations to view the site were sent throughout the organization [Involve Everyone]. We encouraged users to review the site and send any questions and comments to the EA team.

Volunteers from various departments assisted in putting up flyers in common areas [Ask for Help]. This material ranged from facts about the EAP with the elevator pitch and accompanying details, to information about accessing the discussion boards, to contact information for the EA Team members, to meeting announcements, updates, and hot topics. We paid special attention to encouraging participation on the discussion board to generate interest in EA and address any misunderstandings brewing in the organization [Myth Buster].

Engagement in the discussion board was slow, so I sent personal invitations, asking people to review the EA site [Personal Touch]. A schedule was attached with upcoming meetings for the next month, including the time/ date, topics, presenters, and a promise that we would do food. As the town hall meetings continued, the food made it easier for people to stay longer and have some rich discussions. With a well-focused agenda at each meeting, I helped attendees understand the value of each item and did my best to listen to their concerns and empathize with their issues [Emotional Connection]. We continued to use each meeting to keep sustained momentum, taking time for reflection to evaluate our most recent baby step and celebrate our small successes. We regularly evaluated our evolving vision, changing milestones and adding or removing tasks when necessary. This not only made implementation easier for me, but even more importantly helped create a group identity with participants who provided valuable suggestions and took ownership of tasks.

While reflecting on a prior EAP attempt years ago, we decided that the failure was caused by forcing a square peg into a round hole [Time for Reflection]. Therefore, constraining the organization into a rigid framework was not only impossible in the time we had, but didn't make sense to me, the EA team, or the organization. Feedback from participants helped me with the difficult task of creating a roadmap for phasing in the EAP. I was able to discover what everyone needed in the first iteration of the program [Personal Touch] and adapt their suggestions to fit the needs of the organization [Tailor Made].

However, skeptics were still around. Three of the 18 EA team members held on to their negative attitudes about EAP during most discussions. They even complained about the snacks, the length and frequency of the meetings, the topics on the agenda, the website, and things outside of my control. They often sat next to each other, trying to convince others to join them in their resistance. I didn't take time to address their skepticism at every meeting [Pick Your Battles], but eventually recognized they were raising some issues worth considering. So, in an attempt to capture their concerns in a more constructive way, I asked the most open-minded resistors to take on the role of champion skeptic. The problems they pointed out helped us understand that EAP was not a "silver bullet" but rather had some challenges we needed to address as soon as possible.

Throughout our journey, resistors continued to appear throughout the organization. I helped them understand that what they were currently doing wasn't working [Wake-up Call] and reminded them of a prior software rollout that had many headaches during the change process but now provides significant benefits throughout the organization [Accentuate the Positive]. I was hoping this would help skeptics relate to prior successes and imagine new ones [Imagine That].

When it was time to introduce some of the new software tools in the EAP, we held a series of brown bag sessions. We began by discussing only two of the tools [Just Enough]. Participants used the Trial Run pattern so that they could experiment and determine what was best for different projects before we released the final process to the entire organization. When people inquired about the other tools that would be rolled out in the future, we referred them to the EAP website and asked them to consider signing up for future trials [Future Commitment].

Following a trial run, one champion skeptic suggested we conduct a survey to see where we could improve. Its results provoked discussions for improving the entire EAP and prompted even more small successes that I was able to share with others [Smell of Success]. The champion skeptic came through for the entire team, not only by suggesting the survey but by also giving us the opportunity to improve the program based on feedback [Time for Reflection]. I took the time to recognize him with sincere appreciation at our next meeting.

Toward the end of week five of the rollout, the CIO contacted the EA team to express his satisfaction with our work. He asked that after we wrapped up our sessions in our current area, we present our roadmap and vision to other departments in the organization. This enabled the team to introduce the same EAP concepts, tools, artifacts, and processes to the parent organization. We decided to use the five-week process we had just completed as a baseline, but to adjust it as needed for the second iteration of the exercise [Baby Steps].

During this first iteration of the rollout, we were able to spread the word about enterprise architecture, make headway in the organization's transition to our enterprise architecture program, and roll out tools to a subset of projects. In addition, my role evolved into a dedicated champion, so I now have more time to continue the transition to new areas with additional tools. In retrospect, I believe that we should have involved a corporate angel early on to create a higher impact and to guide strategic direction. Nevertheless, our goal to introduce concepts and lay a foundation for the EAP was achieved.

Community Initiative

The following fictitious story about a community initiative uses all the new patterns and many from our original book.

Alex had always enjoyed walking around Sunset Lake, a small wooded neighborhood spot, but over the last several months, it seemed to him that there was more trash along the banks. He worried that the water in the lake was becoming polluted.

One day Alex noticed several dead fish that had washed up on shore and saw that a handful of concerned neighbors had gathered around. The discussion was heated, and it seemed that everyone had an opinion about what should be done. Alex realized that it was easy to talk about a problem but taking action meant being willing to invest time and energy.

After spending time for reflection on his own, he determined that the health of the lake was important enough to him to initiate an effort to clean up the lake [Know Yourself]. He wrote a short summary of his goals to help him focus his thoughts and prepare to explain to others the condition of the lake and the actions that could be taken [Elevator Pitch].

Alex set out one evening to visit the neighbors who had also noticed the dead fish at the lake, asking for help to organize a town hall meeting. The group invited everyone in the neighborhood [Involve Everyone] and asked them to bring a covered dish to share [Do Food].

Alex, in the role of evangelist, began the meeting with a wake-up call describing the dead fish and the increasing amounts of trash. He followed that summary by describing a scenario to help people picture how the lake could look if they worked to clean up the area [Imagine That]. Residents who had been in the neighborhood for many years shared their own hometown stories about how beautiful the lake used to be. The sharing of food and stories helped build an emotional connection within the community. A sign-up sheet was passed around to ask for volunteers for various work projects [Next Steps]. Alex observed that even though everyone at the meeting agreed that there was a problem, only a few signed up to begin the work.

Alex decided not to try to convince everyone [Pick Your Battles], but rather began moving forward with a small core team [Just Do It]. The core team met the following week to draw up a concrete action plan with a list of go-to people to organize and tackle various tasks. The project was christened "Saving Sunset" to allow everyone to identify and talk about the cause [Group Identity]. The team decided to begin working to clean up the shore and start a fundraising effort to dredge the lake to make it as clean as it had been when first built. With this evolving vision, the core team created an updated elevator pitch to help everyone in the neighborhood understand the project goals.

The core team began with low-hanging fruit: It held a trash clean-up on the first Saturday of the following month [Trial Run]. Everyone in the neighborhood was invited [Involve Everyone]. In the days leading up to the event, community members were reminded of the planned activity with persistent PR: fliers in mailboxes, emails, phone calls, and, most importantly, personal invitations [Personal Touch]. Even the busiest residents made a future commitment, since the event was several weeks away.

The project was a "small success." Residents who showed up to help were given a "Saving Sunset" sticker [Token] to place on the front door of their homes. A significant portion of the trash was removed and a few more residents volunteered to join the core team. Similar events were held in the following months. After a few more clean-up days [Baby Steps], more "Saving Sunset" stickers appeared around the neighborhood.

The core team then decided to plan the next step—dredging the lake. They investigated which other lake clean-up projects had been done [External Validation] in the area and found some experts [Mentor] to help them in their planning. They learned that dredging the entire lake was too ambitious at that time. Based on the recommendation of their mentor, who pointed out an invasive plant that was killing the lake, the core team updated their evolving vision to address only this issue. Their mentor explained how to remove the plant—an arduous task that would require lots of labor over an extended period of time. The team understood they needed sustained momentum to reach this new goal.

When pushback appeared from those who didn't want to take on this large project, the core team used the Imagine That pattern to encourage people to think about the fun activities that could happen on the lake if the invasive plant was removed. The team also pointed out that home values would increase with a beautiful lake in the area [Personal Touch]. The skeptics were invited to the core team meetings to voice their concerns [Fear Less]. Some of these resistors helped uncover challenges that needed to be addressed [Champion Skeptic]. The core team didn't get all the neighbors interested in helping to remove the invasive plant, but they had enough to get started. To create an easier path, a central storage area was organized to hold the tools that would be needed to do the work—this allowed anyone with a spare hour to make the most of his or her time.

The clean-up went well for a few months before most community members started getting tired of the tedious work. One highly vocal opponent, George, showed his frustration by spreading the word that the project was an exercise in futility. The core team countered with myth buster information and delivered the message personally to George through someone he trusted, his next-door neighbor Fred [Bridge Builder]. The myth buster information was sent to all the residents via the weekly email project updates from the team [Persistent PR^2].

Even though there was still a lot of work to be done, the core team decided to accentuate the positive by holding a neighborhood block party [Do Food] to offer sincere appreciation to everyone who had helped. At this party, which was held on a fall day before the winter began [The Right Time], the core team invited a representative from a local environmental organization [Big Jolt] to congratulate the residents on the work and encourage them to sustain momentum. Posters were displayed sharing all the small successes the residents had achieved so far. Along with data reporting how the lake odor had subsided and how much of the invasive plant had been removed, the posters created an emotional connection with pictures of people who had started to enjoy fun activities in and around the lake.

After the party, most residents were energized about continuing their work. To keep the project alive over the winter months, the core team decided to stay in touch with residents, primarily through a specially designed social media group [Persistent PR]. In the spring [The Right Time], the team held a town hall meeting to consider the next steps. They invited another potential mentor—someone from another neighborhood who was part of a similar project—to talk about how such a project helped the community. The mentor helped the core team evaluate their evolving vision, update their elevator pitch, and create their next concrete action plan.

PART THREE

The Patterns

This part contains all of the patterns—both the 15 new patterns and the patterns from *Fearless Change*. For each pattern, the following information is provided:

- Opening Story (in italics)
- Summary (in bold)
- Context (in body text)
- Problem (in bold)

- Forces (in body text)
- Essence of the Solution (prefaced by "Therefore")
- More on the Solution (in body text)
- Resulting Context (in body text)
- Known Uses (in italics)

Patterns from other sources are also referenced at various points in the text and their sources are listed at the end of this part.

New Patterns

The new patterns are given further, more detailed coverage in this chapter. Here they are, listed alphabetically. The sections on each pattern follow.

Accentuate the Positive
Concrete Action Plan
Easier Path
Elevator Pitch
Emotional Connection
Evolving Vision
Future Commitment
Go-To Person

Imagine That
Know Yourself
Low-Hanging Fruit
Myth Buster
Pick Your Battles
Town Hall Meeting
Wake-up Call

Accentuate the Positive

Allen Carr, former chain smoker, advises those who wish to encourage friends and relatives to stop smoking to help the smoker believe he can stop—this will cause his mind to open. Carr explains, "If you try to force a smoker to stop, he will feel like a trapped animal and want his cigarette even more. Don't try to scare him into stopping by telling him he is ruining his health or wasting his money." Instead, Carr recommends that you give the smoker hope that he can quit by introducing him to ex-smokers who thought they were hooked for life but can attest to how much better their lives are as nonsmokers. Say how proud you are of him during the long quitting process of ups and downs. Point out small successes along the way, such as how much better he smells and how much clearer his breathing is.[1]

To influence others during the change initiative and inspire them to believe the change can happen, motivate them with a sense of hope rather than fear.

◆◆◆

You are an evangelist or dedicated champion. You have been using fear tactics as part of your influence strategies.

Your attempts to scare others are not working.

You may have used a wake-up call to point out a problem you believe is creating a pressing need for change. This has persuaded a few people to pay attention to your idea. This reaction leads you to believe that if a little fear worked, more will work even better. As a result, you may talk primarily about the frightening things that are happening in the organization or the things that could happen if your new idea is not adopted. You think this approach will cause others to become more afraid of the current situation and accept your idea for "saving" the organization.

A wake-up call can jar listeners into immediate action for the short term, especially if there is a clear way to eliminate the problem.[2] For example, a confrontation with a manager who is angry about a missed deadline is likely to prompt an employee to stay late to work on that project.

However, this approach typically doesn't motivate us to take sustainable action. When problems are larger and solutions are more complex, such as the ones found in leading change, the use of ongoing fear tactics is likely to cause people to avoid you. Most aren't attracted to something that creates negative tension. We're not usually looking for yet another thing to worry about in our already stressful lives, so we often shield ourselves from threats by triggering defense mechanisms such as denial or rationalization. When this happens, the people you are trying to convince will simply ignore or disconnect from the situation you are trying to create.[3] Therefore, your attempts to rouse others can produce the opposite effect. You may, instead, cause them to believe they are powerless to deal with the situation.[4]

Dan Pink, in his book *Drive*,[5] points out that this can apply to the commonly used approach of providing negative consequences (or "sticks") to motivate employees to improve. He explains that fear causes individuals to be "near sighted," with a desire to accomplish the task that will avoid the threatened punishment, but nothing else. Pink argues that this does not foster creativity and out-of-the-box thinking because greatness and near-sightedness cannot exist together.

A fear tactic is an external force that is not likely to sustain a strong internal desire. When the reaction subsides, so can the interest in making the change. In contrast, research on the effects of faith and hope has found that a positive feeling about the ability to change is a strong predictor of success.[6]

Therefore:

Inspire people throughout the change initiative with a sense of optimism rather than fear.

Use the Wake-up Call pattern sparingly, to uncover the need for change. Then, start a discussion about a clear, obtainable solution—stress the benefits rather than the downsides to allow people to feel they have control over the problem. Use the Personal Touch and Tailor Made patterns to point out the organizational and personal assets, strengths, and skills that will help the challenges to be addressed and the change to become a reality.

Use the Imagine That pattern to show what it is possible. Provide external validation. Individuals are likely to draw strength from the comforting and reassuring testimonials of those who have been through a similar change. You may also want to create an elevator pitch with an inspirational message.

Identify typical scenarios that are likely to produce negative reactions. Plan ahead for them so you are prepared to react with confidence.

When you feel discouraged, look for the bright spots among the challenges that surround you. Don't hesitate to ask for help and find your own shoulder to cry on when you are overwhelmed or discouraged. Many times during a difficult change initiative, you may struggle with what you are saying about the future, but you should say it anyway. In addition to helping others, a positive attitude can help convince you, too. But make sure your view isn't distorted: If your predictions are not obtainable, this pattern will backfire. Never promise instant success or enormous benefits. Author and psychotherapist Virginia Satir[7] warns of a dip in productivity that always follows the introduction of something new. Savvy evangelists are prepared for this outcome.

Create emotional connections: Build strong relationships and a group identity to allow everyone to feel safe to express their concerns. Be proactive—and stay on the lookout for negative emotions. Provide support and a shoulder to cry on when needed. If the morale is getting low, schedule a town hall meeting for an update and some time for reflection. Stay in touch with persistent PR—highlight the small successes and everything that has been accomplished in the change initiative. This will reduce harmful rumors and help sustain hope. Even in challenging times, the message should include something positive—there is always something good to say.

Be aware of your own attitude. If you have a fixed mindset, then you believe people are preprogrammed by their genes; in that case, there's little hope for improvement, and many people will be resistant or skeptical. This belief can limit your ability to lead change at any level—organizational, team, or personal. Conversely, if you believe that everyone, no matter where they are today, can grow and improve, then you will be much more likely to be successful. Displaying a warm smile and a willingness to be nice even when negativity surrounds you can go a long way.

= = = = = = = = = = = = =

Use of the Accentuate the Positive pattern helps to build a sense of hope that the new idea can become a reality. Rather than being fearful and overwhelmed by the many challenges in the change initiative, people will be led to become more optimistic that the problems can be solved. Focusing on the positive also helps to keep up your spirits as the leader during the long journey.

However, if you report that everything is going well when it really isn't, you will lose a lot of ground and sacrifice a great deal of credibility. Misguided optimism or irrational exuberance can promote artificial happiness, discourage critical reflection, and leave you and your team ill equipped to deal with setbacks.[8] Keep yourself grounded in reality by asking questions and accepting feedback. When something goes wrong, be candid about the problem and take responsibility by creating a concrete action plan for addressing the issue.

Dr. Edward Miller, dean of the medical school and CEO of the hospital at Johns Hopkins University, points out, "If you look at people after coronary artery bypass grafting two years later, only about 10% of them have changed their lifestyle." Dr. Dean Ornish, founder of the Preventative Medicine Research Institute, raised that estimate to 77%. He observed that providing health information is not enough, and that motivating patients mainly with the fear of death wasn't working, either. For a few weeks after a heart attack, patients were scared enough to do whatever their doctors said. But death was just too frightening to think about. Denial eventually returned, and they went back to their old ways. Instead of trying to motivate his patients with the "fear of dying," Ornish reframes the issue. He inspires a new vision by convincing his patients that they can feel better as they enjoy the things that make daily life pleasurable, like making love or taking long walks without the pain caused by their disease. Weekly support groups with other patients, as well as attention from dietitians, psychologists, nurses, and yoga and meditation instructors, help to point out the "short-term wins" that reassure faith in their ability to lead a healthier lifestyle.[9]

Jonathan led an arduous two-year transition to an initiative in his organization. It was especially difficult because employees viewed this effort as taking limited funds away from other projects in the organization. Even during the especially difficult times, Jonathan consciously wore a smile on his face and delivered the most positive, yet realistic message about the ways in which the employees would benefit from the initiative once it was in place. At the end of the two years, following a successful implementation, employees still commented on how much they appreciated Jonathan's positive attitude that never seemed to wane.

Sandra, a college professor, gets irritated when her students perform poorly on exams or assignments. She is often tempted to create panic by threatening them with a potentially low final grade or a possible failure. However, she has learned that fear lasts only until the next distraction appears in their lives. More importantly, a repetitive fear tactic makes her sound frightening rather than approachable. Sandra has learned that it is sometimes necessary to give a brief wake-up call in which she explains the impact of a bad grade, but she follows it with a commitment to help students change their study habits and attitudes. She doesn't do the work for them, but rather makes herself available to assist students who have the desire to improve. She encourages them with stories of students who struggled but succeeded with a good grade in the class and cheers them on by pointing out their small successes along the way.

A 2010 Gallup poll reported that 48% of Americans believe that global warming concerns are exaggerated. In 1997, 31% of Americans thought the concerns were overrated. The increase might have to do with the framing of the issue. Researchers surveyed individuals, measuring their skepticism about global warming and their belief in the justness of the world. Participants were asked how much they agreed with the following statements: "I believe that . . . people get what they deserve," and "I am confident that justice always prevails. . ." Half the participants read news articles that ended with dire warnings about the consequences of global warming; the other half read more positive pieces focused on possible solutions to the problem. Those who received more positive messaging trusted the science. Subjects who read the "doomsday" messaging were skeptical of global warming; those who thought the world is generally a fair place had even stronger doubts about global warming after reading the negative messaging. While many tend to use fear-based messaging, in the case of global warming our reaction to such message may be to dismiss it.[10]

Concrete Action Plan

Rather than the vague goal of "working out more" or "living a healthier lifestyle," Sally decided, "On Tuesdays and Thursdays, I will walk around the block three times after dinner." Rather than attempting to "cut back on my caffeine consumption," Alan got very specific: "When I get a craving for coffee in the afternoon, I will get a glass of lemon water." Rather than attempting to "have more control over my anger," Anna decided, "When I start to get angry, I will breathe deeply for 5 seconds."

To make progress toward your goal, state precisely what you will do as you take the next baby step.

You are an evangelist or dedicated champion. You have a vision for change.

Leading a change initiative, with its many twists and turns and ever-growing list of things to do, can make you feel out of control.

You've probably experienced the frustration of setting goals, only to see them fade away. The end points are so far out that you can't seem to reach them. Goal setting makes you feel good for a while but then, if nothing happens, you feel discouraged. Often, you never think seriously about those goals once you've written them down.

Gabriele Oettingen and colleagues explain why people can get stuck in this way. In their research on Mental Contrasting with Implementation Intentions (MCII), they found that people tend to use three strategies when setting goals, even though two of these don't work well. Optimists favor "indulging," imagining the future they would like and vividly envisioning the resulting good things. This feels good when you're doing it, but it doesn't correlate with achievement. Pessimists tend to use "dwelling," thinking about all the things that will get in the way of accomplishing goals. Dwelling doesn't correlate with achievement, either. Mental contrasting combines elements of the other two methods—concentrating on a positive outcome and simultaneously concentrating on the obstacles. The next step is creating a series of "implementation intentions"—specific plans in the form of if/then statements that link the obstacles with ways to overcome them. MCII is a way of setting rules for yourself, which helps you sidestep the internal conflict between what you want and your tendency to resist change. Rules provide structure, preparing for encounters with temptation and focusing our attention elsewhere. Before long, the rules become automatic.[11]

Most of what we do every day is done on "automatic pilot." We need new triggers that will elicit behavior that moves us to do something new. Peter Gollwitzer argues for the importance of phrasing "implementation intentions" in concrete terms, such as "if this <particular thing> happens, then I will do that <particular action>." This increases the success rate of adopting good habits while easing difficult decision debates.[12,13]

To know where you are going in the change initiative, you and your team are likely to define a vision and the milestone goals to be achieved along the way. This will give you a good idea of *what* you are doing. But it will not tell you *how* you will complete each intermediate goal and eventually realize your vision. You need to define those small steps in concrete terms.

Therefore:

Describe the next small step for reaching a milestone goal in terms of concrete actions that include what you will do, where, and when.

Make sure your steps are defined in SMART terms—specific, measurable, action-oriented, realistic, and timetabled. Don't simply make vague promises; focus on accomplishments. Clearly define what, where, and when specific behaviors will be performed. Keep it simple and make sure that your goal is achievable in the time period to which you are committing. If your plan includes regular activities, schedule them as you would anything else on your calendar.

Write down the concrete actions and display them. When you do this, magic happens because you and your team will understand where you are going.

Emphasize the actions you will take as well as the learning you will do along the way. As Jerry Sternin notes, "It is easier to act your way into a new way of thinking than to think your way into a new way of acting."[14] Rather than believing that increased knowledge will change your attitude, which will then create change in your behavior, allow your concrete action steps to become the inspiration for changes in your attitude.

Consider your plan for each small step as an experiment. Take time for reflection to see what is working and what you want to do differently. Use the experience as feedback for your next experiment. When you are not successful, tweak your plan or move your efforts toward the next small step that you can control. Consider your plan to be a living list. Reevaluate and adjust concrete steps as you move toward your evolving vision.

Celebrate small successes to help keep your focus on what has been accomplished rather than everything you may still need to do.

= = = = = = = = = = = =

Enacting the Concrete Action Plan pattern helps you move from planning mode to action mode and makes it more likely that you'll keep the promises you made to reach your goal. You and your team will be better prepared to avoid procrastination, overcome distractions, and carry out your resolutions. Also, because you have defined exactly how you will reach a goal, you will be in a better position to evaluate how your plan is going along the way.

However, having a specific plan is no guarantee that you will follow it. It's not enough to set up new triggers and hope for the best. You will also have to include an allowance to help you deal with possible wayward slips. Our tendency is to give up everything after even the smallest transgression. Be patient and be willing to forgive missteps. If you "fall off the wagon," look for a shoulder to cry on to help you and your team take time for reflection about what you can do differently—and then move forward.

The National Novel Writing Month website (http://www.nanowrimo.org/) supports writers as they create a novel in a month. The success rate is high because those who join the site commit to, and receive support for, a concrete action plan: "Your goal is to write a 50,000-word novel by midnight, local time, on November 30."

Stephen was struggling to learn about his new role as the team manager. He made mistakes and had difficulty apologizing. He would say to himself, "I'm going to do better next time," but that mea culpa didn't seem to help. Finally, his mentor, Jake, sat down with him and said, "To say you are sorry takes real courage. Even the worst behavior can be forgiven if you are willing to do three things:

1. *Apologize, with sincerity and without self-justification.*
2. *Talk about what you've learned from the experience.*
3. *Say what you will do differently."*

Now instead of making a big promise to himself about an ill-defined goal, Stephen has a few simple steps he can take to address his problem.

David Armstrong—the fourth generation of his family to run Armstrong International—wanted his company to innovate, change, and grow. He decided to start by getting his staff to stop being negative about new ideas. He needed to create a concrete action plan. He wanted to introduce a new heat-sensitive paint that changes color with temperature but guessed that the initial reaction of his senior engineers and salespeople would be a negative one: "It's too gimmicky. We sell engineered products. Our current paint is good enough. Why would we ever want to fool around with that?" His action plan was to say at the meeting that staff members were there to discuss new ideas. He gave everyone an M&M, saying, "You are allowed one negative comment during this meeting. Once you make that comment, you must eat your M&M. If you don't have an M&M in front of you, you can't say anything negative." His plan worked well. The staff caught on quickly and jumped on any negative comments with "Shut up and eat your M&M!" They got a new product idea out of the meeting—steam traps that change color when they stop working.

Karen's nutrition counselor told her, "It's not good enough to just promise yourself, 'No more junk food.' Instead, say, for example, 'I'm not going to walk into the kitchen as soon as I get home and start to snack so that I've eaten 1000 calories before supper. Instead, I'm going to change into exercise clothes and walk around the block. I'm also going to have fresh fruit and veggies ready to eat as I am cooking dinner.'"

Easier Path

In 2011, Pelle G. Hansen and his students from Roskilde University came up with a litter-reducing nudge that they tested in Copenhagen. The team handed out 1000 candies to pedestrians. All the nearby streets, including garbage cans, ashtrays, and bike baskets were examined for the distinctive empty wrappers, and the wrappers discovered there were counted. Then the process was repeated, but in the second trial, a trail of green footsteps leading to nearby bins was stenciled on the ground. This led to a 46% decrease in the number of wrappers that were thrown on the ground. "The green footsteps certainly caught people's attention," says Hansen. "I think they create an atmosphere where the public feel more conscious about litter . . . and perhaps there is also a subconscious inclination to follow the feet." Hansen's remarks echo findings from a recent trial at an office block in Amsterdam that was designed to encourage visitors to take the stairs rather than power-hungry elevators. Beginning at the lobby entrance, members of Dutch environmental NGO Hivos laid a series of bright red strips along the floor leading up the stairs. During the 24-hour sample period that followed, the frequency of people entering the building who opted to take the stairs leapt by 70%.[15]

To encourage adoption of a new idea, experiment with removing obstacles that might be standing in the way.

◆◆◆

You are an evangelist or dedicated champion. Individuals are saying, or you sense, that there may be things holding them back from making the new idea a reality.

What can you do to make it easier for people to change?

The environment can present a multitude of hurdles. Some are obvious and people complain about them, but others are more subtle and often perceived as a normal part of doing business. Whether obvious or subtle, these hurdles can make the change process more difficult for those whom you are trying to convince.

Innovation efforts can be mentally and physical taxing because it is more time-consuming to be in the "mindful" state of learning something new than in the "mindless" state of doing the familiar.[16] This can encourage skeptics to focus on the barriers as an excuse for not becoming involved.

A basic idea from ergonomics is that physical and cognitive "nudges" can help individuals think about and use something more easily. Innovative organizations apply this logic by designing and spreading affordances that make it easier for people to change. Many times a problem can be solved not by forcing others to adopt a new behavior, but by creatively eliminating the obstacles in the environment so the desired behavior happens naturally.[17]

Changing the environment can be like drawing new painted lines that show how to drive down a highway. As Robert Cialdini, psychologist and author of *Influence: The Psychology of Persuasion*, points out, "Our brains are designed to go into autopilot once we've established a routine that works for us."[18]

Therefore:

Change the environment in a way that will encourage people to adopt the new idea.

Use the Personal Touch pattern to find out what is standing in the way. It may be hard for individuals to know and clearly articulate why they are struggling to make the change. Ask questions, listen carefully, and ask more questions. Look around—see what others are doing. Think about how the innovation could alter their daily routine and make things more difficult for them.

Look for barriers. Are they physical—that is, will the innovation create hurdles in the working environment? Are they systemic—that is, will the innovation require complications in the flow of work and how jobs are done?

Are they something else?[19] In his book *To Sell Is Human*, Dan Pink refers to this process as giving people an off-ramp.[20]

Once you discover a stumbling block, ask for help to find ways to get past it. It can be difficult to uncover a creative solution. You need diverse input. Innovators may be a big help, but involve everyone who may be a good problem-solver. Use the External Validation pattern to find useful techniques and best practices that might spark ideas. You may want to present a variety of options for overcoming difficulties, but be aware that offering alternatives can sometimes confuse or burden people with too many options and work against you.[21]

Make small changes instead of throwing out current approaches and completely replacing them with something new. Consider ways to piggyback on the way your organization is already working successfully. Let these little experiments help you help others move in the right direction. Iterate through the learning cycle—sustain momentum as you just do it, take a baby step, provide time for reflection, and celebrate small successes. These experiments should be part of your concrete action plan.

If your experiments are successful and you uncover ways to make life better for people, you can sell the new idea as a way to an easier path. Often people make long lists or increase process and monitoring to reach their goals. All of these efforts increase cognitive load; think instead of a change as a subtraction exercise. Remove tasks to make the environment simpler.[22] The innovation should be a way to free up time and resources to improve lives instead of a heavier burden on already busy people.

Given that many obstacles in the environment can be too large for you to tackle, look for the low-hanging fruit. Move slowly and deliberately to avoid overwhelming everyone and defeating your efforts. Share successes in hometown stories and invite mentors who can help those who are still struggling.

Keep a sustained momentum. Occasionally an experiment will work instantly and sometimes it will fail, but the results always provide a learning opportunity. After a success, it may be tempting to relax and feel that your work is done. As the innovation spreads across the organization, however, new roadblocks are likely to appear—so you must always look for ways to make things easier for the new adopters. Continue to use the Personal Touch pattern to learn about the people and the Tailor Made pattern to learn about your organization.

= = = = = = = = = = = =

Implementing the Easier Path pattern builds an environment that is more supportive of the new idea. It can help make the transition process quicker, easier, and potentially even cheaper for everyone, including you.

However, this approach is just one tool for paving a path toward change. By itself, it doesn't usually result in complex change, such as fully sustainable living. The effect of creating an easier path can be short term so, when the novelty wears off, take baby steps by tackling another obstacle that is standing in the way of success.

Gerry wanted his students to do a service project but heard one excuse after another from them. Finally, he decided to address one of the excuses he heard over and over: Many of the students didn't have cars so they didn't have an easy way to get off campus to the site of the project. Gerry posted a "ride list" for students with cars to sign up to drive the ones who didn't. The majority of the students then agreed to go. He was amazed at how that one thing got the service project to happen.

In one change initiative, many staff members complained that they did not have time to attend the brown bag lunches or the town hall meetings. So the evangelist asked managers if she could attend their department meetings and have a small amount of time to report what was going on and address questions. Since people couldn't come to the discussion about the ideas, the discussions came to them.

Soon after the university's new exercise facility was built, it became very crowded around 5:00 in the evening because most of the staff on campus worked until 5:00 or 5:30 and then rushed into the facility. Students were also winding down their day around this time. The facility was so crowded that many stopped going. As a result, management decided to open the facility before work hours. Most students didn't want to be up so early, but it was a convenient time for many of the staff to exercise. Members of the campus Center for Creative Retirement were also given a pass to the facility. However, they didn't want to go because they didn't like the music and found it to be too loud. Management responded by creating "quiet hours" every day when no music was broadcast—and now the retired folks love it.

The folks at amazon.com have made it easy to make purchases. If you're ready to buy an item, you can use the "1-Click button," which allows you to associate a credit, debit, or Amazon Store Card with a shipping address. You can place orders with a single click of a button. As Amazon pointed out, "Licensing Amazon.com's 1-Click patent and trademark will allow us to offer our customers an even easier and faster online buying experience."

Elevator Pitch

I remember when I came back from a software development conference. I was so excited! I couldn't wait to talk to my team and tell them about all the new ideas that were buzzing around in my head. The first person I saw on Monday morning asked, "Hey! How was the conference?" Words started tumbling out and thoughts began competing for air time. I saw myself overwhelming the poor guy but I couldn't stop. Half of what I said didn't make sense and I "ummed" and "erred" a lot. "OK! OK! I guess you had a good time! Maybe we can talk later!" It was a dose of reality for me. I needed a better way to talk about the ideas I wanted to share—and fast!

Have a couple of sentences on hand to introduce others to your new idea.

You are an evangelist or dedicated champion working on your new idea. You are encountering others who ask about your initiative. They are busy and time is limited.

When you have a chance to introduce someone to your idea, you don't want to stumble around for the right words to say.

We face this challenge all the time. Those we want to influence ask, "What's that new idea you've been talking about?" You have a small window of opportunity to get your message across in a way that makes them want to know more. When someone asks, "What do you do?" most of us struggle with a concise reply. We know so much about our complicated lives that we feel the listener needs a lot of background to understand us. Without a prepared short introduction, however, either we overload our listeners or we talk in circles and provide little worthwhile information.

Today, we are accustomed to sound bites. According to a study by sociologist Kiku Adato, in the 1968 presidential election the average time each candidate spoke without interruption on the network news was 42.3 seconds. By the 2000 campaign, that average had shrunk to 7.8 seconds.[23] Those you want to reach are used to professional politicians, ad makers, and entertainers getting to the point in a matter of seconds. You need to do the same.

Journalists understand this reality. Time constraints prompted the inverted pyramid style of most newspaper stories—where the essentials consisting of the basic facts, conclusion, and lead come first, and details follow later. This style appeared in the days of the telegraph when a story took a long time to transmit—the essentials were sent first because they were more important for getting to press immediately. This approach still works well for providing the overwhelming amount of information we face.

When you have a vision for your idea, you need to be able to communicate it clearly and succinctly. In his book *The Heart of Change*, John Kotter provides advice about sharing your vision with others: "What works? . . . Visions that are so clear that they can be articulated in one minute or written up on one page."[24] David Belasco encourages you to think with even more brevity: "If you can't write your idea on the back of my calling card, you don't have a clear idea."[25]

When you don't have a crisp, concise message ready to share, your knowledge and excitement can cause you to rattle on and on. This can give the impression that you don't know what you are doing or what your goal is. You need to understand your message and have the ability to explain it.

Therefore:

Craft a couple of sentences that contain your key message.

Describe simply and clearly what your idea is all about. This summary could contain the following information:

- What is your idea? Be succinct—try to explain it in one sentence.
- What problem does it solve? Make a connection between your idea and the situation it addresses.
- What is your vision for the end state? Briefly explain where the initiative will take the organization.

Keep it simple. Just enough is always the watchword. What Mark Twain wrote in 1880 applies today: "I notice that you use plain, simple language, short words and brief sentences. That is the way to write English—it is the modern way and the best way. Stick to it; don't let fluff and flowers and verbosity creep in." Beware of jargon, buzzwords, and long convoluted sentences. You will be a more effective communicator if your message is presented in a clear and straightforward way. It's a bad sign if you can't condense your message.

Think about starting with a question, such as "Did you know . . . ?" You could use the Imagine That pattern to end your pitch with a question that points to possibilities, such as "Can you imagine . . . ?" Individuals tend to receive statements passively, but when hearing a question, they produce their own reasons for listening.[26]

Highlight the most important information. If the list of things you want to say is too long, no one will remember it, much less have a desire to be part of the change initiative. Ask yourself why you are enthusiastic about your new idea; you'll think of a host of good reasons. Everything you could say may be true, but it might not add up to a clear story.

Practice your elevator pitch out loud until it flows smoothly and conversationally. Don't search for the right words. At the same time, try not to sound too rehearsed. Make sure your personality and enthusiasm come through.

Stay humble and unpretentious. Be careful not to sound too glib or too self-confident. Don't come across as a salesperson just trying to make a sale. You will turn people off.

Once you deliver your elevator pitch, allow time for questions. Don't crowd your listeners by pushing them to agree with you. A short pitch is informative but not necessarily persuasive. End with an invitation for further inquiry.

Your pitch is only the first step. Its purpose is to share information and open the possibilities. To be persuasive, continue the conversation.[27] Be sure to stay in touch to address any issues that might arise as a result of your brief introduction.

Post your elevator pitch on your website and around your office. Most people are likely to need more than one exposure to your pitch before they ask for more information.

Here are two different examples of elevator pitches:

> Our company is getting so large that we are having problems giving our clients the personal attention we once could—we are losing clients who are looking for this type of attention. Therefore, I would like to encourage our company to purchase customer relationship management software. This will allow us to find and attract new clients, nurture and retain them, entice former clients back to our organization, and reduce the costs of our marketing and customer service.

> I keep your company out of the Dilbert comic strip! I'm a management consultant specializing in change. If your company is experiencing rapid growth or change, I can offer experience and wisdom to keep your employees happy and your profits in the black.[28]

Initially, your short speech will be the same for everyone. When someone wants to know more, use the Personal Touch pattern: Continue with a customized message that meets the specific interests and needs of that particular person, such as a manager, administrative assistant, engineer, marketing specialist, or human resources staff member.

Review and update your pitch on a regular basis. You will always talk to new audiences and learn more about your idea. Working on your elevator pitch will help you clarify your evolving vision.

= = = = = = = = = = = =

The Elevator Pitch pattern will help you start a dialogue that will support your cause. You'll increase your credibility with your audience because you'll make it easy for them to understand the core message in your idea. You will get everyone on the same page and begin to think about tailoring meaningful responses to follow-on questions.

However, your short pitch may cause listeners to make snap judgments about the idea. Also, if the person is distracted, he or she won't hear your brief message before it is over. Stay in touch and communicate additional information with persistent PR. Your pitch is just one portion of your complete communication plan.

Betsy was working on a climate change project that required her to talk with natural scientists, social scientists, business people, and the general public. She devised the same elevator pitch to begin her conversation with each person—a summary of the project, the problem she was addressing, and her vision for how her work would contribute to the issue. She quickly learned the questions each type of professional was likely to ask, so, when someone requested more information, she had individualized responses that followed her core elevator pitch.

I was on a panel at a conference recently. To open, we were each asked to give a 30-second definition of the Agile software process. Preston was good—he started with a problem statement about not meeting customer expectations and then presented his concise solution. It was short. It was convincing. It told me that he had thought about it and had his answer at the ready. The rest of us were good, but we stumbled around and lost the audience. Preston grabbed their attention and kept it—for a brief, convincing moment.

Dr. Ron Reece's psychology shingle has been hanging since 1975. He focuses on closely held businesses to help them deal with the unique aspects of relationships, business demands, generational transition, and management issues. Ron's brief elevator speech on his website and the answer he gives when someone inquires about his work is this: "I keep people from destroying businesses and businesses from destroying people."[29]

Emotional Connection

One CIO explains that he was very fortunate early in his career "to learn all anyone really needs to know about meeting clients' expectations." After personal interviews with business, corporate officers, and general management, he reported, "Let me say what those clients were telling me in a single sentence: 'I probably won't remember what you say to me, I may not even remember what you do for me, but I'll never forget how you make me feel.'"[30]

Connecting with the feelings of your audience is usually more effective in persuading them than just presenting facts.

You are an evangelist or dedicated champion who is working with a new idea. You are getting ready to, or have already tried to, talk with people about the initiative.

As you share information about your new idea, you might believe that logical argument is enough to persuade people.

You may be getting better at communicating the facts. You may have a snazzy PowerPoint presentation with lists of bullet points. You may have prepared your elevator pitch and created some persistent PR. These are good strategies at the beginning and throughout the change initiative. After all, your audience must know about an idea before they can be influenced to accept it. But facts are not always persuasive.

You may believe that your listeners will be persuaded to support your idea based on a well-organized collection of data. Yet, individuals interpret information to support their own deep-rooted belief systems and, if a fact doesn't fit that system, they often challenge, dismiss, or ignore it. As a result, they are likely to respond with "She isn't making any sense" or "Interesting, but I don't really care." They are likely to feel uneasy about how the change initiative will affect them and could even become angry if they don't see any evidence that you care about their feelings or are addressing their concerns.

Persuading people requires more than a good logical argument. We are not exclusively rational beings, even those people with great logic skill. We are also emotional beings. One of the areas of our brain that is crucial for decision making is also involved in processing emotion—the prefrontal cortex, where information and emotions converge to help us make choices. Therefore, our brains do not simply do the logical type of processing a computer does. We can evaluate a list of facts and calculate the numbers, but eventually the decision must feel right to us.

Studies have shown that damage to the prefrontal cortex of the brain leads to poor decision-making skills. Individuals who experience such injuries retain their cognitive abilities, but the damage disconnects them from their emotions and causes them not to care about their decisions and actions.[31] One such example is Phineas Gage, who famously survived an iron rod blasted through his eye. Owing to the damage to his prefrontal cortex, however, Gage was no longer able to act decisively or responsibly. Another study of patients with prefrontal cortex lesions revealed that despite their normal cognitive abilities, they showed insensitivity to the consequences of their decisions.[32]

This emotional component in decision making makes life more efficient. We can't evaluate every option; therefore, our feelings allow us to make a decision and move on. When evidence is complex, large, or incomplete, these feelings may be the only way a decision can be made, for better or for worse.[33]

Despite the evidence, some may disagree with you on the role of their emotions; they may think they are more like Mr. Spock and can rationally explain their decision-making process. Research shows that we're not usually correct about why we make choices: We often point out completely rational reasons and ignore what we were feeling when we made the decision.[34] Therefore, when we react or make decisions because of what we are feeling, we later tend to rationalize those actions with logic and reason.[35]

Research reported in *The Heart and Soul of Change*[36] has found that the chemistry in emotionally charged relationships is a key factor in inspiring hope and a desire to change. If you understand what others are feeling, you can inspire them to look more closely at the possibilities in your new idea.

Persuasion tactics must consider what people are logically thinking as well as what they are feeling. Leaders of change often forget the latter point. Harvard Business School professor John Kotter explains, "Changing organizations depends overwhelmingly on changing the emotions of the individual members . . . Thinking and feeling are essential . . . but the heart of change is in the emotions."[37]

Therefore:

Create a connection with individuals on an emotional level by listening and addressing how they are feeling about the new idea.

Before you try to persuade individuals, build relationships that help you to identify their interests and address their underlying concerns. Be willing to listen more and talk less to help you understand them. Be patient—we're not always aware of our own emotional ties to an issue. It takes time to get to a deeper level of what others are feeling.

Concentrate on what individuals passionately care about. Build the initiative around a cause that will generate excitement. Focus on the "why" rather than the "what." Look for common concerns in the organization and the ways in which you agree. Inspire everyone by sharing your dreams rather than your specific plans. As you listen carefully to others' dreams, build a group identity with supporters who will be motivated by a common goal. Express your sincere belief in each person's value and unique ability to contribute to the initiative.

Customize your interactions with use of the Personal Touch pattern so you are no longer just a talking head with a good idea. Tell your story of how and why you became convinced of the importance of any problems you have identified or any visions you are proposing. Share your own experiences and be honest about your shortcomings. Remain humble when you express a sincere enthusiasm for the big possibilities in your little ideas.

Think about how you can engage the senses of your listeners. Make the facts more memorable by including images and stories with names, places, and events that are meaningful and credible to them.[38] Ask others to visualize a better outcome by utilizing the Imagine That pattern.

Include a wake-up call that will stir emotions. But don't dwell on the negative—rather, accentuate the positive by getting people intrigued by potential solutions. Build an environment in which people will have a desire to act because you have helped them believe the problem can be solved.

If you become aware of any strong negative emotions, investigate the reason. It may be that while you are talking about what will be gained from the new idea, listeners are focused on what they will lose as a result of the change. Give them a shoulder to cry on. You can address negative attitudes by using the Fear Less pattern, but be patient: Feelings such as fear, anger, or resentment often prevent people from being willing listeners. You may need to delay conversations until the initially intense emotions have diminished. This waiting period may be especially important for the early majority who want to know how others feel about the idea before they will accept it.

Most importantly, know where the boundaries are and be careful not to cross them. Keep the discussions focused only on feelings surrounding the new idea and the change initiative rather than on unrelated personal matters or topics.

= = = = = = = = = =

The Emotional Connection pattern will help create a relationship that will help you become more persuasive. You will bring the participants more deeply into the initiative and make it possible to have more enlightening discussions about the changes you are proposing and how you can work together to make your idea even better.

However, this pattern is difficult to put into practice. Presenting facts gives you a solid foundation and safety, and it is certainly easier and more comfortable than digging deeply into feelings. If you realize you are going to have to struggle with this issue, ask for help. Find other evangelists and bridge builders to make the emotional connection with people while you work on ways to prepare and present various kinds of information. Using this pattern does not mean that you abandon logical argument. Keep that bullet list handy, because many people will want to see it.

During Startup Weekend in Asheville, North Carolina, teams of budding entrepreneurs had 54 hours to build a business idea and pitch it to a team of judges. Following the pitches and the selection of the winner, all mentors and judges were asked to offer advice to the participants. One of the judges talked about how the large amount of market survey data presented by most of the teams did not convince him. Another said, "If you didn't sell me on an emotional level early in your presentation, I shut down . . . Give me an emotional connection to your idea. I will make the decision here" (as he pointed to his heart).

Kathy was trying to persuade Melissa to take on a role in a research project a student was leading. She gave Melissa all the information about the project but Melissa was still hesitant. It wasn't until Kathy told the heart-warming story of seeing the student at the local mall, getting excited about a new suit she was buying for her project presentation, that Melissa finally smiled and agreed to participate.

Before he became a U.S. senator, Frank Lautenberg was a corporate CEO. His firm was a pioneer of the computer age, and, like most business people, especially those in technical fields, Frank thrived on facts. As a senator, he became a champion of the environment, mastering the technicalities of environmental legislation. When it came time to run for reelection, Lautenberg had a hard time translating his many environmental accomplishments into language his constituents could understand. He would stand in a town hall meeting and wonder why his audience would fall asleep. Amy Knox was a little girl who lived in Mt. Holly, New Jersey. Amy was battling cancer, a disease she believed she had contracted because she lived near a toxic site. Amy was a tough, brave kid. She had started a community group called PUKE (People United for a Klean Environment) and had written to her senator asking for support. Lautenberg had offered help and encouragement, doing everything a good senator should do. As a result of this experience, Lautenberg removed the jargon from his speeches and replaced it with stories of the little girl's courage. "When I'm on the floor of the Senate," he would say, "and the big polluters and their pin-striped lobbyists are trying to use our state as their dumping ground, I think of Amy Knox." This connection allowed Lautenberg to communicate his message in a way that inspired listeners.

Melinda is a dean in the School of Arts and Sciences. She schedules 10-minute meetings with every individual in her school on a regular basis, to ask where each person sees himself or herself in the university. Why does she do this? "Because," she says, "I see the employees as people first."

Scattering smashed watermelons around the Stanford soccer field before the players arrived was just the first action that students in a class experiment took to sway the athletes to wear bike helmets when cycling around campus. The group also plastered posters around the field of apparently unconscious, helmetless students lying on the ground with smashed watermelons by their heads. Placing smashed melons next to unprotected heads of soccer players provided a vivid, visceral comparison. Emotions are contagious, especially when they are conveyed in face-to-face exchanges. The soccer players found smaller versions of the posters when they returned to their bikes. The images were coated in plastic and attached to their handlebars. The students crafted a slogan for their campaign, "Love Your Lobes" with a tag line, "Love your life and serve your team by taking care of your brain." Appeal first to emotion, then to reason: The students also offered safety statistics that supported their campaign. Galvanized by the images, the players were convinced to sign a pledge to wear their helmets and post pictures of themselves and teammates wearing helmets on the Watermelon Offensive's Facebook page.[39]

Evolving Vision

Susan made a New Year's resolution to run a marathon in June. She kept up with her tedious workout schedule for about a month, but then got busy with other things. So she started over and realized that if she did two short workouts during the week she could keep going and make progress. After several weeks, she changed her goal to a half-marathon—she realized this would be achievable. In June, as friends cheered her on, she crossed the finish line.

While taking baby steps through a change process, periodically set aside time for reflection to reevaluate your vision.

You are an evangelist or dedicated champion leading a change initiative. You and your team have defined a shared vision.

A lofty vision can seem attainable in the beginning, but can become unrealistic when the world changes during the process.

Whether as a leader of change in an organization or when working on a personal challenge, we often set goals that are too unrealistic. We start with high hopes and when we don't make sufficient progress, we believe success is impossible. Our impatience and frustration tempt us to just give up.

When the vision is overwhelming, it's easy to fall into a trap of "learned helplessness."[40] We can become paralyzed when we start focusing on all of the pieces at once, emphasizing the things that will stand in the way and why our plans won't work.

You are busy. Even if you have passion, all the tasks you and others need to do can make you wonder when, how, and even if you can fit in everything. Perhaps you need a reality check.

Some of the things you thought were important may appear less so over time, while other elements of the original plan become even more vital. At the same time, some elements that weren't considered initially should become part of the strategy as you move forward. The goal changes as you learn and test the idea against reality.

Therefore:

Use an iterative approach to learn about and refine your vision.

Rather than putting together a detailed plan to reach a long-term goal, move slowly with baby steps—that is, define one or more smaller, short-term milestones with end dates and measurable results. After you reach a milestone, take time for reflection to see what you and your team have learned about the long-term vision. Is it still realistic? If not, redefine it. Ask for help and involve everyone.

Sustain momentum and aim for progress, not perfection. It doesn't matter how small the steps are as long as you are learning and reevaluating the vision along the way.

Be happy with small successes. Any accomplishment during each step can be an acceptable solution in itself. Use the progress as a way to spur communication. Publicize the results with persistent PR. Make sure everyone, especially management, sees the link between any short-term goal accomplished today and the shared vision the organization hopes to achieve in the future.

= = = = = = = = = = = =

Using the Evolving Vision pattern creates an opportunity for the team to evaluate its shared vision during the long journey of leading change. Rather than being caught up in striving for what may be an impossible dream, you and others in your organization will be happier achieving measurable progress and being open to making appropriate adjustments as you learn how the goal will fit in your organization. Evaluating a vision helps you and your team determine whether to narrow your efforts or possibly add new opportunities to increase effectiveness and impact.

However, some impatient people may get nervous when you don't have all the milestones clearly defined at the beginning or when the vision must change.

Consider involving these individuals as champion skeptics during milestone planning meetings. If you or members of your team become discouraged when it is necessary to restructure the vision, find a shoulder to cry on.

Proctor & Gamble initially positioned Febreze as a "removing odor" brand by packaging it to look like other household cleaners and placing it in the laundry aisle next to such powerhouses as Tide and Downy. The company then introduced Air Effects, moving Febreze toward a "clean the air" brand. In early 2006, P&G introduced Febreze Noticeables, a plug-in air freshener that alternates between two scents. P&G has obviously moved squarely into the air freshening market. It has done so in a series of stages, learning at each step and changing the big goal for products based on feedback from the market.

Lily Yeh tells us in The Village of Arts and Humanities: *"For the first project I wanted to do an art park on abandoned land in the city. Children on the street came to help me, and then adults, usually without jobs or without highly developed skills. Suddenly I was looking at many social issues without even addressing them. I was converting an abandoned lot into a garden. I was dealing with abandonment of land in the city. And then children came in from wandering on the street. I was doing a children's program without intending to. Then adults came in and I was looking at joblessness, job training, and food."[41] Lily's original vision was an art project but, over time, she realized the vision needed to include much more.*

Those of us who are older than 60 and still semi-serious about bike riding have noticed that the bike riders who stayed with the activity realized that they weren't going to be the greatest and fastest any longer. They did their best and rode as well as they could and were happy with that. I think this is the secret to growing older. It's realizing your limitations while not simply staying home and giving up, but rather getting out there with a renewed vision that changes to reflect your capabilities and limitations as you age.

Future Commitment

Max is often asked to review journal articles. He chuckles when he explains that he will agree to a request if the due date is a month or two away, even though he tends to write the review a day or two before the deadline.

To make it more likely that you will get help in the change initiative, ask others to do something you will need much later and wait for them to commit.

You are an evangelist or dedicated champion. You know you can't carry out the change initiative on your own. You have a to-do list that includes tasks that could be done later, and you know there are people in your organization who could help.

You need help, but people are busy.

When you ask for help, individuals are likely to think about all the things they must do in the upcoming days or even weeks and reply, "I'm sorry, I don't have the time right now." However, research shows that we are bad at estimating what we will do later, so we are more likely to sign up for tasks to be done at a later date. The illusion is that there will be more time in the future. When individuals agree to do a specific task on or by a specific date, they are even more likely to live up to this agreement.[42]

Dan Gilbert, in his book *Stumbling on Happiness*,[43] notes that when we think of distant events, we create a high-level image of what will happen. That is, our brain sees an "object" that looks smooth and lacking in detail, with stressors and costs that appear smaller and insignificant. We often fail to realize that the detail-free event we are imagining now will be the detail-laden event we will ultimately experience.

In contrast, when we think about the near term, we tend to be concrete and make plans with more detail. This leads us to consider more carefully whether we can do what needs to be done. When we make future plans, we tend to think in higher level, more abstract terms—we pay more attention to whether taking action will result in good things for us. Because of this bias to think about an event down the road more in terms of why we want to do it and less in terms of how it will get done, we tend to embrace goals and plans with potentially rich rewards that turn out to be logistical nightmares. For near-term events, we tend to make the opposite mistake: We turn down something fun or rewarding because it seems like too much of a hassle.[44]

Therefore:

Approach individuals with an item that isn't urgent so they can put it on their to-do list on a future date.

Take the time to plan ahead. Work with your team to create a concrete action plan for the list of things the change initiative will need in the upcoming months. Next to each item, write the name of a possible go-to person. Approach the person with a specific task and the time period in the future in which that task must be completed. If possible, the two of you may even want to negotiate the specific due date.

Wait for your targets to say "yes," but don't worry about trying to get them to agree right away. Even those who initially react negatively to helping may eventually come around. Use patience and draw them in little by little—stay in touch with information that will encourage them to become more interested in the change initiative.

Once the individual agrees, solidify the commitment by recording the date and sending it in writing or by email. Send gentle reminders periodically along the way. Even though these reminders can help people stick with a promise, they can also be annoying—so include an exciting update of what is happening and where those individuals will fit in.

= = = = = = = = = = = = =

The Future Commitment pattern provides a solution for the natural response you often get from busy people. Suggesting a later date is likely to be the hook that will draw them in. Even if it's a small commitment, it can inspire the person to do bigger things.

However, this approach doesn't work all the time. Those who over-commit in the present are also likely to over-commit in the future. Just because you have agreement from individuals, it doesn't guarantee that they will follow through. Send gentle reminders but have a backup plan in case they can't deliver on their promises. Always be on the lookout for new team members—involve everyone.

Amanda was leading a two-year project at a university. Recognizing she would need to depend on academics who always have many balls in the air at any time, she periodically took the time to look ahead and make a list of things that would be needed later as well as to identify the go-to person for each task. She approached each person to ask for help as far as possible ahead of time, usually during a semester break when academics tend to feel less overwhelmed (use of The Right Time *pattern). During the lead time before each person's expertise was needed, she would gently remind the individual of what he or she had agreed to do. This was a great way to involve these busy people.*

Janice tries to encourage women to host "parties" for her jewelry business. She discovered that most women replied with stories of their busy lives to explain why they couldn't find the time to prepare and host a party. When Janice changed her approach and suggested they host a party several months down the road, the women were much more likely to agree.

When an upcoming task surfaces during a team meeting, Christina makes sure the deadline is set before everyone leaves the meeting (use of the Next Steps *pattern).*

She does this by asking the team members to consider the parameters and then setting the date that works for them. She has observed that this approach allows the team members to "own" the date and makes it more likely the task will be completed on time.

This website claims to offer the smartest way to set and achieve your goals: http://www.stickk.com/. Individuals can sign up to commit (commitment contracts) to a personal change goal by a certain date. By signing and agreeing to a specific date, they have made a commitment to the goal.

Go-To Person

"You know," said the newly appointed CEO of a large company, "I have more than 1000 people in my head office organization; 900 can tell me something's gone wrong, 90 can tell me what's gone wrong, 9 can tell me why it went wrong, and 1 can actually fix it!"[45]

Identify key people who can help with critical issues in your change initiative.

You are an evangelist or dedicated champion who is willing to ask for help. There are people in your organization who have the expertise you need.

Once you've identified areas where you lack expertise, how do you start asking for help?

There are many things to do during a change initiative. Your list will keep growing. Given that you are the leader, you may believe you are the best person to do everything. Even if you have this passion, you probably don't have the time, skills, resources, or talent to tackle all of the action items by yourself. Consequently, you need supporters who can be trusted to provide a particular service or deal with a particular problem.

Craig Freshley, in *Good Group Decisions*, points out that groups are terrific at generating ideas, but it is individual leadership that brings the ideas to reality. Things tend to get dropped if no one is directly responsible for them. Identifying someone to lead a task gives the person a sense of responsibility and makes it more likely that the task will get done.[46]

Therefore:

Make a concrete action plan with a list of the things you need to do for the next milestone. Next to each item, write the names of those individuals with the specific expertise or resources to help you accomplish the task.

Those persons whom you identify should ideally have the necessary skill and knowledge; should have the authority, influence, and/or ability to cut through red tape; or should have access to the connections that can open doors to tackle the job. They should understand the task you are bringing to them and be willing to make the solution happen.

Ask for help in finding resources. Connectors are likely to know who you may need. If the person you wish to approach for help doesn't know you, solicit the assistance of a bridge builder. Be mindful of any well-established processes, so you don't ruffle any feathers.

Make sure each go-to person has the time and motivation to help. Cultivate these individuals' interest in the project and the task you are asking of them. Have your general elevator pitch ready, but use the Personal Touch pattern to address their questions and concerns. Try to establish an emotional connection that will draw them in and get them excited about the task.

Give each go-to person a well-defined, achievable task. Respect those individuals' schedules by providing as much lead time as possible. If you don't need their help immediately, request a future commitment. Try to schedule the request at the right time for each person. This will make it more likely that they will dedicate their energy to the cause.

Publicize the upcoming needs in the change initiative—let everyone know you are looking for volunteers and give those who are interested a chance to contribute. Involve everyone. When individuals express an interest in helping, add their names to the growing list of go-to people you are likely to need someday.

If you can't find the perfect fit for a task, consider cultivating new talent—ask someone who has expressed an interest or a person you sense would like to get involved and is willing to try. Someone with a willingness to work hard may produce better results than a person who appears to have the expertise but doesn't necessarily have the time or desire to work hard at it. A new talent might do a better job with a little guidance.

Think about those people who may not necessarily carry out a task, but whose support—or lack of it—can have an effect on whether the task gets done in a timely manner. Make sure your go-to list includes the "crucial conversations" you need to have.

Show sincere appreciation on a regular basis to help the go-to people feel good about what they are doing and what they have accomplished for the change initiative. Allow them to serve as examples to others by publicizing the small successes they have made possible through their assistance.

= = = = = = = = = =

The Go-To Person pattern can help expedite important tasks. Rather than becoming overwhelmed by all the work ahead, you identify key people who will help you move forward. Having others involved will also provide more momentum for the effort.

However, be careful about relying on just a few individuals. They can burn out and you might lose them. Keep a backup plan with an evolving list of potential go-to people. Be on the lookout for others who might be interested.

Sally was planning a "big jolt" event for the change initiative. She was amazed at the number of tasks that needed to be accomplished, so she started making a list of those who could help. She knew it would be a challenge to secure an appropriate location and develop a budget for food, but if anyone could figure it out, the administrative assistant, Jennifer, could. After some investigation, Sally decided to ask Adam to lead the technical support effort and enlist William and Lisa to spread the word among the key people on their teams. She also thought of Harry's interesting artwork as a potential gift for the speaker. Sally also knew that her lack of artistic skills would require her to find someone to help with the promotional materials. Then, she set off to talk with each of the go-to people on her list.

"Yes, Norm is the one I should ask," thought Karla, as she realized that she would need someone with user interface design skills to help with her new project. At the same, she had noticed that Steven had been learning a lot about user interface design and had been pairing with Norm to improve his skills: "I'll ask both of them for help, and it will give Steven a chance to work on new stuff." Months later, Karla was talking to a colleague who said how surprised he was to see that Norm had been helpful on the new project, but it was Steven who had worked overtime and done extra research to make the user interface design such a huge success. It wasn't what Karla expected, and she was glad she had invited Steven as an afterthought, because he was the one who had saved the day.

Tom knew that his great idea for the next software release would help the team work more efficiently, but he also knew that his testing skills were not impressive. He started thinking about who might help him with his plans. He thought about a couple of experienced testers who might be willing to support him, but then he realized that many testers on other teams might want to be involved with something innovative. He sent an email to the testing group and was happy when some new names appeared in his inbox. It occurred to him that he might have found more enthusiastic team members by asking for volunteers rather than just involving the "usual suspects," who were always too busy.

Imagine That

The ABC News Special titled "Earth 2100," depicted an imaginary, but possible, scenario. ABC introduced it as follows: "To change the future, first you have to imagine it."

To kick-start the change initiative, engage others in an exercise to imagine future possibilities.

You are an evangelist or dedicated champion who is talking about a new idea.

It can be difficult for those you are trying to convince to see how a new idea will fit into the work they will be doing.

Most of us find it easier to remember the problems of the past and concentrate on the challenges we face in the present. This can inhibit our ability to understand how a new idea can impact our future. But you want others to believe that a new beginning, a better world, is possible and could be just around the corner. You want them to *understand* the past, but *focus* on the future.

You don't always have the resources to do a trial run and you rarely, if ever, have the ability to perfectly simulate what a new idea will provide. Even so, a visualization, a mental rehearsal, is always possible.

Therefore:

Ask people to imagine a possible outcome with the new idea. Begin with "What if . . . ?"

Encourage them to think out loud and fill their mental imagery with many different kinds of sensory details. How will things look when the new idea is a reality? Which kinds of things will we hear? What will it allow us to do?

Tell the story. You could start by talking about the difficulties in the present (use the Wake-up Call pattern). Help your audience feel the frustration and then imagine how events could unfold by describing potential ways a new idea could address the current problem(s). Keep it simple, avoiding details that are not likely to happen. If there were successful change initiatives in the past that relate to what you are proposing now, include these examples as a reminder that success is possible. Be sure that the story is tailored to what the organization or the individuals can and cannot do.

Move past a logical collection of facts and features toward an emotional connection. Prompt your listeners with "Imagine if we could . . . " and then ask them to consider how they feel as they think about this scenario becoming a reality. Do they feel relief? Satisfaction? Excitement? Confidence?

Involve the participants in uncovering the possibilities for moving forward. Let their imaginations run wild as they talk about their ideal situations. Once all the ideas have been expressed, help them dial back to realistic options and an outline for a concrete action plan.

You may also want to encourage people to imagine the risks of *not* addressing the problems in the organization. Include realistic scenarios with possibilities of what could happen if the change does *not* occur. Encourage them to think about and compare the costs of making a change versus the costs of not making it.

Ask for help if you are not a good storyteller or are not skilled at leading discussions. Also, if you don't have a connection with the listeners, you could be dismissed as a salesperson. In such a case, look for a bridge builder to help you plan and deliver the sessions.

Keep in mind that this pattern won't work for everyone, especially those who are not comfortable with visualizing the future in this way. This is only one persuasion strategy that should be combined with concrete data.

= = = = = = = = = =

Using the Imagine That pattern enables you to examine how a new idea might work in the future. It prompts listeners to leave behind old ways of thinking and imagine how new possibilities might be relevant to their daily existence. By focusing on the future, individuals may be more motivated to let go of the past.

However, it can be easy to get carried away. Imagining can be fun and, as a result, you may tell a story about an unrealistic future. This will turn off your listeners, rather than intrigue them, and it will create problems for you later if the imagined future does not match the reality. So, in addition to uncovering the positive outcomes of the change initiative, ask your listeners, "What else? Which problems might we face? Which other scenarios could happen?" Don't dwell on the limitations at this point, but do include a discussion of the side effects that could surface, and think about what everyone might be able to do about them.

To get employees interested in using new project management and social networking software, the CIO's presentation included a variety of specific scenarios describing when, where, and how this software could be used in existing and future projects. The attendees nodded and responded with potential scenarios of their own: "Oh yes," they said, "and I can also see how this software can be used here, too."

A church was facing a new, uncertain future after the unexpected loss of the minister. The deacon held a town hall meeting in which he requested that all attendees choose to participate in one of three groups that represented their personal feelings: anger, confusion, or hope. The "hope" group was asked to spend time imagining a new, better, and exciting future for the church. When this group reported the outcome of their exercise, smiles and nods appeared among the people in the other two groups.

Years ago, when cable TV was soon to become available in the Tempe, Arizona area, one group of prospective customers was presented with the upcoming features while the other group was asked to imagine how the new service would be of value to them. The message for the second group included the word "you" throughout; in addition, rather than talking about abstract benefits, it focused on personal benefits and asked readers to visualize how they would feel about the new service. The result: 10% of those in the first group who received only the informational message subscribed, while 47% of those in the other group who were asked to imagine the possibilities subscribed.

Gary, a personal coach, often does an imagery exercise with his clients who are depressed. He asks the person to close her eyes and describe herself—what color is she wearing, how does her facial expression (e.g., eyes, mouth) look, how does her stature appear, how are her friends reacting to her, what does she do every day, and so on. Then, he asks this person to imagine herself in a year, prompting her with the same questions about facial expression, stature, lifestyle, and so on. Afterward, Gary and his client have a discussion about which of the two images is preferable and how the person can create a concrete action plan to begin moving toward the more desirable image.

Know Yourself

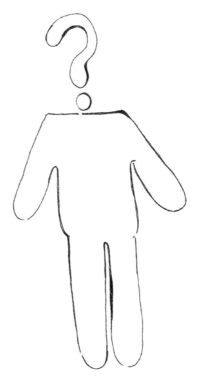

Bob is an innovator who easily gets excited about new opportunities. When a new project comes on board, others in the organization know about Bob's eagerness and often solicit his help. All too often, Bob has found himself agreeing to things that would take a lot of his time without first evaluating if he had the time or the long-term interest to carry it to completion. Eventually, his overbooked schedule began to create frustration both for him and for the people who counted on him. Bob has learned that when he is offered a new opportunity, he needs to curb his enthusiasm and logically evaluate his available time and potential for long-term commitment before accepting it.

Before you begin, and throughout the long journey required to lead a change initiative, consider whether you still have a real and abiding passion and the talents and abilities to make it happen.

◆◆◆

You would like to be an evangelist. You are enthusiastic about an idea that you believe is worth pursuing.

How do you know if you should take on the role of an evangelist?

You know that you believe in your idea now, but do you have the long-term interest to make it happen? Can your passion be sustained throughout the difficult process of change? Opportunities and problems are all around. It can seem that even the best intentions, the hardest work, and the greatest abilities are no match for the challenges we face. Do you have the fortitude to get through the challenges in leading a change?

Eknath Easwaran, in *Conquest of Mind*,[47] says, "In Sanskrit we have a word which means 'heroes at the beginning': people who take up a job with a fanfare of trumpets but soon find that their enthusiasm has tiptoed down the back stair. Those who go far . . . are the ones who keep on plugging. They may not be very spectacular; they may never hear a trumpet. But they keep on trying day in and day out, giving their best in every situation and relationship, never giving up. Such people are bound to reach their goal." Are you the type of person who can get past being merely a hero in the beginning?

We all have limited resources. Even when we recognize that a change effort will take a great amount of time and energy, it will likely take more internal resources than we realize. Will your priorities allow you to have all the energy, time, talent, and patience you will need?

When we don't take the time to develop a realistic understanding of ourselves, we're open to being pulled in different directions. We sign on for too much, believe we can do it all, and set ourselves up for potential failure.

Therefore:

Set aside time for reflection to evaluate and understand your own abilities, limitations, and personal resources. Identify your values, principles, likes, dislikes, strengths, and weaknesses. Examine the beliefs and qualities that define who you are and what you will be able to do if you choose to lead this initiative.

A good way to start your reflection is with a list of questions. For example, see those discussed in the books *What Color Is Your Parachute?*[48] or *The*

First 90 Days.[49] These types of questions will help evaluate your strengths, weaknesses, preferences, priorities, habits, and past experiences. For instance:

- What are your real interests?
- What would you do if you had lots of money and could do pretty much anything you wanted?
- What are the key values in your life?

Have a dialogue with yourself. Talk out loud—even better, walk around! Take different roles and perspectives. Most of us use only one strategy—thinking silently. In fact, numerous studies have shown that overreliance on this approach leads to a negative, self-defeating pattern of thought that makes matters worse, especially when we are depressed or in a bad mood.[50] Tell your story. Begin with: "I'm the kind of person who <describe your strengths and weaknesses>." Strive for a balance between ego and humility.

Try writing with pen and paper—it can produce surprising results. Psychologist James Pennebaker, author of *Opening up*,[51] has shown the powerful insights that can be uncovered by journaling. Create a mind map or concept map of your plans; you can use small cards to help you see what is most important to you.

Have conversations with trusted others. Cognitive psychologists tell us that it's difficult to understand our own motivations.[52] Scientists also say we are hardwired to be optimistic about our own abilities.[53] Talk with a friend or colleague who has known you for a long time and has seen your ups and downs; that person will provide a more accurate assessment than the colleagues who believe you can "do anything."

Set priorities. Even when you have a true and abiding passion and the ability to make your new idea happen, there are often forces in the environment that can push you in another direction. Look for the low-hanging fruit to maximize your limited resources.

Uncover areas where you will need to ask for help. Knowing yourself means being able to assess your capabilities—your strengths and your weaknesses. While it may be tempting to stretch beyond your limits, target the roles you can expect to play well and identify areas in which a go-to person can improve your effectiveness.

If you decide to move forward, periodically ask yourself if you still have the passion for your cause. Evangelist isn't a job title—it's a way of life. Are you willing to continue learning about yourself, about your initiative, and about your organization? Your effectiveness depends not only on you, but also on the environment, and both are always changing. The learning process never ends.

= = = = = = = = = = = =

The Know Yourself pattern will help you develop a better understanding of who you are—your talents, abilities, and preferences, as well as the settings in the past when you have taken on too much. You'll have a clearer understanding of your limits and know when to ask for help. You'll be better equipped to make a decision about whether you should take on the change initiative and whether your passion for the new idea is likely to last through the long-term commitment necessary to see that initiative through to the end. It's important to know yourself not only so you can be true to your own values, goals, and needs, but also so you see others more clearly. Until we reach a better understanding of our own motives, we will waste a lot of energy projecting our feelings on those around us.[54]

However, if you identify essential skills you don't have, this doesn't mean you should give up. Everyone has a unique contribution to make in any setting. If you aren't a perfect match for the requirements you identify, that might mean you will have to work harder and look for other evangelists to help you. Your personal challenges can give you the valuable opportunity to show what you can do. If you have a tolerance for risk and uncertainty and a spirit of adventure, this will help, but a willingness to work hard and learn along the way can often move mountains.

Anna was asked to lead a new initiative in her organization. She believed in the benefits of the change, so her initial reaction was to accept the opportunity to be the project manager. Rather than immediately responding with a "yes," however, she evaluated whether she had an interest in developing the negotiation and report-writing skills that would be required to lead this project. Anna didn't mind moving out of her comfort zone—she had done it many times before—but she had learned through past experiences that when she didn't have a sincere interest in a project, it would not get her best effort. During her time for reflection, Anna recognized she wasn't as strong as other people believed she was in the specific skills needed for the job, and she didn't have a strong motivation to learn them. Ultimately, she turned down the position. As she watched the initiative progress under the leadership of another manager, she knew she had made the right decision.

At the beginning of President Bill Clinton's first term, he spent his time investigating anything and everything. His physical and intellectual energies were nearly limitless. His resources were, too. For example, when you're president, if you want to know everything there is to know about the wool and mohair subsidy, the Assistant Deputy Administrator for Wool and the Vice-Under-Secretary for Mohair will be in the Oval Office in 5 minutes. At the same time, Clinton was trying to work on a few big things— his economic plan, his healthcare plan, and his crime plan. But the endless work was exhausting him. Finally, he realized that he needed to understand the limits on his time and energy. He stopped, reassessed, streamlined, and began setting priorities. That left him with time to think, read, and focus on the things he cared about. One of the keys to Clinton's comeback was likely his ability to maintain a strategic focus rather than a tactical focus.[55]

Zarah and Fred were trying to start a day care center for the children of the employees in their organization. They begged Dan to help because they knew he was a hard-working individual. Dan agreed only because he was a friend of Zarah and Fred; he didn't want to let the couple down. However, as the months went by, Dan became less and less interested in the project and often found an excuse for not pulling his weight. After a heart-to-heart talk with his friends, Dan finally admitted to them (and to himself) that he didn't have the essential passion for the day care center and dropped out of the project.

An extract from an interview between Jane Goodall and Harvard Business Review (HBR) shows how Goodall found her way by knowing herself:

> **HBR:** You've often taken a pragmatic, incremental approach to changing the world.
> **Goodall:** Part of me says, "Gosh, I'd love to join the most violent and destructive groups out there who want to go and raid labs and release animals and do all sorts of dreadful things," but it wouldn't help.
> **HBR:** How do you find the right balance between your ethics and what's possible in the short term?
> **Goodall:** With difficulty. If I'm perceived as a tree hugger, I won't be able to talk to the people who can make the decisions. But then I get criticized from both sides. So I have to be tough enough. And "to thine own self be true."[56]

Low-Hanging Fruit

With little or no budget, you can take simple steps that go a long way in saving energy and reducing costs. Most utility companies recommend setting thermostats to 78 degrees Fahrenheit or higher in summer and 68 degrees Fahrenheit or lower in winter. Each degree below these recommendations in summer, or above them in winter, represents about a 4% increase in the electric portion of your utility bill. Fans are a low-cost option in the summer—they can make you feel about 6 degrees cooler and often use less energy than a 100-watt bulb. In commercial environments, turning off lights that do not contribute to the workspace and are not used at the end of the day can reduce operating costs by saving energy and reducing the number of lamp replacements. These are easy tasks with significant outcomes.

To show progress in the change initiative, complete a quick and easy, low-risk task with wide impact and then publicize the results.

You're an evangelist or dedicated champion. You know there are possibilities for easy wins.

Given all the tasks you have to accomplish in your change initiative, how do you decide which one to tackle when you feel pressure to make progress?

Your change initiative is a series of baby steps. Even when your time and energy are limited, you still need to show you are moving toward your goal. You may have managers or executives invested in the initiative who are monitoring your progress and expect results. You may need to choose between tasks that are "almost" done, or you may need to create a report that shows progress in a large ongoing project.

John Kotter has been studying organizational change for two decades and stresses that change leaders must provide enough visible, unambiguous, short-term wins in mission-critical areas to persuade skeptics and marginalize cynics. "These are concrete successes," Kotter says, "ones that an objective group of people would agree are clear evidence of progress." Short-term wins allow a better chance of completing a change effort if they are visible to many, the terms are unambiguous, and the victory is closely related to the change effort.[57]

The focus on small things with large impact that avoids burdening others in the organization is an example of what Karl Weick calls a "small wins" strategy. In Weick's classic 1984 article,[58] he says that we often respond to big problems by doing nothing because meaningful progress seems impossible. Conversely, approaching even daunting problems with a plan for a small intermediate success encourages us to take action.

Therefore:

As you prepare to move forward, occasionally look for a quick and easy win that will have visible impact.

Find a small piece with minimal risk, and just do it. To move closer to a tipping point, these wins should be necessary actions that you need to perform to accomplish bigger things.

Ask for help from anyone who may be able to identify easy wins. Involve everyone. For example, a guru on your side may know of "low-hanging fruit" opportunities and innovators might help with bursts of activity that have short deadlines.

After you achieve a small success, advertise your progress as part of your persistent PR. Schedule a hometown story. Stay in touch with your supporters—never assume that news of your progress is known across the organization.

When you feel "stuck," look for low-hanging fruit to help you keep sustained momentum. You can always do something. Even when you don't think a small task will matter much, you never know what its unintended consequences might be. Doing one small thing can have a ripple effect across the organization.

= = = = = = = = = = = =

The Low-Hanging Fruit pattern can provide evidence that can be convincing for members of the early majority and others who need to see success before they are willing to try the new idea. The results can build momentum, calm the critics, and boost morale because employees can see the successes of the change in small doses. This allows them to envision the overall success of the goal in the future. When you see what works, you and other evangelists will learn more about the new idea and about your organization. This will give you valuable information that is tailor made for the organization.

However, often you need to tackle the big, complicated issues and be willing to trudge along with no easy wins. Make sure the change initiative includes a healthy balance of low-hanging fruit and more significant progress. Take time for reflection to determine what you can do after you have exhausted the easy wins. Spawn more evangelists across the organization so you can work together to accomplish bigger things.

Renae was assigned to lead a large project in her organization, one in which there was little history and experience to draw from. There didn't even seem to be the kind of talent she needed to build a team. But Renae needed to do something—she wanted to show the organization that she was willing and able to get started. Her small, initial group drafted a timeline with a rough draft for the project, posted it on the organization's internal website, and asked for feedback. It was an easy-to-complete task that sparked good discussions for getting the project off the ground.

Mark was a mentor, struggling to work with one resistant team in a large organization. He finally suggested that instead of tackling a full-blown change to a new software development process, the group just start having daily stand-up meetings. The team reluctantly agreed, and the first stand-up meeting was held the next day. The first person to speak said, "I've been working on that nasty database problem and . . ." He was interrupted by someone on the other side of the circle who said, "Hey! I've been working on that database problem! I thought you were working with the libraries!" It was an enlightening moment—and only the first of many during that initial meeting. Mark was amazed at how such a small addition to each day, a short stand-up meeting, would uncover problems that if left unresolved would fester until the end of the project. The team also observed the value in this simple technique. As a result, they became more open to considering the addition of other new techniques in their software development process.

Fran wanted to learn Italian but with two small preschoolers at home, she did not think she had the time or energy to do so. She was really discouraged until she had the idea of putting sticky notes on a few household objects, labeling them with their names in Italian. Every day she did a few more until the house was covered. Over time, the children and her husband also learned a little Italian. Her mother-in-law was so impressed that she volunteered to babysit a couple of evenings each week so Fran could take a beginning Italian course at a local community college. The moral of this story: Even when things seem hopeless, there's always an easy, simple thing you can do to make progress toward your goal.

Saint Goran's hospital has enthusiastic adopters of "Lean management"—an idea that was pioneered by Toyota in the 1950s and has since spread from car manufacturing to services, and from Japan to the rest of the world. The hospital is organized on the twin Lean principles of "flow" and "quality." Doctors and nurses used to keep a professional distance from each other, concentrating solely on their field of medical expertise. Now they work (and sit) together in teams and are responsible for suggesting operational improvements as well. One innovation involved simply buying a roll of yellow tape. Staff used to waste precious time looking for defibrillator machines until a suggestion was made to mark a spot on the floor with yellow tape and ensure that the machines were always kept there. Small and easy things can make a big difference.

Myth Buster

The great enemy of the truth is very often not the lie—deliberate, contrived, and dishonest—but the myth—persistent, persuasive, and unrealistic.

—John F. Kennedy, 1962

Identify misconceptions surrounding the change initiative and address them in a timely and forthright manner.

You are an evangelist or dedicated champion. Despite your best efforts communicating the new idea, rumors are flying around the organization.

If we hear someone express an incorrect assumption about the innovation, we usually address it head-on with the person who is expressing the concern. However, a false impression in one person's mind is usually a sign that this viewpoint is shared by others.

When we learn something new, we struggle to understand it and may hold on to incorrect information along the way. Because we build new knowledge on current understandings, our misconceptions can have a serious impact on the views we are forming.

Often inaccurate information about a new idea is repeated until it achieves a certain mythical status. Betty Sue Flowers, a scenario planning expert and editor of the book *The Power of Myth*, states: "A myth is a view of the nature of reality, so prevalent that it goes unseen. Although myths are conceived by people, they can feel like they are the only reality."[59]

Rumors need to be debunked before they take root and create significant concerns and anxieties during the change initiative.

Therefore:

To get the word out about what the innovation *isn't* as well as what *won't* happen as a result of its introduction into the organization, create a simple list of the myths paired with the realities.

Address current misunderstandings as well as any that may be looming. Each bullet point can include the following information:

> The <innovation> is not . . . because . . .
> The change initiative will not . . . because . . .

You may wish to create a two-column list, with one column holding a short description of the incorrect information and the other column providing the correct information. Whatever design you choose, make sure it displays information clearly. All people are open to suggestions. Calling attention to negative things can validate them, so make sure your list is designed in a way that unmistakably points out the myths are *not* true.

Give just enough explanation. Keep it brief, and include the name of the go-to person or other resources the reader can consult for additional information.

Use constructive language. Don't criticize others for what they believe. Consider developing a catchy slogan or helpful phrase that will gently debunk the myth.

Ask for help from champion skeptics and others to create the list. They are likely to know about the fears and other negative talk surrounding the innovation.

Include this myth-buster message as part of your persistent message. For example, you can include it on your website and in emails that address the change initiative. Mention the myths at the next town hall meeting and ask that relevant myths be discussed in a hometown story. You might also want to prepare a one-page handout to share at the right time with anyone who approaches you with incorrect impressions and suspicions about the new idea.

= = = = = = = = = =

The Myth Buster pattern can help create a clearer understanding of what the new idea is and what it is not. It allows others to build on the truth rather than on their misunderstandings. In addition, your use of this pattern shows that you are willing to shed light on, rather than simply ignore, any concerns about the new idea.

However, no one likes to be proven wrong, and we tend to cling to our beliefs despite evidence to the contrary. When people are convinced, an attempt to change their minds may have the opposite effect: It may strengthen their position. Even so, this effort gives them food for thought and they may come around later. Create an emotional connection and use the Fear Less pattern.

Patricia was six months into leading a change initiative when she began hearing comments and questions that revealed many misconceptions infiltrating the organization. Because she was required to give regular reports, she turned one of these into a mythbuster presentation. She made it lighthearted and even a bit funny at times. Patricia saw smiles from audience members, so she guessed she had given them a chance to laugh at themselves, which made it more likely they would remember the information.

During the battle for healthcare reform in the United States, rumors and misunderstandings often created fear about things such as "death panels" or the rationing of care. President Barack Obama, in his weekly radio address to the nation, sought to debunk the more outrageous claims. In addition, websites such as the following attempted to bust the myths: http://harryreid.com/content/reform-myths/.

The "5 Misconceptions in Elementary Mathematics" website (http://teachertipstraining .suite101.com/article.cfm/5_misconceptions_in_elementary_mathematics) aims to help elementary students eliminate their tightly held beliefs. The site states that "elimination of mistaken beliefs about math concepts is critical."

To investigate 16 claims that surfaced after the terrorist attacks on September 11, 2001, Popular Mechanics magazine assembled a team of nine researchers and reporters who consulted more than 70 professionals in fields that form the core of the magazine, such as aviation, engineering, and the military. The resulting report, "Debunking the 9/11 Myths: Special Report," stated that they were "able to debunk [the] assertions with hard evidence and a healthy dose of common sense . . . Only by confronting such poisonous claims with irrefutable facts can we understand what happened on a day that is forever seared into world history" (http://www.popularmechanics.com/technology/military_ law/1227842.html).

Pick Your Battles

Matthew was a serious bike racer and entered a number of races. In those races, he often saw Kevin, an overzealous, extremely competitive rider who couldn't bear to be left behind. Kevin was an aggressive but not very tactically savvy rider who would burn out because he forced himself to always be at the front and, as a result, would exhaust all his energy before the race was over.

Before you expend your energy in conflict, ask yourself whether you believe the issue is really important and if you have the resources to carry your fight through to the end.

You are an evangelist or dedicated champion struggling to introduce a new idea into your organization. You see a need for change and you are working hard to spread the word about your ideas, but there are skeptics who are relentlessly opposing your attempts.

You can't spend time and energy addressing every bit of resistance you meet.

It's hard to compromise when it comes to things you care deeply about. You always want to do what you believe is right. Yet, you can easily become distracted by all the little annoyances around you and lose your focus on the big picture.

We would all like to live in a conflict-free environment. Perhaps getting to this point is a matter of figuring out what is really important, what is worth fighting for (and what is not), and, perhaps, being a little more open-minded and accepting of those around us. This may involve reevaluating our priorities. But, for most of us, it's uncomfortable to question and compromise our ideals. We may believe that these priorities define us and that being flexible with them destroys an important part of who we are.

Even if you feel you are compromising deeply held principles by not taking on a struggle, it may be more important to live to fight another day. It's not about the battles fought and won; it's about making progress in reaching your goals. Even if you have the time and the energy, you will lose credibility if you try to become the person who must emerge as the winner at any cost. In addition, those who support your ideas will be reluctant to get caught up in every little disagreement or will get worn out trying to act as mediators or confidantes.

Community organizer Ben Thacker-Gwaltney explains in the book *We Make Change*, "I think organizing is a pragmatic profession. If you're too idealistic, you're not going to make it. You're going to get disillusioned. You have to cope with failure and compromise on all the rest."[60]

You are at risk for making a real enemy by not being open to considering something that might be very important to someone else. Allowing others to have something to hang on to will help them become more comfortable with the new way of doing things.

Therefore:

Stop. Take a deep breath and think for a minute. Ask yourself if the current conflict is worth it. Overcome your initial emotional reaction and make a conscious decision to fight only for those things that will make a difference. Maintain your integrity so that at the end of each decision point you are proud of yourself.

Ask yourself:

- Can I win? If there is no hope for victory, what will you really gain? Choose wisely. Know yourself. Ask which abilities and resources are needed in this situation and whether you have them. This may be a battle worth fighting, but do you have what it takes to carry it through to completion? In particular, make sure your idea is a good, workable solution and you're not headed into battle with no strategy.
- Should I win? Consider the importance of the relationship with your opponents. It might be more valuable to support this relationship than to win the current conflict. You may block your progress if you hold out for a win. Are you really sure that you are right and the others are wrong, or can you make a small concession to keep the initiative moving forward? Often it takes a bigger person to simply let the conflict go. This can be a turning point—if you let the opponent win, you may win a convert.
- What's it all about? Maybe it's a simple misunderstanding. If it's worth fighting over, it's worth spending time to understand what the real issues are. Check your words—make sure your opponent really said what you heard, and make sure your opponent really heard what you said. Things are rarely black and white; try to see the many shades of gray. Be more open and accepting when others' values are different from yours. Try wearing De Bono's Six Thinking Hats[61] to help yourself consider all sides. You can learn a lot about your cause.

Plan ahead. Use these three questions to form a clear understanding of what you believe is worth fighting for. Decide ahead of time which items are mission critical and which will make little or no difference if they are adjusted.

When evaluating the questions, ask for help from other members of your team because it can be difficult to decide which battles can and should be fought. It's easy for our brains to deceive us about whether we can win because we are often overly optimistic about our abilities and rarely objective about our motives. It's easy to see in others, but hard to do for ourselves.

Even before you start a discussion, think about which needs are vital and which points allow room for negotiation. This will help you remain focused on the things you must accomplish.

You may want to vent with the help of a friend or a trusted colleague, someone who can talk you down or provide insight into why another person is behaving a certain way.

Appreciate the view of the resistor (using the Fear Less pattern). Send a clear message that everyone is on an adventure together. There are few, if any, "rights" or "wrongs." Instead, progress is a series of baby steps where everyone is always learning. Look for common ground and places to compromise along the way.

To address the concerns of someone who is resistant to your cause and making a lot of noise, consider a small concession that will show you acknowledge the point of view and the contribution of that person. Sometimes you can make a concession early or make a large concession to reach agreement, but negotiation experts warn that doing so often drives parties further apart by raising the expectations of the other side about even more concessions. Make only small concessions, make them only after due consideration, and always ask for something in return. Consider a trial run for ideas you see as possibilities. Set clear expectations—establish a concrete action plan with the length of the trial and the evaluation criteria for the concession. Learn what you can from every experiment and be flexible about adjusting your ideas.

= = = = = = = = = = = =

The Pick Your Battles pattern will help create a more peaceful existence and will likely strengthen your interpersonal relationships. You will have more time to work on the things that matter because you will not be worn out by battling constantly. Focusing on important issues will help you achieve your long-term goals because you'll be more effective in winning battles that are important to you and your team. This pattern encourages respect for individual differences and preferences. If you are able to compromise, it's likely that resistors will become more open not only to your idea, but also to a more respectful relationship with you.

However, your decision to avoid tackling a certain battle may be the wrong one and have significant impact. History tells many stories of those who chose "peace at any cost." Ask for help when deciding which battles to avoid and create a backup plan for the possibility that you and your team made the wrong choice. It's also possible that, even after you compromise on the sticking points, a skeptic will remain resistant. You might consider this person to be an effective champion skeptic, someone who takes on the role of pointing out all the downsides of the new idea.

A group of activists were standing on the street, attempting to get as many signatures as possible on a petition to legalize gambling in North Carolina. When passersby reacted negatively to their ideas, they did not argue with the resistors. In some cases, they took time to listen to their concerns, but usually, they chose to politely thank the naysayers and move on to the next pedestrian, who might be a potential advocate for their cause.

Dan was coaching a team that was moving to Agile software development. The plan was to move the team to an open environment with individual offices for anyone available on an as-needed basis. Fred, one of the team members, was insistent on keeping his old cubicle. It seemed like this roadblock would hold everything up until Dan suggested that for the next few months, they could let Fred keep his cubicle. The rest of the team members would follow the new plan. They would evaluate the results at the end of a trial run and see what had been learned. It's amazing how well that worked. Because Fred felt that his concerns were being addressed, he was not so openly resistant; in just a short while, he realized that having the individual office available whenever he needed it would work for him. He began to spend more time in the open environment. The rest of the team didn't make a big deal out of it, but just welcomed him whenever he decided to join them.

As a parent, I have to recognize and respect that peer pressure is real and I have to deal with it. Constantly fighting with my child is counterproductive. If I criticize everything my child and his peers are doing, I risk shutting the door on communication permanently. It's not easy to live with an outrageous hairstyle or a sloppy wardrobe, but it may be better to let these things slide and to save my strength for the more important life struggles, such as stealing, alcohol use, or drug abuse.

Town Hall Meeting

When members of Congress return home for their annual August recess, many representatives and senators hold in-district town hall meetings to hear from their constituents. The American Diabetes Association sent an email to remind people that "these meetings are a great opportunity to speak directly with your elected officials. They listen to the pulse of their constituents. Show them that Diabetes Advocates are a vocal part of their community."

As early as possible and throughout the initiative, schedule an event to share updates about the new idea, solicit feedback, build support, uncover new ideas, and bring in newcomers.

You are an evangelist or dedicated champion who wants to explore the issues in a change initiative. You may be at the beginning of your journey, interested in identifying problems and possible solutions. Alternatively, you may have experimented in your own work by deciding to just do it, or you may have completed a trial run and are now willing to discuss the progress report and thoughts about the next steps to take. You have something to report about the change initiative, and you are willing to listen to what others have to say about it.

It is difficult to stay in touch and involve everyone during the long period of time that is often necessary for a change initiative.

Feedback is essential—you don't want to work in a vacuum. It might seem easier to trust your own judgment and do what you think is best, but in doing so you risk taking actions that do not provide real help for the organization. You might even be far enough removed from the day-to-day operations that you have lost touch with the real needs in your organization. You don't want to miss important information or run the risk that people will feel ignored.

Use of the Personal Touch pattern will help you understand how individuals can use a new idea and how they are feeling about the change. While individual conversations throughout the change initiative are important, one-on-one meetings with everyone in the organization are likely to take more time than you have. This type of contact will be especially difficult, or even impossible, in large organizations. The Persistent PR pattern is useful for communicating information, but it has limitations for creating a dialogue where emotions can be uncovered.

Therefore:

Hold a meeting to solicit feedback, build support, get new ideas, intrigue newcomers, and report progress.

Use the Personal Touch pattern to individually invite as many people as you can. Involve everyone—encourage attendance by participants with diverse backgrounds and ideas. Make sure you give particular attention to those who are most affected by the change.

Before the meeting, talk to skeptics (that is, use the Fear Less pattern) to avoid being caught off guard. Use the Corridor Politics pattern to influence the tone of the meeting before you open the discussion to a large group.

Send out an agenda ahead of the meeting. Begin by focusing on the purpose of the meeting. Give a brief history and status report of the change initiative (in other words, use the Just Enough pattern). Solicit feedback and brainstorm new ideas. Check your ego at the door and explain that you are there to increase everyone's understanding, including your own.

Demonstrate leadership—because if you don't, people with an agenda of their own might potentially create chaos. Be clear about the rules for conducting the meeting (for example, how questions and comments will be handled).[62] Watch out for ineffective discussions and endless debate. Be willing to politely put these matters in a "parking lot" for later or for offline discussions.

End the meeting by summarizing the next steps and welcome volunteers to be go-to people. Be sincere when you ask for help. Sometimes a group will expect a leader to provide all the answers. There is a fine line between appearing incompetent or weak and performing the vital task of bringing others into the conversation.

After the session, stay in touch. Continue the conversation and post progress updates for everyone to follow.

= = = = = = = = = = = =

Using the Town Hall Meeting pattern will build visibility for the new idea and provide for a "pulse check" of the community. You can solicit feedback and collect other ideas. This pattern also gives you a chance to gather support and build a group identity. Most importantly, everyone has the opportunity to get an update and become involved in the initiative. People are less likely to complain later and more likely to take ownership if they are kept informed and have been given a say in the changes that could be made.

However, attendees may want the meeting to reach a consensus or they may expect their individual suggestions to be followed. If disappointed, they could get angry and work against you. Be sure to set clear expectations at the beginning of the meeting, and gently remind everyone periodically about the intent of the meeting. Be honest about your ability to please everyone; make sure they understand you can't do everything. If individuals are passionate about their suggestions, you may wish to encourage them to become evangelists and make their ideas happen—this is a good opportunity to bring in more volunteers.

Ralph, the head of a library, was retiring after 30 years of service. The administration decided that it was a good time to examine the organization's structure and procedures to determine which changes could be made. One representative from each department was invited to a series of meetings where these issues were studied. Their rough ideas and recommendations were then presented in a follow-on meeting with everyone in the library. The results of these meetings formed the basis for the new leadership as Ralph's retirement drew closer—changes in the org chart, decisions regarding Ralph's replacement, and modifications to some processes and library facilities.

Alice was hired as the new president of a university. It was a time for change. Alice saw issues that needed to be addressed. Her staff scheduled a series of meetings to gather input for a strategic plan. Everyone on the campus was personally invited over email or phone to attend one of the sessions. Each meeting began by setting the expectations for the session and the suggestions that would be gathered. During the meetings, Alice presented a list of specific questions. The responses were recorded, and a summary of the results was sent to each participant. Everyone was kept current on how the summaries were being used in the strategic planning process.

When Congressman Chip Cravaack held an invitation-only, $10-per-plate luncheon, protesters were there. Cravaack asked the crowd if they wanted a town hall meeting and they responded with an enthusiastic "yes." "OK," he replied. "We can hear each other and have a good dialogue." During the meeting, one college student challenged Cravaack's assertion that programs must be cut to spare taxpayers, while another asked why he wasn't raising taxes on people who could afford it. The questioners and the congressman didn't come to an agreement, but in the hour-long meeting nobody threatened anyone, which was later referred to as "progress on the civility front."[63]

Wake-up Call

"Hey, we've got a problem here." The message from the Apollo 13 spacecraft to Houston ground controllers at 10:08 p.m. EDT on April 13, 1970 initiated an investigation to determine the cause of an oxygen tank failure that aborted the Apollo 13 mission.

Alias: "Houston, we have a problem."

To encourage people to pay attention to your idea, point out the issue that you believe has created a pressing need for change.

You are an evangelist or dedicated champion who has identified a problem and sees a need for change.

People in your organization seem to be comfortable with the status quo. They don't see the need to change the current state of things.

When you talk about your idea, you are proposing a solution to a problem. But if no one is aware of the difficult situation, it's likely that your idea will be viewed as merely an interesting possibility rather than something urgent that requires action. As a result, your proposal is met with complacency, pessimism, or defiance, or everyone simply ignores you.

We are creatures of habit. When we are settled into a routine and are satisfied with the way things are, we're not likely to see an impending threat. You will need to help others understand that the world has changed and that they must change as well.[64] It can be difficult to face this reality. We can feel overwhelmed and hopeless when facing a challenge—yet most of us want to make things right. Therefore, we are more likely to take action if we feel a certain amount of tension brought about by, for example, a need to eliminate a potential risk, a desire for safety and comfort, or a wish to fulfill a goal. If you can create this kind of tension, people are likely to seek a resolution.[65]

An upbeat style of leadership encourages optimism, but when it becomes excessive, it distorts reality. Individuals will believe everything is going well. They will stop asking questions and avoid considering feedback that could lead to improvement. This "excessive optimism" or "irrational exuberance" can leave an organization ill equipped to deal with inevitable setbacks. You need to be courageous enough to bring potential problems to light and encourage periodic critical reflection in areas that are not doing well.[66]

According to John Kotter, the first step in real change is to "get the urgency up." He explains that showing people a compelling need for change will energize them to make something happen—it will get them "off the couch, out of the bunker, and ready to move."[67]

In *Weird Ideas That Work*, author Bob Sutton points to research on social movements, showing that the hallmark of scalable ideas is for leaders to first create "hot" emotions to fire up attention and motivation and then provide "cool" rational solutions for people to implement.[68]

Thomas Friedman, author of *The World Is Flat*, reminds us: "Where there is a problem, there is an opportunity."[69] Your idea can be that opportunity.

Therefore:

Create a conscious need for change by calling attention to a problem and its negative consequences in the organization.

Do your homework to understand the "pain points" and their impacts. Prepare concrete information. Double-check your facts. Describe the situation in a compelling and powerful way. Let the numbers talk, but remember to include the human side as well by establishing an emotional connection. Ask for help from those who are also aware of the issue to help you understand how it affects different people in a variety of environments.

Use corridor politics and talk with key individuals. Once you have supporters who agree that the threat is real and needs to be addressed, they can help you in a town hall meeting, where you can spread the information to others in the organization.

Tell your story. Explain how you recognized the issue, but don't get carried away with details that could keep everyone consumed with the problem. Focus their attention by explaining just enough.

Have a solution that people will care about implementing. Relate it to the goals of the organization (using the Tailor Made pattern). Use the Personal Touch pattern to help individuals answer the question: What's in it for me?

Point out what could happen if the problem is not solved, perhaps with various scenarios (use the Imagine That pattern). But don't just tell horror stories: Accentuate the positive. You want to inspire hope to encourage everyone to discuss potential solutions.

Don't outline a complete strategy for the solution, because then the initiative could become all about you. Even if you think you have a good idea, you will get more buy-in if you present it as a rough proposal and then ask for help in creating a concrete action plan.

Stay in touch. Once you have helped others recognize the issue, don't allow the urgency of reaching a solution to decline as people get busy with other things.

= = = = = = = = = = = =

Use of the Wake-up Call pattern helps to create awareness of the current reality in the organization and the problem(s) that are responsible for it. Listeners will stop and think, "Wow, I didn't know that!" You will likely bring to light issues that many didn't see or may have been denying. You are preparing them to open their minds to new possibilities and recognize the need to take action. This allows you to propose your ideas for change.

However, you are not likely to get everyone to care about the problems you raise. You should be careful about dwelling on existing predicaments—there can be serious political ramifications from such an emphasis. You can come across as a troublemaker, especially if the old way is owned by those with influence. If too many people are not responding to your wake-up call, you may have to pick your battles and move on.

Max became the manager of the customer services team in a large manufacturing company. Even though the team was considered to be the "premiere" leader in the sales division, Max noticed gaps. Rather than approaching the team with "This is what I see," he tried to help team members reach their own conclusions. He called a meeting and began by asking them to rate their customer support as good, very good, or great. The group declared they were "great" and listed all the wonderful things they were doing. Max encouraged them to dig deeper with a follow-up question: "What makes a customer support team great?" As they discussed the question, Max prompted the team members to think about their personal interactions with customers and benchmark them against other companies that have great customer service. This allowed the team to identify important qualities in customer support, including empathy, sound professionalism, and the willingness to take responsibility to meet expectations. Max sounded a wake-up call by asking if there were any gaps in these qualities. The team decided that while a "very good" customer service team has empathy and seeks a complete answer by taking ownership of each problem, a "great" one builds relationships to create trust with their customers. Their concrete action plan pinpointed the notion that customer service representatives should be, among other things, more proactive by reaching out to customers they had not heard from in a while to inquire if there was anything they can do for them. The exercise allowed everyone to "wake up" and acknowledge that they weren't working at their highest possible level and to identify opportunities for improvement. The team was able to recognize when they were simply meeting or truly exceeding their customers' expectations.

The system for assigning faculty to committees at one university was tedious and outdated. Ellen drafted a new system that needed to go to the Faculty Senate for approval. Unfortunately, she didn't use the Corridor Politics *pattern, so Senate members raised many questions and concerns following her presentation. When Ellen realized that her proposal was not likely to pass, she politely stopped the discussion and back-peddled with a detailed explanation of the problems in the present system. Senate members reacted with surprise. They had not been aware of the difficulties and were immediately more willing to support her. Ellen then suggested a trial run of her new system, and the motion passed in her favor.*

Paul Levy was appointed to head the BIDMC hospital system, the product of a difficult merger between two hospitals. To signal the need for a new order, Levy developed a bold message explaining that this was BIDMC's last chance to make improvements. Pointing to his private discussions with the state attorney general, he publicized the real possibility that the hospital would be sold. He knew this bad news might frighten staff and patients, but he believed a strong wake-up call was necessary to get employees to face the need for change.[70]

Josie King's senseless death started with a hot bath. The one-and-a-half-year-old girl climbed into a tub and burned herself in January 2001. Her initial recovery, at a large hospital, seemed promising, but then the toddler began experiencing insatiable thirst. Nurses told her mother not to let her drink and said her vital signs were normal, even as she sucked washcloths to quench her thirst. Then, despite a no-narcotics order, a nurse gave Josie methadone, which led to cardiac arrest. Two days later, she died in the intensive care unit. Josie's mother, Sorrel, gave this heartbreaking wake-up call in December 2004 at an event kicking off a campaign to reduce by 100,000 the number of patients who die each year in US hospitals because of preventable errors. A small nonprofit called the Institute for Healthcare Improvement (IHI) was behind the 100,000 Lives campaign. By June 2006, the hospitals enrolled in it had accomplished this goal. Although the organization lacked formal authority over the hospitals and operated with a tiny staff and modest resources, it helped save 100,000 lives by inspiring and guiding executives, physicians, nurses, and a host of other staff members in the 3000 hospitals (representing more than 75% of U.S. hospital beds) that joined the campaign.[71]

The Original Patterns

The patterns from our first book are included as they originally appeared. Any changes in a pattern's abstract are presented in the table of summaries in the Appendix.

In addition, some of the patterns have an additional "Insights" section, where we share what we have learned about a particular pattern since it was originally published.

Here are the original patterns, listed alphabetically. The sections on each pattern follow.

Ask for Help

Baby Steps (formerly
   Step by Step)

Big Jolt

Bridge Builder

Brown Bag

Champion Skeptic

Connector

Corporate Angel

Corridor Politics

Dedicated Champion

Do Food

e-Forum (now part of Persistent PR)

Early Adopter

Early Majority

Evangelist

External Validation

Fear Less

Group Identity

Guru on Your Side

Guru Review

Hometown Story

Innovator
Involve Everyone
Just Do It
Just Enough
Local Sponsor
Location, Location, Location
Mentor
Next Steps
Persistent PR
    (formerly In Your Space)
Personal Touch
Piggyback
Plant the Seeds
The Right Time
Royal Audience

Shoulder to Cry On
Sincere Appreciation (formerly Just
    Say Thanks)
Small Successes
Smell of Success
Stay in Touch
Study Group
Sustained Momentum
Tailor Made
Test the Waters (now part of Just
    Do It)
Time for Reflection
Token
Trial Run
Whisper in the General's Ear

Ask for Help

Markita Andrews has generated more than $80,000 selling Girl Scout cookies since she was seven years old. She does not propose to be smarter or more extroverted than other people. Rather, she claims the difference is that she has discovered the secret of selling: Ask, ask, ask! The fear of rejection causes many people to fail before they begin because they don't just ask for what they want.

Since the task of introducing a new idea into an organization is a big job, look for people and resources to help your efforts.

◆◆◆

You are an evangelist or dedicated champion working to introduce a new idea into your organization.

The job of introducing a new idea into an organization is too big for one person, especially a newcomer who doesn't know the ropes.

The single biggest failing of many change agents is that they do not look for help. They believe they can do it themselves, or they feel they can't ask for help because this would reveal their own inadequacies. Yet the likelihood of success is directly related to their ability to ask others for help.

David Baum, author of *Lightning in a Bottle*, has observed that a leader who appears invulnerable, never showing anything but complete confidence and certainty, will eventually create a workforce with a somewhat warped view of reality. Conversely, a leader who admits his vulnerability will find that people will move to support him in surprising and generous ways.

We all need help at times. People who set a high goal will eventually find that they cannot achieve it without other people. It can take effort to find help but the return can be worth it. Taking the steps to identify which resources are available will allow you to take advantage of them.

Often we feel it would be easier to just do it ourselves, but involving others will bring extra benefits in addition to the help. Involvement leads to growing support for your new idea. It can also encourage people to take partial or complete ownership of the project—this is especially valuable for a change agent who hopes to spark the idea and then pass it on to others to implement.

Some people are not quick to volunteer their help or advice. It could be because no one ever asked them. Most people are more likely to help when they are asked. Most people want to be connected, invited, and involved. Most people will have energy and commitment if they are given the opportunity to be players and to influence an initiative's outcome.

Therefore:

Ask as many people as you can for help when you need it. Don't try to do it alone.

Get the help, advice, and resources of people who care about you and/or the things you care about. Look around and talk to everyone about the innovation. You may think you don't know anyone who can help you with your dream but keep talking and then talk some more. Ask them at the right time and remember to offer sincere appreciation.

Sometimes it takes digging—you might have to talk to someone who knows someone, and so on, before you get the help you need. Every organization provides some kind of support: web development, graphic design, special printing, free advertising, corporate publications, secretaries, and assistants. Help can be there for the asking. Sometimes just wandering over to a support area and stopping at someone's desk can help you discover what's available.

If a person is hesitant to agree to your request for help, turn it around. Explain how this opportunity can be an advantage to him, such as allowing him to learn something new, make new contacts, or even add a line to his end-of-year report.

Don't become discouraged if the help is slow in coming. Even a small start can help you promote your ideas, leading to more resources in the future.

= = = = = = = = = =

This pattern builds support from people who will now feel part of the effort. Small contributions from a variety of individuals can create small successes and can add up to significant results. Most importantly, each time you ask for help, you'll bring in more interested individuals.

The risk is that asking for help can be seen as a sign of incompetence, especially if you are part of an organization that fosters a "You should be able to do it yourself" image. You can overcome this difficulty by creating a group identity and involving everyone who has contributed to the initiative.

Someone told Samantha, "No one knows you. If you talk to Mark or Greg, they know how to get things done and I'm sure they'll help you." He was right, and it made a big difference. Mark told her how to reach the editor of the online daily newsletter to announce upcoming events. Greg introduced her to the tech support person who could set up a bulletin board for the new idea. They were both available when she had questions. She felt like she had a chance of achieving success after that.

Writing computer programs in pairs is part of the new Agile software development approach. Programmers say that pairing makes it easier to admit they don't know something. In the pair programming relationship, individuals lose the embarrassment that typifies the lone cowboy coder who would rather try to muddle through on his own. Asking for help has become a natural part of the software development process.

INSIGHTS

We thought this pattern was about getting someone to do something for you, but now we see that it's also about bringing in other points of view. Invite new people but also include those individuals whom the new people know and will talk to about the innovation—their networks are potential supporters. The pattern emphasizes that the problems in a change initiative can't be solved by you and a select few. The most effective change agents are willing to give away their ideas to encourage contributions from others. Involvement breeds commitment.

Here are good times to ask for help: when someone does something you want to know about; when there is something you know you don't do well; when you don't know who to ask for help!

Often leaders of change have a history of being proactive. It's hard to stop saying, "Let me show you how to do it." Learn to let go. When you know yourself, you realize that you have deficiencies and need contributions from others.

Plan ahead. Don't wait until you need something. Keep a list of go-to people who may be able to help in the future. You never know when and where the best ideas will surface. If you are willing to learn from anyone, you'll often get good ideas that will surprise you.

You'll be more successful at recruiting if you ask people to do things they enjoy doing. Give them opportunities to show off their skills, and you will have supporters who are more likely to stick around.

Someone once asked, "Why should I bring in a new idea if I'm not going to get credit for it?" Here are several ways to think about this problem:

1. You have lots of ideas. If you have one good idea, no matter whether it works, you'll always have another one.
2. You will always know that it was your idea. You don't need external validation for that.
3. Over time, the power brokers may learn who brings in the new ideas.
4. Find someone you want to honor who has the power to get recognition for the idea and let her introduce it.
5. You'll like it when your own ideas come back to you!
6. Your ideas are 80% good. They get 95% good when you listen to others.
7. People are so busy they don't often know what others are doing. This is true in any social situation. Many of us don't do a good job of communicating. Speak up for yourself. Don't assume that everyone knows what you've been up to.

In some situations, asking for help can be seen as a sign of weakness. You may have to consider what's more important—that others think you're weak or that you got things done and brought in more people.

It may be difficult to ask for help, especially if you're a strong person who is used to doing things your own way. The message here is that there are larger goals around everything you do. It's not just about getting an item off the to-do list; it's about building an initiative and growing community.

Baby Steps

E. L. Doctorow once said, "Writing a novel is like driving a car at night. You can see only as far as your headlights, but you can make the whole trip that way." You don't have to see your destination or everything you will pass along the away; you just have to see two or three feet ahead of you. This is right up there with the best advice about writing, or life, I have ever heard.[72]

Relieve your frustration at the enormous task of changing an organization by taking one small step at a time toward your goal.

You are an evangelist. After applying the Just Do It and Time for Reflection patterns, you realize that there is interest in the new idea in your organization.

You wonder what your plan should be for introducing the new idea into your organization.

"If we can see the path ahead laid out for us, there is a good chance it is not our path; it is probably someone else's we have substituted for our own. Our own path must be deciphered every step of the way."[73] There are no shortcuts to anyplace worth going.

It is impossible to instantly convert everyone to your way of thinking. An attempt to create a master plan for the change initiative is probably setting yourself up for failure because there are too many unknowns in any organization. The very nature of a complex problem can bring you to your knees and cause you to make no progress at all. Yet, to climb a ladder, you don't leap from the ground to the top. Rather, you climb slowly and surely, one step at a time. Similarly, organizational change happens not with a giant leap, but in small, sometimes hardly noticeable steps. People are less resistant to small changes than to large ones, but lots of small changes will ultimately create major shifts.

We can become discouraged and find it difficult to maintain enthusiasm for a single goal that is so far into the horizon that it's hard to imagine you can ever reach it. There's an advantage to setting short-term goals and seeing clear progress. It's definitely more exciting to identify small steps and celebrate when you reach each one than it is to outline an overpowering vision that will take months or years to achieve.

The most common mistake change agents make is to take on too much, too soon. They are often like anxious gardeners standing over their plants, imploring them, "Grow! Try harder! You can do it!" Of course, good gardeners don't try to convince a plant to grow.[74] Instead, they realize that significant change starts slowly and evolves steadily over time. In organizational change, as in nature, new developments should spread quietly at first, so that the leaders can learn from the failures and build on the successes.

Therefore:

Use an incremental approach in the change initiative, with short-term goals, while keeping your long-term vision.

Focus on a few meaningful problems. Create a compelling vision, but keep it broad enough to increase your chance of success. You may wish to list the things that need to happen to achieve your vision, but you don't need an exact plan specifying precisely *how* you will make these things happen. Rather, set a few short-term goals and be prepared to adjust your expectations as you learn what works and what doesn't.

Identify things you can achieve quickly, then implement some small portion of the initiative. Work toward early wins that bring about any change. Use your initial successes as stepping-stones to reach increasingly ambitious gains. Remind yourself each time you achieve a short-term goal to celebrate the small successes.

Encourage people to experiment using a trial run even for a small part of the new idea. Make small changes that don't disrupt the system, and trust that the collection of small changes will ultimately result in big change. Before you go tearing in to change something, step way back, calm down, and think about the least perturbation you can introduce and still get the result you want. Over time, with enough little efforts, a new order will emerge—one you could not have planned no matter how many flip charts you hauled out. Help what wants to happen, happen. Rather than attempting a complete system overhaul, remove just one little obstacle or add one little ingredient. Launch your first step and then take time for reflection to decide what to do next.

As new evangelists come on board, let them plan their own part of the journey. They'll have more success by doing what's appropriate for their part of the world, and you won't have to know everything there is to know about every part. The change is bigger than you: It's not important that you personally travel each path to the goal. The important outcome is that the goal is reached, and that will happen as a result of a coalition, not one person's efforts.

Be wary of promising specific deadlines by which goals can be achieved. Cultural change tends to be organic and hard to predict. Be suspicious of people who promise big changes on a cultural level in some specific time frame—they're blowing smoke.

Remain optimistic even if you take one step forward and two steps back. Find a shoulder to cry on. As pointed out in Brian Foote and Joe Yoder's Piecemeal Growth pattern, mistakes are inevitable and growth is a slow and continuous process that cannot be achieved in a single leap.

= = = = = = = = =

This pattern builds an incremental approach to your change initiative. Because you can't possibly know everything that could happen, this approach gives you the chance to learn as you go. You can take advantage of what you learn along the way to adjust your plans accordingly.

Some people might think you don't know where you're going. Help them understand that the goal and the path to get there are not the same thing. Even though you don't know the exact path, devise a clear goal and continually communicate it with your current plans. This pattern doesn't suggest you shouldn't plan ahead at all. After all, Noah didn't wait until it started raining to build the ark.

From 1992 to 2001, the University Hospital of North Norway gradually introduced a digitized radiology system. This effort was successful because the system "grew" into place. First it was a small, customer-built image managing system; then a patient flow handling system; and finally an upgraded common version in all 11 hospitals in northern Norway. The gradual approach let developers alter the system based on user feedback without spending large sums and involving too many users. A more robust and well-tested system could then be introduced to a wider user group.

The leaders of RiverLink started with a 10-year plan to revive the French Broad River and turn the region into a place where people could live, work, and play. But after many unexpected challenges, such as a fire in one of its central buildings and the loss of some land, the plan had to be altered many times. Eventually, the members of RiverLink began constructing strategies with shorter time frames. As a result of the short-term plans, "people are more likely to believe that this can happen." In addition, the executive director noticed that the ability to readjust "has, I think, ended in a better place than our original plan."

INSIGHTS

We have decided to change the name of this pattern to Baby Steps because it is a better description of the process you will follow as you introduce your new idea. One reader referred to it as a "leap and learn" because the process of taking one little step followed by another allows learning to occur. Sometimes the move forward can be a considerable advance when an "aha" moment occurs. When a setback occurs, the learning is about what didn't work. It's easy to get discouraged when no "aha" results, but remind yourself that you are learning—that's an important goal for each step you take.

This pattern is based on the powerful influence strategy called commitment or consistency. Once we take even a small step in a given direction, we tend to keep going in that direction. The more steps we take, the more likely we are to stay on that path. Cognitive psychologists suggest that this approach builds new neural pathways in the brain. It also overcomes the brain's inborn fear of change and new things.[75]

You may ask, "What if I fail?" Perhaps it is better to recognize that there will be setbacks in the difficult journey of change and to prepare for the inevitable. Ask yourself, "After I fail, what then?" Seth Godin suggests, "Well, if you've chosen well, after you fail you will be one step closer to succeeding, you will be wiser and stronger and you almost certainly will be more respected by all of those that are afraid to try."[76]

Mario Livio in his book *Brilliant Blunders*[77] states, "Blunders are not only inevitable but also an essential part of progress in science. The development of science is not a direct march to the truth. If not for false starts and blind alleys, scientists would be traveling too long down too many wrong paths. . . . blunders have all, in one way or another, acted as catalysts for impressive breakthroughs—hence, their description as 'brilliant blunders.' They served as the agents that lifted the fog through which science was progressing, in its usual succession of small steps occasionally punctuated by quantum leaps." This observation about the progress of science is the same for progress in any effort.

Chip Heath, co-author with his brother, Dan Heath, of *Switch: How to Change Things When Change Is Hard*,[78] recommends, "Whatever change you're trying, shrink it." Imagine that person who forces herself to exercise for the duration of one song on her iPod when she doesn't feel like working out at all. When she makes that one small step, however, she usually continues exercising during the next song.

We often think about our change journey as starting with a clean slate. In reality, the stepwise journey must begin from where the organization currently is and the question we must answer is where to take the next step. We are always continuing onward from where we are now. Not all parts of the organization will adapt at the same rate. Taking small steps allows one part of an organization to learn something that could help another part later.

A serious consequence of this pattern is that a baby steps approach may cause enthusiastic supporters to become discouraged and lose heart because they are expecting to see great things happen quickly, but instead see only small progress. Recognizing and celebrating small successes along the way will help keep spirits high.

Linda's story provides an interesting argument for a baby steps approach:

Since I wore braces late in life, I like hearing how this technology has changed in the last few decades. It used to be that those who suffered through braces had to watch in horror when their braces were removed, as their teeth slowly moved back to their original positions. Orthodontics used to be about big shifts, but now it's about smaller changes—lighter, gentler forces ease teeth into alignment with much less discomfort. As one dentist said, "A common comment I get from patients is, 'Make it tighter, doc. I want to get my braces off faster!'" It's tempting to think that tighter adjustments will move your teeth faster. While a certain level of force is necessary, orthodontics is a delicate balance. Too much force may cause teeth to move but not result in stability. With the old technology, teeth often reverted to their original position—a discouraging outcome and a waste of everyone's time and energy.

Big Jolt

I was invited to give a presentation at a company in another city. Afterward, the local evangelist said, "You didn't say anything I couldn't have, but more people will listen to you. Your talk will have greater impact than mine would and then they'll come to me for more information."

To provide more visibility for the change effort, invite a high-profile person into your organization to talk about the new idea.

You are a dedicated champion working to introduce a new idea into your organization.

You've been carrying out some activities to give your new idea some visibility in your organization, but at some point you need to attract more attention to the effort.

Some people might be too busy to attend your presentation, but they will take time to hear an expert in the field. When a speaker has credibility, people are influenced by what he has to say.

Even those who have adopted the innovation need to have their interest reinforced. They need something to re-energize their interest and strengthen their commitment; otherwise, they may fall back into old habits or forget the new approach.

Therefore:

Arrange for a high-profile person who can talk about the new idea to do a presentation in your organization.

If funding is not available, entice the expert by pointing out that his visit is an opportunity for publicity for his latest project or book. Increase the probability of significant audience attendance at his presentation by providing lots of publicity before the event and by personally inviting and reminding people. Tell connectors. "Big name" people usually expect a big audience and may consider it an insult if they don't get one at your organization. This is especially important if the speaker is not being paid.

Schedule a pre-event meeting so the speaker can tailor his talk to the needs of the company. Give him some insight into the attitudes surrounding the new idea, the local power structure, and the organization's true priorities. Make certain he understands the types of individuals he will be speaking to. Well-known experts may wish to talk about something that most people in the organization are not prepared to understand, so encourage the visitor to use the Just Enough pattern to speak at a level the organization can absorb.

When advertising and introducing the speaker, highlight his experiences that relate to the innovation. This is likely to impress even the people who are not familiar with his name and make them more interested in what he has to say.

If the speaker will agree to do more than just a presentation, arrange a royal audience to reward those who have helped with your new idea or to make an impression on a corporate angel or local sponsor.

Get permission to videotape the presentation for people who can't hear the speaker live. Later, you can schedule some group viewings—be there to answer questions. Use both the presentation and the video sessions as an opportunity to plant seeds.

= = = = = = = = =

This pattern creates an event that will increase awareness of an innovation and provide some training for it. A big-name speaker will catch the attention of even the busiest people and will raise your credibility because you arranged for this person to visit the organization. Even those who cannot attend may be influenced by the publicity before the event and the talk about it afterward.

The risk is that such an event can create more enthusiasm than you can handle. Make sure you have people to help you after the speaker has gone. Without appropriate follow-up, the enthusiasm is likely to fizzle. Also, dealing with the visitor may involve a lot of extra overhead, divert resources, and distract you from higher-priority tasks, and it may not contribute to your long-term community development. Make sure this event is held in the context of a larger plan.

Barb invited a well-known speaker to talk about a new idea in her organization. Immediately following his visit, she saw a difference between those who had heard the talk and those who did not. Most of those who attended were willing to hear more, while most of the others were still skeptical.

David said, "We use this as much as we can. For some reason, people don't believe the in-house experts as much as a visiting 'dignitary.' We've had several big-name speakers pay us a visit, and it never ceases to amaze me the number of new people who sign up afterward. It's not like we don't have our own in-house training or resident mentors. I'm learning about the impact of outsiders!"

INSIGHTS

This pattern was originally about the appearance of a noted guru, but we've learned that holding *any* kind of significant event draws attention to your innovation.

Bridge Builder

I knew better than to try to convince the guys in Human Resources that our proposal for increased minority hiring would help the company in the long run. All I had to do was walk into that meeting room and our hopes were dead. Instead, I sent Bob to represent our team. He wore a suit and was our Ivy League recruiter. He didn't have the reputation for being a "bleeding heart" like the rest of us. He could speak their language. They listened and our proposal was accepted, no problem.

Pair those who have accepted the new idea with those who have not.

You are an evangelist or dedicated champion working to introduce a new idea into your organization. Some people in the organization have accepted the new idea, while others have not.

Some won't listen to even the most enthusiastic proponent if it's someone they don't know or trust.

In many cases, people may be suspicious of the evangelist and not the idea itself. Many hard-boiled veterans will not listen to a newcomer, no matter how knowledgeable that person may be. Veterans need to hear from one of their own, someone they trust. People like people who are similar in opinion, personality, background, or lifestyle. They enjoy interacting with others who understand where they're coming from.

Even trivial similarities between individuals have been shown to create a greater openness to new ideas and a willingness to try new approaches.

People are often skeptical because they see the world differently than the person who is talking about a new idea. Those who have already accepted the new idea can help with this, especially if these adopters are considered to be thoughtful and discerning in their decision making.

Therefore:

Ask for help from early adopters, connectors, or gurus who have already adopted the innovation. Introduce them to people who have interests similar to theirs and encourage them to discuss how they found the innovation useful.

Match a skeptic with an adopter he knows and respects. Ask the adopter to use the Personal Touch pattern to inform and address questions of the more skeptical partner. While the goal is to try to convince the non-adopter, this may not be possible when talking with a strong skeptic. In this case, it may be just as important for the bridge builder to allow the person's viewpoint to be heard by someone he respects.

It can take a lot of time and energy to find the right bridge builder for everyone, so you may want to reserve use of this pattern for only the key people. However, if you know someone who is "hot" on the innovation who has a buddy who is a skeptic, you might just simply ask, "Will you talk to <skeptic> about your experiences with <the innovation>?"

Don't become discouraged if this pattern does not work for everyone. The last to come around—the laggards—usually accept an innovation only after most or all of their co-workers have adopted it. Even then, they may do so only under pressure. Therefore it might be the best use of your limited resources to simply wait for them to come around, if they ever do, rather than putting a lot of effort into trying to persuade them.

When someone takes on the challenge of being a bridge builder, remember to offer sincere appreciation.

= = = = = = = = = =

This pattern builds a bridge between two people who can talk about the new idea. Someone who wasn't receptive to you is now more informed, thanks to the help of someone he will listen to. In addition, the person you asked to be the bridge builder becomes a stronger part of the effort because of the contribution he is making.

The risk is that a strong skeptic may make the adopter think twice about the innovation and you may lose both of them. Make sure that the bridge builder is someone who is truly convinced of the innovation and strong enough to work with a potentially argumentative skeptic.

I was a dedicated champion, with a cubicle right next door to a skeptic whose opinions were respected in the organization. I tried to influence him without success. Finally I found someone the skeptic respected, someone he had worked with at the company for a long time, who supported the change initiative. I asked for her help in convincing the skeptic. She agreed, and now the former skeptic is a supporter.

Lisa needed a favor from Bill. Although she knew she could probably get what she wanted by asking him, she also knew he really liked a good friend of hers. So she asked the friend to solicit the favor. Not only could Lisa be sure that the favor would be forthcoming, but she also knew it would make Bill happier to do it for the friend—and that's exactly what happened!

INSIGHTS

This pattern was originally about finding *people* to be bridge builders, but we've learned that organizations can also build connections, as in the following story.

Atlanta learned how to build relationships among the city's sectors. "CODA was the bridge," explains Clara H. Axam, CEO of the Corporation for Olympic Development in Atlanta. "There's no way the business executive is going into the neighborhoods. And the neighborhood folk are not comfortable in the boardroom. CODA could go either place. We learned how to translate conversations to each party. We are the bridge." The test comes now, post-1996, with Hot Atlanta cooled back to earthbound temperatures. Will the relationships stay connected around that table? Will the community rebuilding jump-started by CODA continue? If so, it will be relationships that make the difference. There's no discernible structure there to lean on.[79]

Brown Bag

One of the engineers stopped by my cubicle the other day. "You've had such great success with <the innovation>—I wonder if you would help me. I have an idea but I don't know how to get started." I told him that I got things going by announcing a brown bag and talking to people who showed up. It was a small beginning, but the people who came were interested in the topic and were willing to help me take the next steps.

Use the time when people normally eat lunch to provide a convenient and relaxed setting for hearing about the new idea.

You are an evangelist or dedicated champion who would like to call a meeting to introduce a new idea. Members of the user community are free to attend or not.

People can be too busy to attend optional meetings held during work hours.

There is always other, more important work to be done. Even though most people have a natural curiosity to hear about new ideas, it can be hard to take time during the workday to sit and learn. This makes it difficult to find a time when people can attend discretionary meetings. But since almost everyone eats in the middle of the day, a meeting over lunch will often find more people with time available. Lunchtime meetings are not as likely to be viewed as wasting time that could be spent doing "real" work, since the time would be spent eating anyway.

Therefore:

Hold the meeting in the middle of the day and invite attendees to bring their own lunches.

You can increase attendance if you find the right time. Consider spending a little of your own money to use the Do Food pattern. Advertise the event with persistent PR. Talk it up with connectors or a friendly guru.

Use the Next Steps pattern near the end of the event to help keep interest alive, and don't hesitate to ask for help. Tell people where they can find more information and who is using the innovation in the organization.

Hand out a token to help people remember the new idea that was discussed during the session.

= = = = = = = = = =

This pattern creates more awareness for the innovation. When the participants take time and bring their own food, it shows a willingness to invest a little of themselves that can grow over time.

While a noontime meeting can attract more people than a meeting at mid-morning or mid-afternoon, there will be others who won't attend because they view lunchtime as their break time. You will need to arrange other events for these people. Also, some cultures are not open to having meetings over lunch. Make sure that people will accept the idea of a brown bag before you begin your plans.

Brown bag lunch discussions started in Brian's organization so testers could network, share ideas, and learn more about testing topics. The events are held biweekly from noon until 1:00 p.m. The meetings range from free-form discussions to formal presentations. Topics have included demonstrations of products they test and how they test them, conference experiences, software testing certifications, what kind of testers they are, and the organization's testing process.

Initially Brian came up with a few topics, but he soon began asking for feedback from peers. At the year mark, he formed a committee to request topic ideas from peers, set up agendas, find speakers, and bring in snacks and supplementary materials. In the beginning, most attendees were testers. Information about upcoming brown bags was sent to everyone in the company, in addition to those who received a notice of the meeting. The events have attracted a variety of people—managers, developers, and others who are interested in software testing.

David organizes brown bag conferences. His recommendations:

- *Have a presentation every day at lunchtime for one to two weeks.*
- *Ask for help to create a program committee to organize the event.*
- *Invite attendees to bring their own lunches.*
- *Draw presenters primarily from inside the organization.*
- *Invite corporate executives to host a session and introduce the speaker.*
- *Advertise the conference so it is perceived as an event.*
- *Track who signs up and attends each session.*
- *Send reminders to participants who registered.*
- *Have tokens or door prizes and snacks at each session.*
- *Take time to reflect and ask attendees to evaluate each session.*

INSIGHTS

An event doesn't have to be held over lunch. It could be an afternoon tea time, an after-work gathering, or even a breakfast before work.

Champion Skeptic

Astronomer Carl Sagan said that we need a balance between two conflicting needs—the most skeptical scrutiny of all hypotheses that are served up to us and a great openness to new ideas. If you are only skeptical, then you never learn anything new. You become a crotchety old person who is convinced that nonsense is ruling the world. (There is, of course, much data to support you.) Conversely, if you are open to the point of gullibility and do have not an ounce of skeptical sense in you, then you cannot distinguish useful ideas from the worthless ones.

Ask for help from strong opinion leaders, who are skeptical of your new idea, to play the role of "official skeptic." Use their comments to improve your effort, even if you don't change their minds.

You are an evangelist or dedicated champion trying to involve everyone. You are using the Fear Less and Bridge Builder patterns to try to interest skeptics in your new idea.

Some of the resisters to the new idea are strong opinion leaders in your organization.

Skeptics who are both gurus and connectors know and talk with many people across the organization. If they are vocal about their reluctance to accept your new idea, this will stifle your efforts unless you change their minds, limit their impact, or ask them to help you. The first option may not be possible—you may not be able to bring them over to your side. But if they are offered a role in the initiative, they could change from a skeptical outsider to an insider who could make a positive contribution. They do this by bringing a "devil's advocate" approach to decision making: A solid argument is made and then subjected to grilling by another person or group. Proponents report that this approach allows only the best plans to survive.

A certain amount of opposition can be beneficial. If there are several strong opinions that provide different points of view, there is likely to be more thought and discussion. As a result, you can work toward a consensus of all the ideas.

Therefore:

Ask for help from a skeptical opinion leader to play the role of "official skeptic" or "official realist."

Encourage him to point out the problems he sees with the new idea. Invite him to all meetings and presentations, but if he can't attend, give him an opportunity to talk with you personally. Make sure he understands that his opinions should not stand in the way of progress. Rather, explain that his role is to anticipate problems so that these issues can then be addressed.

Use the information the champion skeptic provides. For example, when you talk about the new idea, mention the problems that still need to be tackled so that people know you have a complete view of the new idea. The information can also help set realistic goals that deliver real value.

Offer sincere appreciation when some point you hadn't thought of is brought to your attention. It may be your opportunity to be corrected before you make a serious mistake.

Don't take the idea of champion skeptic to the extreme. A moderate amount of disagreement is acceptable, but avoid people with strong personalities who are openly hostile.

If there is more than one skeptic who should be involved, you might consider creating a "Greek Chorus," a forum where skepticism is featured. This could be a one-time workshop or a group of people who regularly contribute to meetings.

= = = = = = = = =

This pattern creates a relationship with a vocal, influential skeptic who can't be included in any other way. The invitation to become a champion skeptic will encourage the skeptic's involvement and give him an opportunity to learn more about the innovation. Assigning this role can also feed the skeptic's ego. Recognizing and validating the ideas of an argumentative person will give him positive reinforcement, and may possibly make it no longer as much fun for him to argue.

If the skeptics are a strong influence in the organization, amplifying their objections could result in the non-adoption of your idea. You must be resilient—be prepared to handle criticism and negative statements.

A couple of people in Dave's firm are good at "being critical." Even though they are difficult people to please, they are highly respected throughout the organization. So Dave makes a point of having at least one of these folks on any steering group. He says that they keep him from getting carried away.

When one department has a meeting or discussion, they expect Susan to take the negative side. No matter what she truly believes, she is excellent at playing devil's advocate. She seems to hate everything, but once she starts to use something she usually likes it. Her initial skepticism but openness in the long run makes her credible. Susan has an important role. Although the team sometimes feels as if she is working against them, she keeps them honest in the long run. Without her insights, the other department members might not consider all the possibilities.

INSIGHTS

The original pattern suggested that the champion skeptic could be anyone who disagrees with the new idea. We have learned that you might want to be more selective. A good champion skeptic complains not just to whine, but rather to make things better. Provide clear guidelines describing what and how contributions can be made. Look for skeptics who are willing to speak in a respectful manner. Avoid those who have a "holier than thou" attitude or believe that their point of view is superior; they will go overboard to bring everyone into a negative space.

This is a "devil's inquisitor" role—not a devil's advocate, who simply argues against the status quo, but someone who, like a good lawyer, challenges the testimony of those who advocate for the majority. By asking questions, not simply arguing an alternate point of view, a skeptic can encourage people to look for evidence beyond their normal channels. This is a good way to avoid groupthink.

Confirmation bias explains our tendency to pay attention to information that confirms our current beliefs. While being aware of this bias can help, one of the best ways to counter it is to invite those who see things differently to share their opinions and then try to be open to what they have to say. Otherwise, we risk making a lot of bad decisions simply because we can't see evidence objectively. Take advantage of a good skeptic who will not only point out potential biases, but also offer ideas for addressing them.

In the original version of the pattern, the role of champion skeptic was described as a participant in a meeting. This is just one implementation suggestion. There are many ways to involve a champion skeptic—for example, as a bridge builder to other skeptics.

Champions come and go. One of the side effects of this pattern is that the current champion skeptic will say, "I don't want to be the negative guy anymore." When it's part of the job, it's not as much fun! In his book *Slack*,[80] Tom DeMarco suggests that everyone take turns playing this role—as did Edward de Bono in his book, *Six Thinking Hats*.[81]

The biggest lesson in this pattern is that instead of ignoring a skeptic and hoping he will go away, encouraging him can lead to your acquiring a tremendous asset and perhaps a major contributor to your change effort. The following story describes exactly that kind of person and the special contribution.

Losing My "Champion Skeptic"[82]

by Alan Dayley

During the time I have been advocating changes to Scrum and Agile I have encountered many skeptics. One excellent engineer was such a strong opponent of Scrum, I feared he would derail all change efforts. For a while, I also feared talking to him about his objections because:

- *He was very skilled in the craft, with knowledge and the ability to create great software.*
- *He had a strong personality, able to decide what he wanted and work for it.*
- *He pulled no punches, stating his opinion with conviction.*
- *I admired his abilities and work ethic.*
- *I didn't know him, personally, very well.*

To face him I had to know what I was talking about and put my beliefs in the line of fire. One day, I asked him why he objected so strongly. A difficult and rewarding conversation followed. It was the beginning of understanding, of many more conversations, and of working better together. In a private moment with the objecting engineer I informed him that he was my "Champion Skeptic." Surprise: He was skeptical. Months have passed and our discussions were more helpful than he knows. He suggested task card improvements, important impediment removal, and improved build processes, among other things. Most important to me, he helped me improve myself. I was able to present ideas better and improve my arguments for Scrum and Agile practices. He helped me understand more deeply his points, and my own. We became more friends than just co-workers. This week he announced that he is leaving the company for other adventures. The technical loss of his skills to the team and company will be felt for a while. The loss to me as Scrum and Agile evangelist is also significant. I now need to find another "Champion Skeptic" against which I can hone my skills as change agent. I'll need to find someone to talk straight and cut me down to size when my thoughts and ideas fall short. Oh, I can find people who don't "believe" in Agile, but one who also provides open, truthful conversation is not easy to find.

Connector

When I'm in search of something or someone in my large, complicated organization, I know who to ask: Mary. She seems to know everyone, or at least someone, in all the divisions and departments. When I explain my problem to her, she seems to think for less than a second and then replies, "Oh, yeah, you need to talk with. . . ." It always saves me a lot of time to ask Mary first.

To help you spread the word about the innovation, ask for help from people who have connections with many others in the organization.

You are an evangelist or dedicated champion trying to introduce a new idea into your organization. You're doing some things to give exposure to a new idea, but you know there are others who might be interested.

Your organization is too big for you to personally contact everyone.

Studies have consistently pointed to the importance of informal networks. This is how people learn about new ideas, coach one another, and share practical tips and lessons over time. The information that passes through these networks has credibility. When people we know talk about something new, we naturally pay attention.

Over 25 years of research shows that many people are more likely to turn to friends, family, and other personal experts than to use traditional media for ideas and information on a range of topics. Making a decision means having a conversation.

Word-of-mouth epidemics are created when connectors talk with others. These special people see possibilities in everyone they meet. They know many types of people in different social circles and have a gift for bringing the world together. The closer an idea comes to this type of person, the more opportunity it has.

Researchers have identified a special subgroup of connectors, the influentials. They make up approximately 10% of the adult population in the United States. They are interested in many subjects and are connected to many groups. They know how to express themselves. Because of their connections in the community, workplace, and society, their opinions are heard and they can influence decisions among many people. Almost certainly you know one. Chances are you seek out an influential when you have an important decision to make. Influentials often know the answer to the question you have. If they don't, they know someone who does. Influentials tend to be two to five years ahead of the rest of us on many important trends, such as the adoption of major technologies or new ideas.

If word of mouth is like a radio signal broadcast over the country, influentials are the strategically placed transmitters that amplify the signal, dramatically multiplying the number of people who hear it. The signal becomes stronger and stronger as it is beamed from influential to influential, and then broadcast to the nation as a whole.

You have to work in the formal structure of your organization, but you can't overlook the ability of other communication networks to spread the word. You'll improve your chances for success by taking advantage of the many informal relationships in your organization.

Therefore:

Ask for help in spreading the word about the innovation from those who know and communicate with many others in your organization.

Look for individuals who can connect with others. They will be easy to locate because they know so many kinds of people, including you! You may be more likely to find them among the early adopters—this group is generally more social than the innovators and more likely to be members of many different social circles.

Use the Personal Touch pattern to convince them of the value in the new idea. If they are innovators, it should be easy to persuade them. If not, it will be well worth the extra time, because once they become interested, their connection to others will decrease the effort you will need to spread the word. Connectors do not need to be close friends with everyone. They will have "strong ties" that typically share their interests or proximity, as well as many "weak ties" that link them to other social circles. Encourage them to talk with both their "strong" and "weak" ties about the new idea. Connectors will also know the skeptics, so ask them to be bridge builders. Remember to offer sincere appreciation when they tell you about any contact they've made.

Be wary of connectors who don't support the innovation. Connectors who are influentials can spread the word about a new idea in persuasive ways. Few important trends reach the mainstream without passing through the influentials in the early stages, but influentials can stop a would-be trend in its tracks. They give the thumbs-up that propels a trend or the thumbs-down that relegates it to a short 15 minutes of fame. Consider giving connectors with a thumbs-down attitude the special role of champion skeptic.

= = = = = = = = =

This pattern makes connections with people you might not otherwise reach on your own. Once the connectors are convinced of the new idea, they will spread the word faster than you can by yourself.

But connectors can also bring in more people than you have time to handle—so make sure you have interesting things to tell them and some plan of action in place so that the new people don't become intrigued, only to find out that there really isn't anything interesting going on.

The people who were the most helpful to Pat when she started introducing a new idea were the secretaries. They knew everybody and everything. They were the power behind the managers who made important decisions. They knew who to talk to about any issue. They became Pat's most powerful resource.

There are many connectors at one company because it funds organizations that encourage activities such as the music club, the flying club, and the golf club. The company also has a group that plays bridge at lunchtime and goes out for a meal every other week on payday. Most of these people have known each other for years—both at work and outside work—but even outside work, they talk about work, of course.

INSIGHTS

Connectors can be members of any subgroup in the organization—for example, those who work out together, eat lunch together, or even smoke together. Consider this: Smokers have to go outside the building to a small area, where they normally talk to a wide variety of colleagues. They often hear a lot of company news during smoking breaks.

The connector role is not just played by a person who can help you do a set of things—this role is vital and must be part of your effort from the beginning. Without a person with connections, who knows how to help with persistent PR, and who has a lot of weak and strong ties throughout the organization, you are less likely to be successful. Of course, it's good if you are also a connector, but if not, then make it a high priority to engage one.

Corporate Angel

My boss stopped by my cubicle and said, "I hear you've been giving brown bags on <a new idea>. I think you should give a presentation to the vice president. His staff meeting is in a couple of weeks." I agreed, but I didn't understand why the high-level managers needed to hear about this particular idea. I thought it was a good idea for the technical people in the organization but that was it. I was so wrong. That presentation brought training and the purchase of cases of books and, eventually, a new job description for me that allowed me more time to work on introducing the innovation. My ideas wouldn't have gotten far without buy-in from upper management.

To help align the innovation with the goals of the organization, get support from a high-level executive.

You are an evangelist or a dedicated champion trying to introduce a new idea into your organization. You've been giving brown bags and have won the approval of your local sponsor.

Support from local management will provide some attention and resources for the new idea, but you need high-level support to have a more lasting impact.

Enthusiasm at the local level can go only so far. Big-ticket items—training, books, conferences, and visiting gurus, such as a big jolt speaker or mentor—are needed if interest in the new idea is to grow. But resources can be limited because each level of management has authority to spend only in a certain area. A high-level supporter who believes in the importance of the innovation and will lend appropriate coaching and direction can make many inroads easier. In addition to resources, he can provide the collaboration and encouragement to align the new idea to the broader goals of the organization. This is vital to a successful change effort. It is this alignment that will make the initiatives last beyond any changes in local management.

The higher you go in your organization to reach and convince others, the more secure your effort will be. An analysis of the best technology-transfer practices of a broad cross section of government agencies, research institutions, and national and industrial laboratories identified the importance of *angels*, high-level executives who protect start-up projects until they mature.

Therefore:

Enlist the support of a high-level executive who has a special interest in the new idea and will provide direction and the resources to support it.

Talk to high-level executives about the new idea as early as possible. Explain how the innovation is tailor made to match the needs of the organization. If the corporate angel (or his staff) is hesitant and wants more information, you might suggest that he call for a guru review.

Look for high-level supporters who are respected across their organization; otherwise, their involvement could hurt your cause. The wrong kind of executive support can give the impression that the new idea is being "railroaded" through the organization. Be wary of those who embrace the new idea simply because of personal interest—the initiative may not survive if the executive moves to a different role or organization.

Make sure that the upper-level position is not brought in to dictate behavior. The role of corporate angel is similar to Peter Senge's "Executive Leader"—a protector, mentor, and thinking partner. This is not an authoritarian role. David Baum suggests that a simple statement from a leader, such as "We're all going through an amazing amount of change," can create a sense that everyone in the organization is facing the struggles together. This alone can help.

Keep the corporate angel interested. Stay in touch and offer the chance for a royal audience when an appropriate big jolt visitor is planned.

= = = = = = = = =

This pattern establishes high-level executive support for the innovation in the organization. The process of introducing the innovation becomes easier because lower-level managers and others in the organization are usually open to directives from the top. The corporate angel can also ensure that your interests and the plans of the local sponsor are aligned with that of the organization to avoid competition and limit any confusion.

The risk is that high-level support can give the impression that the innovation is being imposed or is simply just the "buzzword of the week." If you suspect this could happen, it may be better to concentrate on growing more grassroots interest first.

The team that worked over a three-year period to earn Division I NCAA Certification for their university's athletic program found that the support of the chancellor was vital. Although he was not involved in doing the large amount of paperwork, his occasional attendance at the team meetings was uplifting because it showed the hard-working members that he was willing to listen and participate in some of the discussions. He frequently mentioned the ongoing effort during campus meetings to the faculty that was not historically supportive of athletics. At the conclusion of the effort, when the athletic program received recertification and an outstanding report, the chancellor continued marketing athletics on the campus by making the announcement and pointing out that the institution should be proud that they fared better than most institutions.

Every time Helen brought a new proposal before her organization's decision makers, she faced a long discussion and a low probability that her proposal would pass on the first attempt. However, it was a different story when the vice president attended one meeting and took a few minutes to thank Helen for her hard work in making some needed changes in the organization. Her two proposals passed that day in a record amount of time.

Corridor Politics

I'm on the board of directors for several nonprofit organizations, so it happens all the time: When I see the caller ID of a fellow board member, I know that I'm in for an earful. I learn a lot, though. I get the inside scoop, and in the end I almost always wind up supporting the guy who called me. I figure he's taken the time to call and thinks I'm open to his argument. Besides, next time I might be the one making the phone calls when I'm preparing for an upcoming vote on the board.

Informally work on decision makers and key influencers before an important vote to make sure they fully understand the consequences of the decision.

You are an evangelist or dedicated champion facing an upcoming decision that will have an impact on your effort. The decision makers are peers, or at least approachable.

It's difficult to address the concerns of all decision makers when a new idea is raised in a large meeting.

If you go into a vote without having an idea about what will happen, you risk an unfavorable outcome that may be impossible to change later. It's hard to change the decision of a group once it is made. Yet, decision makers are not likely to agree with a new idea immediately. Their automatic response is usually "no" if they hear about the idea for the first time during a meeting. They must get the opportunity beforehand to voice their individual concerns and ask questions. This is difficult to do in a group meeting, but much easier and more effective to do on a one-on-one basis.

Therefore:

Informally work on decision makers and key influencers one-on-one before the vote. Try to get the approval of anyone who can kill the idea.

Approach the decision maker gently by briefly explaining the issue and then asking if he has any questions. Listen to his concerns and address each one. After you've answered the questions that are foremost on his mind, give him additional details. Present the facts, not just your feelings. Be clear about what you hope will happen. Tell a story to make the issue real. Make sure all decision makers fully understand the problem and the consequences of the decision. Don't distort the facts just to win the vote; that will come back to haunt you later.

Let each person know if a decision maker who is a manager or a local guru has already given support. In many cases, if you talk to the most receptive people first, you can use these people as references for the next person you talk with.

Don't present the issue as controversial. No naming; no blaming. Don't use this pattern for personal issues (e.g., to have a specific individual put on a layoff list—it then becomes a personal crusade and can lead to hard feelings). Don't use this pattern to get around a powerful person. Even if you win the votes and the decision goes your way, that powerful person may become angry if his perception is that the issue is being steamrolled past him. Use the Whisper in the General's Ear pattern to enable a manager to look good in a group setting.

Use the Fear Less pattern to calm skeptics. Even if your argument isn't convincing, you may turn down the heat on the other side.

Know when to compromise—it may be the best way to reach your ultimate goals. Don't be a fanatic. As long as it isn't seen as a trick, a concession will likely stimulate a return concession. Making concessions during an interaction is an effective way to win an argument.

Build a relationship with the decision maker. It may not be possible for a person who is new to the organization to use this pattern until a trusting relationship has been established with others.

If you are short on time, your key contacts should be the fence-sitters, those who are uncommitted and could vote either way.

If the decision doesn't go your way, remember, "No permanent friends, no permanent enemies." Someday, on some other issue of importance to you, the decision maker may come through. In the meantime, don't allow a decision maker to become an active opponent. If you win support for your issue, offer sincere appreciation and pay your debts. If someone supports you, remember to listen when he has an issue that is important to him.

The importance of talking with people before an event is similar to fellow pattern writer, David Kane's No Surprises pattern, which stresses the need to talk with customers before any anticipated changes. In other words, rather than doing damage repair, anticipate what is about to happen and do risk management.

= = = = = = = = =

This pattern creates one-on-one communication with decision makers. It helps you provide information before a meeting to encourage a vote to go your way. Since the issues are understood, the meeting time can be more efficient. There may be no need for discussion since all concerns have already been addressed.

The risk is that the people you talk with will expect a favor in the future. Also, one-on-one discussion before a meeting can be perceived as underhanded politics. You want to be as aboveboard as possible. Using this approach for purely selfish reasons is likely to backfire. The pattern is most effective when it is driven by what is best for the community.

When Bill's company decided to use the Rational Unified Process (RUP), some of the managers were tied to the old software process. So before they voted on the process decision, Bill talked with all the software managers. Then, at the meeting, the vote was taken without any discussion. Bill was certain that if he hadn't met with the managers individually, they wouldn't have understood why the company needed to move to RUP and they would have automatically reacted against it. If the vote had been taken under those conditions, it would have been almost impossible to undo.

Lisa wanted mandatory training for all software developers, which had to be approved by management. She visited each manager in her area and described how the program would work and the costs and benefits. She explained how the training would reinforce the company values and would be useful in the short term as well as over time. By the time Lisa brought the training up at a manager's meeting, it was a done deal. There wasn't any discussion; they just voted.

INSIGHTS

Classic work in psychology, conducted by Solomon Asch at Swarthmore College, provides insight into using this pattern when time is limited. In an experiment, a participant was brought into a room with a number of research confederates and told that he was participating in a study of visual acuity. Two large cards were shown to the group. On one card was a single line, the target line. On the other card was a set of three lines of varying lengths. Each person in the room was asked, "Which of the three lines on this card is the same length as the target line on the other card?" The experimenter always began with the research confederates, asking each to report which line matched. In some cases, all the confederates reported the correct answer, but in other cases, they deliberately gave a wrong answer. When the majority in the room claimed the wrong line matched, one-third of the participants would go along and also state out loud the incorrect answer. Thus one-third looked carefully and reported something they knew to be false just to agree with others in the room.

In another set of studies, Asch varied the number of confederates who identified the wrong line. When only one confederate stated an incorrect line, the number of errors made by subjects was quite low. The subject's error rate increased when two confederates identified the wrong line, and then got even higher when three gave an incorrect answer. Further increases—four, five, and six—added a little to the error rate, but not much. So it seems that three may be a magic number when it comes to influencing people to adopt a point of view. If you don't have time to visit all the members of the committee or group about to make a decision, aim to have conversations with at least three.[83]

In some cases, this pattern is broader and more complicated than a few brief water cooler conversations. Using this strategy can take a lot of time and may require a series of short meetings to get ready for the final approval, as was the case in the following story.

In George Mitchell's book on negotiating peace in Northern Ireland, Making Peace (Alfred A. Knopf, 1999), it seems that corridor politics is about having a lot of small meetings before the big meeting where those small discussions and agreements lead up to the final decision. As Mitchell states, "Once I had the plan clear in my mind, I discussed it with my staff, and with my peers. I then talked with the British officials and the Irish leaders. I met with the delegates. I did the same for all the parties. I went around to all of them several times. Based on their comments, I revised some of the details. By the deadline, I was ready, as were all of the participants. I had spent weeks thinking about the plan and discussing it with them and working to get their support. Before I presented the revised plan for their approval, I knew it would be agreed to unanimously."

Dedicated Champion

What allowed us to depart from our normal manner of business? I believe the most important element was a successful champion who engendered interest in process change. Our champion is a respected team member who is well known for getting work done and for his sincere desire to help lead the organization toward practical improvements.

To increase your effectiveness in introducing your new idea, make a case for having the work become part of your job description.

You are an evangelist who has successfully enlisted a local sponsor or corporate angel.

Effectively introducing a new idea into any organization is too much work for a volunteer.

Without the proactive effort of someone whose job description includes championing the new idea, it can wither and die on the vine. A single, dedicated individual can bring a focus to the activities necessary to maintain a sufficient level of interest to keep the idea alive. A volunteer doesn't have enough time to do this. To get this time, the change effort needs to be recognized as part of your job.

Therefore:

Make a case for including the change initiative as part of your job description.

To convince your manager, consider the following suggestions. Managers are interested in metrics. Track the number and names of attendees at meetings, and those you have signed up for the mailing list. If you have any findings, objective or subjective, from your own experience in applying the Just Do It pattern or the experience of others, this is also convincing information. The support of a local guru will help, especially if it is someone your manager trusts. Offer to schedule a guru review to provide an evaluation of the appropriateness of the idea for your organization.

External validation is also convincing, especially if the publications are in the domain the manager cares about or take the form of business-related books and articles. News about a competitor can make a big difference! A big jolt visitor can be influential if he spends time in a royal audience to address the manager's concerns.

You are "dedicated" if you have (1) devotion to the cause and (2) time dedicated to the task of championing the new idea. You can start with a small percentage of your time and later use the Tailor Made pattern to argue for expanding it if there are business reasons that will be compelling to your manager.

When you become the dedicated champion, keep your enthusiasm and don't neglect any of your current evangelist activities. Even if you are hired as a dedicated champion, you must still take on the role of an evangelist.

Realize that you do not own the success of the new idea. Too often, a dedicated champion, in his zeal to succeed, does all the work rather than facilitating and ensuring that others do their part. Use the Involve Everyone and Ask for Help patterns. Measure success by how many tasks you encourage others to do. You must become comfortable with an emergence of the new idea in the organization, patient as teams struggle to find how the innovation helps them succeed, and secure enough to create opportunities for others to do their part.

=========

This pattern creates a role dedicated to leading the introduction of the innovation into the organization. The new idea is likely to grow in the organization because you now have time, and possibly additional resources, to carry out the necessary tasks in the change initiative.

However, the approval of this role may come with the expectation to succeed. If the success of the innovation is on your shoulders, it becomes important for you to justify your time, track the results and the small successes, and continually demonstrate the benefits. Metrics can be useful. If you note these as you go, you will have them in your "back pocket" in case your boss needs data to justify your new role.

Margaret's primary job in the organization was to introduce the innovation into the organization. Because of this, she had time to do things like talk with people individually, arrange special events, keep the idea visible, and have regular conversations about what was going on with the managers. In other words, the biggest and most important resource she had was time.

A newly hired vice chancellor noticed there were a few areas in the university that had been neglected and were in need of attention. So he appointed one faculty member to each of the areas with the task of making improvements. Because they were awarded some "reassigned time" from their teaching obligations, they had the time to examine the problems and lead the needed changes.

Do Food

Our small team had to prepare weekly status reports. We hated this job and the wasted meeting time it took each week. Someone told me that the next meeting was our team lead's birthday, so I bought chocolate chip cookies. As we gathered for the meeting, I said, "I heard it's Tim's birthday today, so I brought cookies!" It was as though we'd been living in a cave and someone had turned on the lights. People smiled and began telling stories from their childhood. The meeting was fun. We joked about the report and the task we all hated. We finished early. All this from a few cookies.

Make an ordinary gathering a special event by including food.

You are an evangelist or dedicated champion who has called a meeting to introduce a new idea. Members of the user community are free to attend or not. You have resources—your own personal contribution or those of a local sponsor or corporate angel.

Usually a meeting is just another ordinary, impersonal event.

Research shows that we become fonder of people and things we experience while we are eating. Even in ancient times, people understood the importance of breaking bread together. In Christopher Alexander's pattern Communal

Eating, sharing food plays a vital role in almost all human societies to bind people together and increase the feeling of group membership. Food turns a meeting into an event. "The mere act of eating together . . . is by its very nature a sign of friendship."[84]

Therefore:

Make food available at the meeting.

Mention the availability of food when you advertise the event. Ask for help from your local sponsor or corporate angel to furnish the food. This is an important sign to attendees that the organization supports the effort. If organizational funding is not available, you could buy some inexpensive snacks. Both your colleagues and management will be impressed that you believe in the idea enough to put your money where your mouth is.

Be sure you understand the role of food in the culture. In some settings, food and work don't mix and the idea of eating during a business-related meeting would not be accepted. Each company treats food in certain ways during the workday.

Try to be sensitive to health issues. People who struggle with weight problems may find that cookies on the table are too much of a temptation. Someone with an allergy to the one food you offer will feel left out. Think about offering a bit of variety and some healthier choices.

There is no need to be extravagant; the forces are resolved in this pattern even if the food is simple.

Food is also important in small meetings, even between two people.

= = = = = = = = = =

This pattern turns an ordinary meeting into a special event and contributes to a feeling of community among the participants. Because everyone likes free food, this lure can draw people in. It will turn a mundane meeting, presentation, or other gathering into a more special event. If food is offered in the beginning, it starts the meeting on a positive note. If the topic gets controversial, it can put people in a more relaxed mood—they can stand up and get a cup of tea or grab a cookie. Food holds people's attention if the meeting gets slow.

When you begin to regularly have food at events, people will expect it and be irritated when it doesn't appear. If the food budget is depleted, have a brown bag. There are other ways to make a meeting special, such as holding a meeting outside on a nice day, using a different meeting management technique that people are not used to, cutting the agenda in half and letting people go early, or holding the event in a special executive conference room arranged by your corporate angel.

When the company started cutting back on everything, the food budget was eliminated for meetings. So Sue started bringing some inexpensive sweets. Sometimes "scouts" went out before the meeting and reported back to the rest of the group if there was food. It made Sue realize how important food was for the success of the event. When a manager came to her and asked for a retrospective, she would say, "I think it's important to have food at the meeting, so I will personally pay for cookies for the team." The manager would always reply, "Okay, since you obviously think this is important, I'll personally pay for the Pepsi." It never failed. Yes, Sue had to spend a bit of her money every time, but the manager would always ante up his contribution and the team knew it. It actually was better than when the company's budget paid for everything.

When Rachel prepares for leading project retrospective sessions, she always reminds the organizers that they need to supply snacks and drinks during the day. She has noticed that participants often gather around the food for a friendly chat during break time and wander to the snack table when they need a break but can't leave the room. This is important, because it helps to relieve the strain and exhaustion that often develop during the intense retrospective work.

INSIGHTS

Research shows the following downside to this pattern: When you are with one other person, you'll eat 35% more; with a group of four, it's 75% more; and with seven or more people; it's 96% more. Most of us are mindless eaters: When distracted by an interesting presentation or other activity, we will eat more without being aware that we are doing it.[85]

Be sure the food is something the group will appreciate and enjoy; otherwise, the snack will work against your cause.

Even when an organization's budget is tight, you might want to think about using your own money to purchase some simple foods—this can be an inexpensive investment that will pay off in a big way.

e-Forum

When I started on the South Beach diet, I thought, "Here I go again." I read the book and tried to clean out my pantry and refrigerator, but it didn't take long to get really tired of the food on the acceptable list. Then I discovered information about this diet on the website Prevention.com. I had been a reader of Prevention *magazine for years, but the recipes and the tips that others shared on this website kept me going.*

Set up an electronic bulletin board, distribution list, listserve, or writeable website for those who want to hear more.

You are an evangelist or dedicated champion trying to introduce a new idea into your organization.

You need to initiate and maintain regular contact with people who might be interested in your new idea.

It's hard to get information to everyone. People are busy and overwhelmed by too many ideas. They may not find the time to attend every event, but they like to know what's going on. You are busy, too. You want to stay in touch but don't have the time to personally keep everyone informed about the latest and greatest happenings with the new idea.

Electronic forums allow people to keep in touch and keep a new idea on their minds. When you set up a mailing list for the enthusiasts or devotees, you'll get to know some of your most potentially valuable members and give them a chance to meet each other.

Therefore:

Create a publicly accessible electronic, interactive forum. Advertise its existence. Keep it alive, active, and growing.

This can be an electronic bulletin board, distribution list, listserve, or a writeable website. You may wish to use it to distribute electronic resources, announce upcoming events, and connect people who are doing similar things with the innovation across the organization. Create separate "announce" and "discussion" lists, because some people want to participate actively and others want to passively hear what's going on.

This is one way to stay in touch, but it should not be the only way. Use persistent PR. Give regular status reports and tell people what's happening next. Use connectors to send information through their networks. Don't forget to maintain personal contact with individuals who are key to your efforts.

If you monitor the medium, you can use this data to convince a local sponsor or corporate angel that there is sufficient interest to take the next step in the change initiative.

= = = = = = = = =

This pattern creates a place to electronically share information and expectations about the new idea. It keeps you from becoming isolated from those who are interested in hearing about it. The virtual community will help you establish a real one.

If you use it too much, it can have an overdose effect and can even be viewed as spam. Don't get too accustomed to using electronic means. Know your community and know what they are interested in seeing.

The first brown bag meetings Gary held were well attended but a few busy people stopped by and said, "I was held up and couldn't make the meeting. Do you have any handouts?" "Sure!" he replied, "I'll send them to you." While he was at it, he emailed notes to others he knew were interested. That's how it started. The list grew as others heard Gary was emailing notices for meetings and other events. It was the beginning of the community that became involved in the new idea.

Alison used an email distribution list to draw attention to the activities surrounding the new idea. The initial list came from people who attended a hometown story. Later, when training courses were offered, attendees were added. The distribution list was used to advertise upcoming events, like big jolt visits. The list made the recipients feel special because they heard about something before the general population.

INSIGHTS

Although an e-Forum can be an effective way to spread some information about the new idea, we have learned that this is really not a separate pattern. Instead, it is a specific technique that can be used as part of the Persistent PR[86] pattern.

Early Adopter

Geoffrey Moore explains, "Visionaries are that rare breed of people who have the insight to match a [new idea] to a strategic opportunity, the temperament to translate that insight into a high-visibility project, and the charisma to get the rest of the organization to buy into that project."[87] They are the ones who can give your new idea its first break. Even though it is hard to plan for them, it's even harder to plan without them.

Win the support of the people who can be opinion leaders for the new idea.

You are an evangelist or dedicated champion trying to introduce a new idea into your organization. You have a small group of innovators who support your new idea.

To create more impact for the new idea in an organization, interest must extend beyond the initial group of supporters.

Innovators are helpful as gatekeepers for the innovation, but they generally don't make good opinion leaders because people are wary of their attitude toward risk. Innovators tend to be effective opinion leaders only in highly innovative organizations. In other environments, you need the help of people who are more practical, who have a reputation for being open-minded and sensible decision makers. These early adopters follow the innovators on the normal curve of adopter categories. They are just ahead of the early majority in their level of innovativeness and risk taking.

Early adopters are visionaries who care more about fundamental break-throughs than simple improvements. Unlike the more enthusiastic inno-vators who like an idea just because it's new, early adopters consider the usefulness of the idea and attempt to match it to a business goal. As a result, they often have the respect of their peers and make good opinion leaders. For this reason, they are generally sought out by change agents to help speed up the diffusion process.

Therefore:

Look for the opinion leaders and ask them for help.

You can find early adopters among people who have a reputation for discrete, successful use of new ideas. These are people who don't jump on a new idea, but instead react with an open mind and an interest to learn more. Give them as much information and training as possible to convince them of your idea. They are attracted by the smell of success.

Use the Personal Touch pattern and encourage early adopters to look to innovators for experiences with the innovation. To cultivate their interest, you must use the Tailor Made pattern and a down-to-earth approach and show the usefulness of the innovation to the organization. Be flexible and willing to work with them as they try to realize the business value the idea offers.

Once they are convinced of the new idea, encourage early adopters to take on the role of bridge builder. Ask them to lead a study group or do a home-town story after they get some experience using the innovation. They can also help land the support of a local sponsor or corporate angel.

If you find an early adopter who becomes a guru on your side, he may be interested in being part of a guru review.

Stay in touch and remember to offer sincere appreciation.

= = = = = = = = =

This pattern helps establish a group that can serve as opinion leaders for your new idea. The backing of these individuals will reduce the uncertainty that other people, such as the early majority and skeptics, have about the new idea.

The support of this group does not come for free. Unlike innovators, who usually become excited after attending one event, early adopters will ask for more information before they become convinced. But this reaction to new ideas is what earns them a trusted reputation and, in turn, their role as opinion leaders. So any time you take with them is likely to pay off later.

Soon after Kathy started talking about a new idea, she noticed that Carol took the initiative to read one of the well-known books on the topic. Kathy took Carol out for coffee one day to answer her questions about what the idea could offer. Carol was hooked. Because her work and her opinions were respected in the organization, Kathy asked her to talk with others about the new idea. Also, when Kathy planned an event, she always asked Carol for her opinion on the details.

The knowledge management initiative at one company targeted the software developers who would be interested in the long-term goal of building a repository to capture best practices. Those who were involved in the knowledge mining for the repository were the respected, down-to-earth developers who were open to new ideas, not those who were wildly enthusiastic just because it was a new thing.

Early Majority

Marketers of a high-tech product tell this story. In the first year of selling their product, the technology enthusiasts (innovators) and some visionaries (early adopters) quickly jumped on board. During the second year, the company won over more visionaries and signed a handful of truly major deals. In the third year, the company expanded its sales force, increased its advertising budget, opened new district offices, and strengthened customer support. But the sales ended up being far less than expected and the growth in expenses was larger than the growth in revenue. What the company had interpreted as a steadily emerging mainstream market was really an early market. The company failed to recognize that selling an idea to innovators and early adopters is different from selling it to the early majority.

To create commitment to the new idea in the organization, you must convince the majority.

You are an evangelist or dedicated champion trying to introduce a new idea into your organization. You have the support of innovators and early adopters.

The support of innovators and early adopters will spark the new idea, but you need much more to truly have impact.

You begin to build your grassroots effort with innovators who are gatekeepers and early adopters who are the early opinion leaders. But at some point you must win the support of the majority to allow the idea to thrive. The early majority represents about one-third of the population. Once this group is convinced, they are loyal and will often enforce organizational standards to help the innovation succeed.

The early majority are much more deliberate in their decision making than either innovators or early adopters. Before they commit to a new idea, they want to know how others have succeeded with it. They want the innovation to work properly and integrate well with the way things are done. Risk is viewed as a waste of time and money, rather than as a chance for opportunity or excitement. Unlike innovators, the early majority adopts too late to take on the role of gatekeeper for the new idea. Unlike early adopters, they are followers and generally do not hold positions of opinion leadership. Yet, they provide the link between those who adopt early and those who are relatively late to embrace the idea. This link bridges the gap or "chasm" between early adopters and the early majority. You must cross this chasm to get a new idea into the mainstream.

Therefore:

Expand the group that has adopted the new idea rapidly to include the more deliberate majority that will allow the new idea to establish a strong foothold.

Look for individuals who are practical and want incremental, measurable, predictable progress. Use the Personal Touch pattern to show them that the risk is low while the value to their immediate needs is great. Show them the visible improvements that can be obtained with the innovation by applying the Tailor Made pattern. Demonstrate results with the Just Do It pattern and share sources of external validation. Connect them with early adopters and others who have already adopted the innovation. Encourage them to attend a hometown story.

Once they are convinced, encourage them to talk with their peers about the innovation. Since they are the link to the late majority, ask them to take on the role of bridge builder to connect with individuals who are more conservative than they are. Remember to offer sincere appreciation.

= = = = = = = = = =

This pattern establishes a grassroots majority for a new idea in the organization. Acceptance by the early majority defines the tipping point for the innovation. Gaining their support will accelerate the introduction of the new idea because the chasm has been crossed and the innovation has entered into the mainstream. In addition, unlike innovators, who usually move quickly from one new idea to the next, and early adopters, who often see themselves on the fast track, the early majority can offer stability and long-term commitment.

But you can become frustrated with this group because they can be hard to reach by simply talking with them. Be patient. You must have successes before you can begin to convince them.

A faculty member in a neighboring department stopped by Karen's office seeking advice on a proposal he submitted for a new undergraduate major. He explained that he had been encouraged by the initial enthusiasm from some members of his department. So he moved forward with the planning and thought that the other members would eventually become convinced that it was a good thing to do. But this did not happen: The majority of the department was not behind him. Karen suggested that these people needed more assurance that his idea was not risky. So the faculty member talked with each individual about the advantages the new major would offer the department and provided evidence that it would not take large amounts of resources from other projects. The idea wasn't an overnight process, but eventually the majority agreed that he should move forward with the planning.

How do you know when you have built a culture surrounding a new idea? Randy thinks he knew that he had passed a significant point when a high-level manager stopped by his office late one evening. He sat down heavily and began to talk about some problems he was having and then asked, "So, do you think <the new idea> can help me?" This was a manager of a large legacy system. The new idea had never been "pitched" to his department and although anyone could take the training, most of the interest came from the new projects. If this manager was asking to use the new idea, clearly the majority was being won over.

Evangelist

Evangelist and author Barbara Waugh writes, "How I thought it worked was, if you were great, like Martin Luther King, Jr., you had a dream. Since I wasn't great, I figured I had no dream and the best I could do was follow someone else's. Now I believe it works like this: It's having the dream that makes you great. It's the dream that produces the greatness. It's the dream that draws others around us and attracts the resources it takes to accomplish the dream."[88]

To begin to introduce the new idea into your organization, do everything you can to share your passion for it.

You're excited about a new idea. Maybe you went to a conference or read an article or book and, as a result, started learning more. You believe your idea will have value for your organization and you want to spread the word.

You want to get a new idea going, but you don't know where to start.

It's hard to translate enthusiasm into action that has lasting impact. New ideas are always out there, more than we can handle. Even the best ideas still need to be sold. This depends on the enthusiasm of people who are the natural instigators of fresh ideas and practices. They are the ones who can grow an idea into real change for the organization.

159

Therefore:

To introduce a new idea, let your passion for this new idea drive you.

Invest yourself in your cause. In other words, the first person to convince is you. If you don't believe in your cause, it will be difficult to sell it to anyone else. If you're not convinced, then you're not convincing. You must be likeable, believable, and open, but not a fanatic. This is not a role for the fainthearted. Look for possibilities in every situation; take advantage of even small opportunities to get your idea across.

Share your vision with others. Let them feel your enthusiasm. Tell your story—this is the driver for real change. Your story should convey your passion, excitement, and conviction, and inspire others to feel the same way. It's a good idea to have a two-minute "elevator pitch" targeted for different audiences, so you're ready when anyone asks you about your new idea. Show that there's value in your new idea. Don't preach—any improvements should just radiate from you and from your work. With luck, others will notice and inquire.

Learn more about possibilities for the innovation in your organization by using the Just Do It pattern. But realize that you are not the expert. Don't sell yourself that way or expect that you can play the expert role. A little humility goes a long way. Also, keep in mind that you are not the idea. You're a person who has a good idea, but other people can share it. You don't lose anything if others become more knowledgeable, or if others also become evangelists.

Don't worry if you don't have an all-encompassing strategy. Just do it using a concrete action plan. Take time for reflection and learn as you go. Celebrate small successes, be prepared for setbacks, and realize that real change takes time. Get beyond a quick-fix mindset, because progress can be slow. Proceed with baby steps, letting each stage build on the previous one.

Give brown bags and use the Plant the Seeds pattern. Do food at events when you can. Begin to identify innovators and connectors. Set up a mailing list or website.

If there is interest, start a study group. If you have a well-known contact who will come into your organization at no cost, bring in a big jolt.

Use the Personal Touch pattern and remember to offer sincere appreciation.

If you are seen as an innovator, people are less likely to trust what you have to say, since you probably get excited about new things just because they are new. If you are seen as an early adopter, you are likely to be more effective in reaching the rest of the organization because of your reputation for being more down-to-earth in your decision making.

Research suggests that if you are naturally likeable and attractive, your job will be easier because people are unconsciously more open to people they like. If you are introverted or opinionated, people are not likely to trust you, even if you've got the best data in the world. You must be a strong communicator, someone who can build personal credibility. Fellow pattern writer Joe Bergin's Introvert–Extrovert pattern suggests that you can learn to play the role of an extrovert, so that an observer believes you are bold and outgoing. You must recognize when this role is appropriate, gather your resources, and play the part.

Ask for help. It's hard to be a salesperson and a connector and a maven, but all three roles are needed to lead a change initiative. Don't try to do it all. For example, a guru on your side is a good candidate for a maven. Encourage others to be evangelists in their own teams.

Your goal is to earn credibility. Others may not always agree with you, but they need to trust what you say. This is the most important part of being a change agent. Once you've earned credibility, you're in a good position to become a dedicated champion. Be on the lookout for possible managerial support. Real impact will require a local sponsor and a corporate angel.

= = = = = = = = =

This pattern establishes a role for an initial enthusiastic introduction of a new idea. It gets the new idea going and sparks some support from innovators and possibly some interest among management.

The risk is that you can appear too passionate about the new idea and turn some people off. Maintain the enthusiasm, but don't get carried away. Don't let your enthusiasm make you impatient. One of your most powerful qualities may be your ability to be patient and impatient at the same time. Keep in mind that most people need time before they will feel the same enthusiasm you do.

In 1999, after writing a book about improving long-term care for the elderly, Bill Thomas hit the road on a promotional tour. He spoke on radio and television. He also met with public officials, offering his perspective as a medical specialist on the care of the elderly. He stressed what was wrong with nursing homes: They were utterly devoid of hope, love, humor, and meaning—the very stuff of life. He gave lectures on the changes he had in mind, but he also demonstrated why this was no ordinary book and this was no ordinary tour, and why he is certainly no ordinary doctor. It wasn't enough for Thomas to communicate his vision for better long-term care through an imaginative book. He also developed a one-man show based on the tale, traveling to 27 cities in 31 days. For him, the tour never ended. It can't—not if he's going to fix long-term care in the United States. It's an audacious mission and a truly big fix—one that requires more than just fresh ideas. Thomas advises, "You need to have people go a little nuts about what you want to do."

Walt Disney was good at conveying his vision for a new film. He would act out all the roles in front of a large group of his staff. Even though he was not a cartoonist, he knew what he wanted and could get his ideas across. He believed in these approaches: Establish the vision; sell your dream, make it clear and alive; trust your people; don't interfere with their work; and give feedback at critical points.

INSIGHTS

The pattern name "evangelist" was contentious at the beginning because some thought it had a religious flavor. We considered changing the name of this pattern to energizer, but now we realize that "evangelist" is the right choice. In the early stages of introducing a new idea, the evangelist doesn't *know* that it will work within the organization and, therefore, must *believe* it will be a good thing. Belief creates the necessary passion to carry the change initiative forward. Even when you feel you know for sure, always leave a little space for uncertainty so you can continue to learn. As Steve Jobs said in his commencement address at Stanford University in 2005:

> *You can't connect the dots looking forward; you can only connect them looking backwards. So you have to trust that the dots will somehow connect in your future. You have to trust in something: your gut, destiny, life, karma, whatever. Because believing that the dots will connect down the road will give you the confidence to follow your heart, even when it leads you off the well-worn path.*

Ultimately, this role is all about sales. The first person you have to sell is yourself. Often this means overcoming the obstacles that come to mind. We hear many people make excuses for not taking the first step because they don't have resources or knowledge. These are valid concerns, but taking on the role of evangelist is not about having sufficient resources or vast knowledge, but about believing in the importance of the idea enough to work hard and make it happen. It's about passion and belief.

You must be realistic about your vision. Otherwise, you run the risk of being a delusional dreamer who takes on an impossible dream for a day, fails, blames the environment, and moves on to the next delusion. You must remain flexible with an evolving vision that includes a concrete action plan.

One of your important tasks is to look for more evangelists. Help create a culture in which everyone is more likely to succeed by mentoring others and recognizing their strengths. Giving to others boosts happiness and self-esteem, as numerous studies show. Supporting others makes it easier to ensure that they support you.

All evangelists, even those at an executive level, are powerless to force people to change their minds. One high-level executive was asked how he got people to work well together. He gave a simple answer: He ordered them to, and when employees wouldn't change, he fired them. This approach is very effective at getting compliance, but it also creates an environment in which everyone is driven to think the same way. Moreover, when the hammer goes away, so can the initiative. Therefore, we recommend developing commitment. You want other members of your organization to sign up for the new idea because they believe in it. You want their hearts to be in it. That's what the *Fearless Change* patterns are all about.

You will be more successful if you approach the organization with respect for existing processes and techniques. If you step over the fine line and become a fanatic, convinced that you know best without regard for the status quo, you run the risk of alienating the community.

External Validation

I've been trying to convince my dear friend Linda that my hometown of Asheville, North Carolina, would be a great place for Linda and her husband to retire. She would just nod politely when I would tell her about all the things I thought the area has to offer. Then I pointed out some national publications in which the Asheville area appears as "best city" and "best place to retire." Linda now tells me that she and her husband have put Asheville on their list of cities to seriously consider.

To increase the credibility of the new idea, bring in information from sources external to the organization.

You are an evangelist or dedicated champion working to introduce a new idea into your organization. People are writing and publishing on topics related to the new idea.

Before being persuaded to accept a new idea, people want assurance that the idea has validity outside the organization.

The innovation-decision process begins with knowledge. When people become aware of an innovation, they want to understand how it works. This information can come from within the organization but, initially, external

164

sources of information are more important. External publications have more credibility than internal technical reports, which are often write-only documents that are distributed widely but largely unread.

Most people want some evidence that the innovation is not just an impractical notion promoted by a few individuals in the organization; therefore, endorsements from outside the organization will catch their eye. External sources of information are especially important for innovators and early adopters, who are typically the first to adopt an innovation, because at the time they are seeking knowledge there are few people in the organization who have experience with the new idea.

Therefore:

Give people in the organization external sources of useful information about the new idea.

Mass-media sources are a good place to start—books, articles, and web pages with no-nonsense information. Include success stories when you can for those who appreciate the smell of success. Make sure the publications are trusted by the people you are trying to reach. For example, managers read business journals, not technical ones.

Look for opportunities to plant the seeds. Distribute the information one-on-one by following the Personal Touch pattern or on a wider basis by utilizing persistent PR. In addition to the written word, bring in a big jolt speaker.

Consider presenting your work externally in a venue that is recognized by your colleagues. Publish in journals read by the people you want to convince, especially early adopters and anyone who is a guru on your side. You may even want to write a book and get it published by an external publisher.

Although external sources can and should be provided at any time, use this pattern especially in the early days of your efforts, when people need knowledge and there are few opinion leaders in the organization.

= = = = = = = = =

This pattern generates some validation for a new idea in the organization. It shows that the innovation is not just a local phenomenon. Because this is what people need, it is effective in gaining awareness and raising credibility. Management might see this external validation as a sign that the competition is gaining ground in this area. This can spur decision makers to support the innovation.

Sometimes, however, the distribution of external sources throughout your organization can be seen as intellectual browbeating. Sending books or articles up and down the chain can make people feel inadequate because they can't keep up with the pace of reading. Use the Just Enough pattern and present ideas with simple, authentic statements. Provide more background if anyone asks. External publishing also involves risks. Others across the organization might label your effort as "writing only and not working." Make your topics factual, relevant, and useful so your colleagues don't dismiss them as academic.

My manager never paid much attention to my research until one day I showed him a book that referenced one of my publications. He wasn't familiar with the topic of the book, but was extremely impressed that my name appeared in it. I did not expect such an enthusiastic reaction from him, but it showed me the power of external validation!

When we moved from Level 1 to Level 2 CMM (Capability Maturity Model), we asked a few speakers from other companies at Level 2 and 3 to talk about the benefits they had realized in their organizations when they achieved these levels. This helped people to understand what could be achieved, and how these other organizations approached the changes.

INSIGHTS

Have you ever had the experience in your organization where an expensive external consultant was brought in and said the same thing that you've been trying to get across to your colleagues? Why did everyone listen to the outsider but not pay attention to you? It seems we're stuck with this behavior, so the best thing for you to do is to take advantage of it. Improve your credibility by referencing an outside source—something that means something to your organization. It can be an article, a book, a video, or just about anything that shows influential outsiders think your idea is a good one.

Fear Less

In her book Soul in the Computer, *Barbara Waugh says, "I force myself to ask of every obstacle, 'What if this is a gift? What is it that this obstacle or setback is telling me?' Someone who is initially the most skeptical may become my best partner, constantly detecting the hype and fluff and unnecessary complexity in my thinking about what we are doing and what the next steps are."*[89]

Turn resistance to the new idea to your advantage.

You are an evangelist or dedicated champion trying to introduce a new idea into your organization.

Any innovation is disruptive, so resistance is likely.

Every change agent complains about resistance, but if you think *this* is bad, consider the alternative. It's frightening to imagine a situation with no resistance at all. If that were the case, you would be solely responsible to be 100% correct, 100% of the time. Scary, isn't it? But nobody's perfect. We need resistance to test our ideas. So, the first step in dealing with opposition is to appreciate it. Fortunately, contrariness is universal. It's like fungus; it doesn't thrive in daylight. Therefore, once you suspect that there is resistance, your first step is to get it out in the open, rather than let it fester in the dark.

Skeptics can teach us a lot about what we are doing wrong. No matter how determined we are, how "righteous" our cause, we're going to run into obstacles. No course of action is perfect. Skeptics present gifts; they provide us with information about the route we've chosen and how to alter our approach and our goals.

You will eventually have to address fear—both the listener's and your own. Listeners may fear loss of position or status, loss of comfort, or being taken in by hype. Someone may resist change because he is trying to avoid the pain he believes will result or the loss of something positive and enjoyable. Fears typically manifest themselves as resistance. Your reaction is likely to advocate your views even more vigorously. That response, too, is motivated by fear: the fear of looking bad when everyone is watching, the fear that your ideas may, in fact, be wrong. The collision of two fearful people leads to an impasse. Resistance is not the primary reason why changes fail; rather, it's the reaction to resistance that creates problems.

It's hard to listen to people when we don't agree with them. Usually we just elaborate our point of view or repeat what we've said. A better approach is to encourage the other person to say more about his point of view. Sometimes just hearing what another individual has to say will help both of you reach a better understanding.

Therefore:

Ask for help from resisters.

Listen, really listen, to what a skeptic has to say and learn from him. Try to appreciate the differences in opinion. When people disagree with you, stop and think about the value in seeing things from their perspective. Rather than hiding the potential problems, ask for input on ways to address them. When someone makes a critical comment, reply, "What would you recommend?" You don't have to agree with the critics; you can simply recognize them, and then seek to understand their positions. Be sure the skeptic knows you are listening. Acknowledge and validate his expertise. Ask questions. Try to understand his arguments.

Bring the skeptic's concerns to light and address them before he has a chance to use them to stifle your efforts. Include his objections as limitations and topics to consider when you do presentations or lead discussions on the new idea.

While listening to their objections, help resisters understand that learning a new idea does not mean throwing away their experience. Use the Personal Touch pattern to show how the innovation can improve things for them. Sometimes people who are resistant to an innovation can become quite enthusiastic if they are just given the opportunity to try it.

Don't assume that a skeptic's position is fixed. Just because he is initially opposed to your new idea doesn't mean that he can't be open to what you have to say over time. It's a natural human tendency to shy away from criticism, but it can be a sign of a healthy, vital culture when people care enough to air their concerns. Don't avoid opposition, but rather engage it and assess its merits with the critic. If the person is an influential, his ability to sift through information and see benefits as well as problems—as well as revise his assessment when it is merited and to tell others—makes him a valuable complainer. He will likely change his opinion when he sees cause for change.

Invite resistance so that all concerns are heard. Find something to appreciate in all those people who aren't on your wavelength. Appreciation asks for nothing and gives everything. Research shows that it is physiologically impossible to be in a state of appreciation and a state of fear at the same time. Thus, appreciation can be an antidote to fear.

Be humble in your efforts and compassionate toward imperfections, including your own. While you may like some people more than others, keep in mind that a range of personalities lives in each person. The way you operate toward other individuals will elicit the personality you see—the resister you fear or the best person someone is capable of being.

The skeptics must be willing to talk and to listen—if they are not, put your energy elsewhere. It's sad, but some people will never be happy no matter what, and you probably don't want to encourage them by spending a lot of time with them. Sometimes the resistance is due to a personality clash. If others who have adopted the new idea are willing to help, try the Bridge Builder pattern. If some resisters become too difficult, find a shoulder to cry on—you might discover other ways to deal with them.

If you know a resister who is a strong opinion leader, consider giving him the role of champion skeptic.

= = = = = = = = =

This pattern builds a relationship with a skeptic. It allows you to use resistance to your advantage rather than permitting others to wield it against you. Listening to skeptics will bring to light the limitations of the new idea so that issues can be addressed frankly and honestly. Resisters may not welcome the new idea with open arms, but if you have done your best to calm their fears, some will come around or try to be open-minded. Other people who see you dealing respectfully with resisters, and even raising objections in advance, are likely to be impressed with you as the messenger of a new idea.

The risk is that resisters can overwhelm you if you are not prepared to handle criticism. Encourage them to talk with you one-on-one to protect yourself from a verbal attack in public that can end up damaging your cause.

You always know who "they" are—the people who don't show up for your presentations, the people who don't stop by to ask about a new idea, the people who just don't care. So, you slip into denial and focus on the positive responders. You tell yourself that "they" will come around because your idea is so good. That was Roger's strategy until another reorganization and subsequent move put him next to one of "them"—one of those guys who had been with the company forever. Roger was polite and nodded, "Good morning! How's it going, Bill?" One day he heard him over the cubicle wall, "Okay, Roger, tell me about that new idea!" Roger was up like a shot. He spent nearly a half-hour with Bill and got to hear firsthand what the skeptical co-worker thought the problems were. It was amazing that the two men were almost always in agreement. Bill brought up some things Roger hadn't considered, so Roger included these points in his next presentation about the new idea. Roger and Bill still have great discussions, even though they've both left the company.

Lynn was giving a talk about a new idea and someone in the audience was angrily disagreeing with everything she said. After hearing a few negative comments, Lynn decided to ask the guy to have lunch, which was scheduled just after the talk. She sat down with him, pulled out her notebook, and said, "I can't promise to do anything about your concerns, but I want to hear all of them. Fire away!" He kept her busy for the entire meal, and after it was over he said sincerely, "Thanks for listening. Everyone is usually too busy to care and they treat me like a crackpot. I appreciate that you took the time. Thanks." Lynn wasn't sure she had won him over, but she was glad she took the time to hear his viewpoint. That's important for new ideas or anything else.

INSIGHTS

The original version of this pattern emphasized listening, and that's still important—but we stopped short of suggesting that you say nothing in response. Just listening is powerful. You don't have to follow your listening, your silence, with any comment or argument. Let it be.

This pattern is not about overcoming objections; it's about using what others know and have to contribute. Giving up on conquering and giving back the right of colleagues to make up their own minds is likely to be much more effective than using all your energy to convince resisters. Consider a strategy that provokes thought and then allows others to convince themselves.

Part of a good conflict resolution strategy is to separate the person from the problem and to focus on interests, not positions.[90] This is an important part of the solution for this pattern and a good thing to remember in general. Some people will resist your new idea simply because they don't have the bandwidth to think about it, let alone implement it. If you are sympathetic to their plight and your plans include ways to make their lives easier (implementing the Easier Path pattern), this will go a long way toward lowering resistance.

The original pattern didn't stress just how challenging the use of this solution can be. We want resisters to see things our way. We may believe that if we just argue longer or louder or more cleverly that we will win! It's hard to listen and learn and believe that each of us might have a piece of the truth. Just as you wouldn't be angry at your gas gauge for telling you that you're almost out of gas, so you shouldn't be upset if someone pokes holes in your idea. In both cases, use the information as feedback and learn what you can do to improve, whether it's to remember to check your gas level before you head out on a long trip or to seek information on how others will be affected by your ideas.

There's real danger in focusing on the negative. In a recent workshop, the goal was to list all the objections to a good idea and come up with ways to overcome them. By the end of the session, participants seemed to feel they had all the objections and negativity nailed down. They didn't consider that we often resist an idea, consciously or unconsciously, for reasons that are not available to us: It's difficult for us to understand, let alone explain, the root cause for our own objections. Therefore, it's tedious to attempt to address a specific concern—you can play a lot of "whack a mole" by preparing for one thing, only to see something else pop up in response.

When you want to get something going, look for the low-hanging fruit and seek out as many supporters as possible. Don't run up against the negative folks, unless absolutely necessary, until you're well under way. At that point you will likely have some evidence that the new idea works. Spend a minimal amount of time attempting to convince the resisters. If they remain negative, without making useful contributions, then try to work around them or make them a Greek chorus of champion skeptics. But do so only if you have to—if you spend too much time with die-hards, you'll never get anything done. Fear Less is a good pattern but it doesn't work for every skeptic.

Focus your energy on skeptics who have influence. Use your best tool— your willingness to just listen. This is especially important in the early days of the initiative when you have no data or successes to share.

It's OK to feel anger, but when you hear negative comments, use your resentment to help you move negativity in a positive direction. As Seth Godin says, "Use your fear like fuel."[91] Your goal is to sense that the other person is just having a conversation with you because she feels that you are interested in what she has to say. Resist the temptation to fight to the death to prove every point—utilize the Pick Your Battles pattern.

It's worrisome to hear a change agent talk about individuals who disagree with the new approach by labeling them *those* people: "Those people just don't get it" and "Those people are stupid." A change agent often believes that he has great insight and doesn't need to compromise. The following story from Dale Emery illustrates another way:

When Susan finished telling me about the "resisters," I said, "Instead of calling these folks 'resisters,' suppose you think of them as people who are resisting this change at this time." She considered this for minute, then said, "That makes a big difference. When I think of them as resisters, it's as if I have them all figured out, that they're just resistant to change. When I think of them as resisting a particular change at a particular time, I see them more as people. Maybe they have reasons for resisting." I said, "Now, instead of thinking of them as resisting the change, what if you think of them as responding to it?" After a moment, she said, "Thank you! Now I know what I need to do!" I talked with Susan several months later. She had met several times with the company veterans who were most concerned about the change, and focused on listening carefully to what they had to say. She learned that their biggest concern was how they would fit in.[92]

Group Identity

A group of people involved in facilitating project retrospectives gathered in Oregon in 2002 to share their interest in retrospectives and brainstorm ways to increase their use across the software development industry. When the group created a list of action items, the first on the list was: Who are we? What are we trying to accomplish? Do we share a set of common goals? Once these fundamental questions were answered, the group was ready to move forward and make progress. The group is called Retroasis and convenes annually at different locations around the world.

Give the change effort an identity to help people recognize that it exists.

You are an evangelist or dedicated champion. You've had a brown bag or perhaps just an informal meeting in the cafeteria or hallway.

It's harder to introduce a new idea when people aren't aware that the effort exists.

It's easier to recognize and talk about something if it has an identity. This is why organizations often assign a name to individual projects and sports groups give their teams a name. This is why patterns are given a name! When the name is mentioned, people will think about the new idea and know what you are talking about. If they don't know what it's all about, they are likely to ask.

Assigning an identity to a change initiative helps people become aware that it exists and what it is trying to do. The more people hear and see the name, the more likely they are to become curious about it and get involved.

Therefore:

Give the change effort an identity.

A good way to begin is to give your group a name. It can be one that is created by the group itself—this builds camaraderie. The name can also come from other sources. At one company, a new process was introduced called the Product Input and Planning Process. When the CEO decided to champion this effort, he joked, "So the product owner is Gladys Knight and your team is the PIPs!" The nickname stuck, and it gave the new approach instant visibility. Having support from a corporate angel may have had something to do with that!

Use the name often and everywhere you can. Display it when you use persistent PR and when you hold an event.

There are other ways to give a group an identity. For example, a regular meeting signals an organized effort. The meetings can be for planning and other business or incorporated with another activity. Ask for help from those who attend the meeting. The meetings may have few attendees, especially in the beginning, but even a small group begins to build a community. But use the meetings carefully. In some company cultures, holding meetings will give the initiative a negative identity. This is especially true if meetings are run badly.

A web page, a URL, or an email address helps make the group look official.

If the group decides to write a mission statement and objectives, display them where everyone can see. Mission statements and/or group objectives help those involved in the effort focus on what they are trying to do.

= = = = = = = = = =

This pattern establishes an identity for your efforts with the new idea. An identity makes the initiative more visible in the organization, gives it more credibility, and creates something that others can ask about, talk about, and get involved in. It helps create a vocabulary for the group that supports the new idea; this can be the beginning of a subculture.

At the same time, when you label something, people can label you. If they see your group as exclusive, they will develop misconceptions. Be clear about the purpose of the group and involve everyone.

One organization identifies the internal faculty of practitioners who contribute to the company's internal training program as "University Faculty." They have web pages that include their biographies and pictures, and each person is given a new shirt every term with the corporate logo and the title of the training program. This creates a sense of identity for the faculty so that there is pride in ownership and participation.

In the German-based xpedition courses (www.xpeditionstraining.de), the first assignment for the teams of participants is to create a name. During the break, one of the trainers arranges for T-shirts to be printed for each team with their name. Since the training lasts only two days, this speeds up the team jelling process.

INSIGHTS

The formation of every in-group creates a counterpart out-group. As a result, there are serious downsides to this pattern. The minimal group experiments by Henri Tajfel demonstrated that any symbol can be used to define a group, even when it's arbitrarily created. Tajfel randomly assigned subjects to groups, and no matter which group a person happened to be in, he or she quickly began to discriminate in favor of in-group members and against out-group members. Yet, if asked, subjects were not always aware of why they did what they did. In-group members justified discriminating behavior with rational arguments about how unpleasant and immoral the out-group members were.[93] To prevent this type of outcome, do all you can to ensure that the group identity is positive and inclusive. Inspire; don't create barriers for those who aren't eligible or imply that "we get it but you don't." Don't allow a group identity to have an elitist flavor. This will work against the change effort. Instead, do all you can to involve everyone.

The following stories are good examples of positive, non-exclusive group identity.

The Institute for Healthcare Improvement (IHI) is behind the 100,000 Lives campaign. Instead of focusing on the negative problem (hospitals making mistakes that were killing patients), it chose a name for the initiative that was positive and nonjudgmental—100,000 Lives—and set a specific target. At the campaign kick-off event, IHI's CEO, Donald Berwick, said, "Here is what I think we should do. I think we should save 100,000 lives. I think we should do that by June 14, 2006—18 months from today. 'Some' is not a number; 'soon' is not a time. Here's the number: 100,000. Here's the time: June 14, 2006, 9:00 a.m." It was an invitation to the entire community to join—not a label for the enlightened.

For the 2008 presidential election, the turnout rate was approximately 96% among registered voters who first filled out a survey asking, "How important is it to you to be a voter?" compared with 82% for those who were asked, "How important is it for you to vote?" The study was led by Christopher Bryan of Stanford University, who said, "We offered people the prospect of claiming a desirable identity. That's a powerful thing."[94]

Guru on Your Side

After I gave the first brown bag on the new idea, one of the attendees commented, "This is good stuff, but no one knows you. You should talk to Jeff or Randy. If they like it, then others will follow." I immediately went to see these senior programmers and sure enough, at the next brown bag, attendance doubled and most of the newcomers told me, "Jeff (or Randy) said I should hear about this." I was grateful for the help!

Enlist the support of senior-level people who are esteemed by members of the organization.

You are an evangelist or dedicated champion trying to introduce a new idea into your organization.

People in an organization can be reluctant to show interest in a new idea unless it has the support of colleagues they respect.

Most people are continually bombarded with information and are too busy to keep up with the latest and greatest, so they depend on others to help evaluate new ideas. Usually these trusted advisors are senior-level people who are respected by everyone. When these people get behind an idea, it's one of the strongest kinds of approval you can have.

If managers follow the patterns that Don Olson and Carol Stimmel have written, Shameless Ignoramus and Get a Guru, respectively, then they admit they can't keep up with technical matters and have established a trusting relationship with a reliable technical expert. When such an expert is convinced of a new idea, he can help persuade the managers and other people in the organization.

Therefore:

Enlist the support of experienced, senior-level gurus who are respected by both managers and non-managers alike.

Approach gurus with humility. You're there to learn from them, not educate them about every nuance of the innovation. Instead of hitting them over the head with your new idea, use the Just Enough pattern to present it gradually, asking for the guru's opinion about it. Instead of saying, "Wow! I was at this cool conference and I found this great new way of doing things. I'm so excited about it! I thought I'd have a meeting and tell the team," try, "I'm sorry you didn't get to go to the great conference last week. You would have enjoyed seeing all the latest stuff. I heard about this new way of doing things and I wanted to see what you thought of it before I run off at the mouth telling everyone."

Another way to approach the guru is by saying something like, "I know you're the local <topic> guru, but I also know that you're interested in new things, so I thought you'd like to hear about the symposium I attended last week." Research has shown that engineers are fearful of being labeled an expert in an area if it keeps them from learning new things. They don't want past knowledge to limit their potential for future growth.

Take the guru out for coffee. Give an appropriate two-minute "elevator pitch" on the innovation and then be prepared to listen. Someone with a great deal of experience has a lot to share. Use the Personal Touch pattern to show how the innovation can address some of the problems he mentions, and use the Tailor Made pattern to suggest where the innovation would fit in the organization.

If you're new to the organization, ask connectors who these gurus are. It helps if you know a high-level manager or another guru who can make an introduction.

Give gurus a chance to be involved if they find the innovation worthwhile; encourage them to talk with others or invite them to be part of a guru review.

= = = = = = = = = =

This pattern creates a community of people who can supply technical credibility for the new idea. If you can convince them that the innovation is a good idea, others will at least hear you out. Management, especially upper management, often depends on respected individuals to provide an assessment of potential solutions. So once they are on your side, your battles are half over.

But recognize that these veterans can make or break you. If the person thinks the idea sounds like a "pile of garbage," he is likely to share his feelings with others. Encourage him to take on the role of champion skeptic so that his resistance can make a constructive contribution.

Alan was the evangelist for the introduction of Java in our organization. The biggest worries among the skeptics were the fear of the new technology and concerns about performance and scalability. The hardest person to convince was the head of the architecture group. He was a very active, vocal skeptic who had the ear of the vice president. Alan knew that because this skeptic's expertise was respected in the organization, he would be more open if his expertise was validated. Therefore, Alan tried to understand his objections and help him feel less threatened. The skeptic was ultimately convinced by (1) the proof of concept and (2) subsequent discussion of how much more difficult it would be to implement the project in C++. After he said Java was OK, convincing the rest of the team was easy.

When presenting a proposal to the faculty senate, Pamela always glances now and then at the person who is the most respected member of the senate. If she sees anything that indicates approval by this guru, such as a nod or a smile, she winds down her speech because she is quite certain that the hard work is done.

INSIGHTS

The original pattern focused on gaining support so that the guru will help the change initiative. What you really want is to be sure that the guru will not work against you.

Don't count on just one guru, regardless of how influential she is, because she could leave your organization. Try to enlist as many gurus as possible on your side.

The phrase that many people often use when referring to this pattern is "trusted advisor." Managers and executives often have a technical advisor in the organization who provides trusted counsel—this person is the guru.

Guru Review

The managers seemed to have that "Oh no, not another silver bullet" look every time I mentioned the new idea. But when one of them asked me what Garrison thought of the idea and another asked me what Carol thought of it, it hit me that the managers looked to these two individuals for advice. So I asked all the managers if they would help me create a review team for the idea. Each of the managers who agreed appointed one member. When the team met one afternoon, I was there to give a short presentation and to answer their questions. I took notes and wrote a report that the team approved before it was forwarded to management. Not only did this exercise help me convince management that the innovation had merit, but it also uncovered some issues I had not considered. As I recall, there were even skeptics on that review team who were eventually won over to the benefit of all concerned.

Gather anyone who is a guru on your side and other interested colleagues to evaluate the new idea for managers and other developers.

You are an evangelist or dedicated champion working to introduce a new idea into your organization.

Some managers and developers are supportive, but others are reluctant to join in until they have some assurance that this is a worthwhile idea.

Managers and developers are overwhelmed by information. They can't keep up with the latest and greatest. They have probably been disappointed by the promises of the never-ending stream of silver bullets and have become skeptical and reluctant to go along with even the most convincing arguments.

However, they are always interested in something that will help make their jobs easier and improve the quality of their products. They just need solid evidence. Usually, managers and developers will trust the judgment of their local guru, especially if they have a long-term relationship.

Because this guru usually keeps up with the latest trends, he can be referred to as a maven, a reliable source of knowledge. This perception of reliability allows him to influence a large audience, including managers.

Therefore:

Gather a review team of respected gurus in the organization to evaluate the new idea.

Start looking for potential team members among the individuals you have identified as gurus on your side. The team must be respected by management and other influential people and have backgrounds that will allow them to be effective evaluators. Ask for help. Get names from managers or from connectors. Include all the right people. Leaving someone out could hurt your cause. If one of the gurus is a vocal skeptic, you may want to include him as champion skeptic in this group.

Personally invite these individuals to be part of an organized review. Utilize the Do Food and Location, Location, Location patterns if the budget allows. Hold a series of information sessions or a half-day or full-day workshop. Give the team a list of questions or issues to address. Encourage discussion to uncover any areas where there is doubt. Include sources of external validation. Be present when you can to answer questions and address concerns.

Prepare a report for management. Keep the results around to use when a manager wants to know, "What's this stuff all about?" Be ready to answer questions generated by the report and have a plan for the next steps. If this sparks some management support, it may be a sign that now is the right time to take advantage of managers' openness to the idea.

This one-time task force may be willing to continue as an ongoing review committee for the innovation. Such a committee can include gurus who were appointed to the original task force and others who are interested enough to join in. Remember to offer sincere appreciation for any support.

= = = = = = = = =

This pattern produces data about the innovation through a firsthand evaluation from respected colleagues. The report, if positive, can be used to spark more support for the new idea, especially among management.

But use of this pattern can be risky. If the team's report is not positive, or if a few members are vocal about their apprehensions, the efforts to introduce the new idea can be brought to a standstill. Head off this possibility by using the Corridor Politics pattern and use the Stay in Touch pattern during the evaluation process.

The vice president and his staff requested a review after Brad's initial presentation about the new idea. Each member of the vice president's staff named one person for the evaluation team. Innovators who had been involved from the beginning were also invited. After a positive evaluation, management became active supporters of the innovation and the word spread throughout the organization.

Before bringing Lotus Notes into one organization, a cross-functional Information Needs Committee was formed to gather information on the feasibility of the software. After conducting a thorough review, they made the recommendation to implement Notes. Some of the members then created a project team to define which applications to attack first.

Hometown Story

My first two presentations about the new idea had generated some interest among the innovators and the early adopters. But I knew that the early majority weren't likely to accept a new idea until they had heard what their co-workers thought. So my next presentation included some time for people who had used the new idea to talk about their experiences.

To help people see the usefulness of the new idea, encourage those who have had success with it to share their stories.

You are a dedicated champion trying to introduce a new idea into your organization.

People who haven't used the new idea may not be aware that other people have used it successfully.

Hearing the experiences of respected colleagues is the next best thing to having the experience yourself. People are attracted by the smell of success and are curious about what successful individuals are doing. However, we tend to see the same people up front giving presentations. We know others could talk about their experiences, but they don't want to take the time to prepare and deliver a formal presentation. Yet informal, interactive presentations require little preparation and can be very effective. People are more likely to talk about experiences when they can do it in an informal way with little or no preparation.

Therefore:

Encourage individuals to share their experiences with the new idea in an informal, highly interactive session.

Do the legwork to prepare and promote the event. Use persistent PR. Do food or a brown bag. You do not need a large audience. Small group settings can create the atmosphere you want. Be there to help in any way you can, especially if the presenter is not good at leading a discussion.

Although you may wish to ask anyone who has had a positive experience with the innovation to do a hometown story, any guru on your side or early adopter is likely to have the biggest impact because these people are generally seen as opinion leaders.

Use this pattern as often as you can. Make sure a variety of experiences are heard, not just the ones from a few elite groups. Innovators are the only ones likely to get excited about the new idea after hearing just one success story; others will need many experience reports from many different people before they become supporters.

Hand out a token to help people remember the new idea that was discussed during the session.

= = = = = = = = =

This pattern creates an event in which individuals share their experiences. It is likely to increase the appeal of the new idea because most people are intrigued by success stories.

If you choose the wrong person, however, this can run the risk of hurting your cause. For example, arrogant presenters who are likely to drone on about all the wonderful things they did could end up turning people off. Try to encourage individuals who are liked and respected to contribute. If someone with an unpleasant personality insists on doing a hometown story, you can ease his influence by combining his presentation with those from other, more likeable, speakers at the same event.

Sally was a little worried about the presentation she was asked to give about a new technology. She got a lucky break when her co-worker, Steve, stopped by her cubicle while she was working on the slides. He told her that he had played around with the technology a bit. Sally reacted with such interest and excitement that Steve offered to give the second half of the presentation. Even though his experience with the new idea was limited, his presentation ended up being so natural and believable—he just leaned on the desk in the front of the room and told his story. Sally just sat there and smiled. She had put a lot of work into preparing the formal slide presentation, but the real hit of the event was Steve's story.

At Ken's company, success stories were often on the agenda at regular team meetings. The group prided itself on being innovative, so they were always excited and interested when someone on the team tried something new. They didn't even mind if an occasional failure was the topic instead of a success. It gave them the courage to keep learning.

INSIGHTS

The original pattern did not discuss the power of storytelling. In a blog post titled, "What Listening to a Story Does to Our Brains," Leo Widrich noted that stories activate not only language processing areas in our brain, but also other parts normally used when we experience events like the ones in a story we are told.[95] When we hear about a delicious meal, our sensory cortex lights up; when action is part of the narrative, our motor cortex responds. Stories involve our whole brain. To bring people on board, share personal experiences and use the Personal Touch pattern to try to identify with the struggles of your listeners.

Stories can be remembered and repeated much better than a random collection of facts. Be sure that opinion leaders, such as connectors and bridge builders, know the stories around the new idea so that they can share them when given the opportunity.

This pattern is about hearing from a friend or trusted colleague. A story can be even more effective when it comes from someone we know more than from an unfamiliar expert. This is especially true for members of the early majority, which makes up about one-third of a normally distributed population.[96]

Innovator

Roger lived next door, so every time he bought the newest, coolest gadget, I would hear all about it. He would get so excited about his purchases, even when the items were grossly overpriced. But if he convinced me that something was really useful, I would wait and buy it months later when the cost came down to less than half of what Roger paid.

When you begin the change initiative, ask for help from colleagues who like new ideas.

♦♦♦

You are a new evangelist or dedicated champion just starting to introduce a new idea into your organization.

You need people to jumpstart the new idea in your organization.

You can't interest everyone in a new idea all at once, but you need to start somewhere. A community of even a few people who share your interest and want to work together will make a world of difference in the confusion and inconsistencies that invariably arise. Almost every significant change initiative starts with a small number of deeply committed individuals, often as few as two or three.

It's easier to begin with those people who will be most receptive to the new idea. Innovators make up a small percentage of the population. They get intrigued and excited about something just because it is new. They don't need much convincing, just a little information. They enjoy trying to figure out how the latest thing works. This puts them in a good position to help launch the new idea into the organization.

Therefore:

Find the people who are quick to adopt new ideas. Talk to them about the innovation and ask for help in sparking an interest for it in the organization.

Look for innovators among those who attend early brown bags and other meetings where new ideas are being introduced. Some of them will come to you once you start talking about the new idea.

Encourage these individuals to take on the role of gatekeepers. Use the Just Do It pattern to create an early evaluation. Ask for their feedback about the innovation and listen to their suggestions for appealing to the larger community. Because they are the first to come on board, perhaps the innovators could lead one of the first study groups with other people who are curious about learning more. Those who are especially enthusiastic may become evangelists in their own groups.

= = = = = = = = =

This pattern establishes support from a group who can help get a new idea going. It doesn't take a lot of work to interest innovators, and then you won't feel so alone. Because they are willing to accept some of the uncertainty that comes with anything new, they ease the risk for later adopters.

Be aware, however, that you may not be able to depend on innovators in the long term. Their interest in new things makes them move from one thing to another. In addition, their willingness to quickly accept new ideas causes others to be suspicious of their claims. Therefore, they generally aren't good opinion leaders. Count on their help as gatekeepers in the short term. If they offer more, consider that a bonus.

Bill's eyebrows seem to rise to his hairline when he hears about something new. So he was one of the first people Julie talked with about the new idea. He tried it, reported the results, and helped Julie plan a few events to pass the word. His enthusiasm was just what she needed to keep her going in the early days of trying to convince other people whose eyebrows did not rise as quickly.

Some people know when you've returned from a conference and drop by to see which new books you've bought or new techniques you've seen. They wanted to be there but couldn't take the time. Sam always tries to bring something back for these individuals. It is fun to watch how happy these people get about anything because their need to be in on the "latest and greatest" is almost physical. Sam knows what his boss means when he says, "Sure, you can go to the conference, but bring something back for the team!" He is thinking about these guys.

INSIGHTS

It's possible to have a champion-anything, including a "champion innovator." Linda tells the story of a *Fearless Change* workshop she was leading. The group talked about a challenge in dealing with an overly enthusiastic innovator, and decided to create the role of champion innovator. One participant explained what the team did: We scheduled a special time (Friday afternoon at 2 p.m.), provided cookies, and invited everyone to listen to the champion innovator talk about the "new thing of the week," with the understanding that he would not be intrusive at other times. People really did want to hear from this person about new stuff, but not constantly. The weekly meeting was a way of keeping him involved without allowing him to become annoying.

Involve Everyone

Margaret Wheatley, author of Leadership and the New Science, observes that "great things are possible when we increase participation. I always want more people, from more diverse functions and places, to be there. . . . I learn a great deal from other people. I expect them to see things differently from me, to surprise me." [97]

For a new idea to be successful across an organization, everyone should have an opportunity to support the innovation and make his own unique contribution.

You are a dedicated champion working to introduce a new idea into your organization. There are others in the community who might get involved with a little encouragement.

Even when you ask for help, there's a tendency to take on too much. Others—especially those who don't see the value in the new idea—may think of it as "your show."

You're the person dedicated to spending time on introducing the new idea. You want to do as much as you can to help your organization improve, but you don't want the organization to become too dependent on you. Moreover, the corporate picture of the new idea may tend to converge around your own. As a result, there's less definitional discussion because you are setting the stage and the pace.

If you take on too much, you can become the single point of failure. Because people will tend to see the new idea as being about you, your personality and history can color their view. People who might contribute to a discussion of how best to make the innovation work will instead defer to you, seeing themselves as students learning "the right way."

A small group interested in a new idea can become a clique isolated from the needs of the organization. Those who aren't part of the effort may become defensive and withdrawn, afraid of not being able to keep up with the change. Wide involvement is essential for the development of a good implementation strategy. Some things might be less stressful if everyone was alike, but the long-term plan would not be robust enough to stand the test of time.

You can never predict who will be the real enthusiasts for the new technique. In organizations, you can't get far with pristine and hermetically sealed experiments. This is one reason for reaching out to a broad cross section of support. In addition to contributing skills and strengths, a diverse group of people will bring awareness of the limitations and organizational constraints that any successful change effort must transcend.

Leading change is not a one-person job. Increasing the number of people involved means that the innovation belongs to the entire organization instead of just one person or a small group. Because of the extensive participation, the idea becomes everyone's product. Shared experiences can keep others interested. When you share the opportunity to lead, you discover that the extent to which people "own" a project is the extent to which they invest their time and energy to make it succeed.

Ownership is important. It is a term that describes not only literal owners, but more importantly the emotional investment of employees in their work. It describes personal connections to the organization; the powerful emotions of belonging that inspire people to contribute. A tried-and-true maxim of organizational behavior is that "people support what they create."

Therefore:

Make it known that everyone is welcome to be part of the change effort. Involve people from as many different groups as possible: management, administrative and technical support, marketing, and training.

Do the best you can to involve a variety of people from the start. If the innovation is viewed early on as a clique, it may never be able to shake that image. Even when you're not sure how it will work out, and even when you're not sure where things are going, involving everyone creates a stronger community.

Give everyone ownership of some part of the change effort. For example, encourage the innovators to help test the new idea and the early adopters to be responsible for some leadership roles. Find connectors and get a guru on your side to help spread the word. Don't restrict involvement because of any preconceived ideas. Even skeptics can contribute by becoming a champion skeptic.

Try to bring together a diverse group of people from different parts of the organization. Seek out a variety of roles and ideas. Invite people who could hold untapped wisdom—not the same voices, but new and different ones. Alistair Cockburn's pattern, Holistic Diversity, advises creating a team with multiple specialties, and Neil Harrison's pattern, Diverse Groups, recommends including different kinds of members in determining requirements. Give everyone the freedom to express an individual perspective on the new idea.

Create forums and processes that allow a variety of people to have their voices heard about the new idea. Make sure it is not a passive system in which individuals merely say what's on their mind. Rather, create active discussions where people offer suggestions for any problems they raise.

Put the "spotlight on others." Convince individuals to take on public leadership tasks by running an event or telling a hometown story. Help each individual become an effective leader. People have different abilities and interests. Some are not comfortable writing, while others don't like public speaking. Sometimes you can just use the Ask for Help pattern to hear what they would like to do.

If you're appointing someone as a leader, you have to be ready to follow. Prepare yourself mentally to cede ownership of the new idea to someone else.

= = = = = = = = = =

This pattern builds a community of people committed to the new idea, ready to take on leadership roles in the change effort. Increasing the number of people involved in the process results in a movement that belongs to the entire organization rather than something produced by one person or a small group. Your attempt to involve everyone ensures that as many individuals as possible will see themselves as active participants in the change process. People who have this perception will view the success of the innovation as their responsibility. This means that they have accepted the change in some small measure, and you have that much less resistance to overcome. Those who become leaders of the change effort will soon become experts in others' eyes, and they will probably do so as your close partners. Your effectiveness will be multiplied because you have people to talk with and fall back on. They'll tell you which ideas worked out well and which didn't work out so well. They'll tell you which contacts were helpful and which weren't. They'll keep talking to you, and you'll keep learning from them. It's a loop.

Of course, every time you involve another group, you run the risk of getting so many points of view that the multitude of perspectives becomes overwhelming. Acknowledge the differences by utilizing the Fear Less pattern, but put your focus on the common ground. This will allow you to move forward rather than wasting your energy on the countless issues that cannot be immediately resolved. Everyone doesn't need to agree on everything before you can start taking action.

Tim has been actively trying to convince others to become leaders of the change effort for the innovation. For example, he was asked to give a keynote talk on the innovation at a software testing conference. Instead of accepting, he said, "You should ask Elisabeth. She's up and coming, working with the innovation, and a good speaker." That's what happened. Similarly, Tim nudged someone else to be the host of the conference. Neither started out that enthusiastic about the innovation, but they gained enthusiasm at the workshops, and Tim thinks they will get more caught up in it as they play a more public role. Tim has also noticed that encouraging others to become involved makes the innovation seem less like one of his weird ideas, which, he thinks, was initially the impression of some.

Karen is the executive director of RiverLink, a nonprofit organization spearheading the economic and environmental revitalization of the French Broad River. She was asked to identify the one thing that had the most positive influence on the successful progress RiverLink has made over 15 years. Without hesitation, she described the ability to pull together people with a variety of interests, including lawyers, accountants, engineers, architects, bike riders, kayakers, and other athletes. Community outreach was often accomplished through personal visits and more public forums such as focus groups, public hearings, and even a 24-hour brainstorming session. Karen noted that this approach allowed each person to come away feeling that he or she owned a part of the project.

INSIGHTS

This pattern was originally considered to be appropriate for later phases, but now we know that it's important early on and throughout the initiative.

The Involve Everyone pattern is not only appropriate for the change effort, but can also be a part of how you look for solutions during a meeting. Lead the group in a brainstorming session to generate possible ideas. After some discussion in which you identify "themes" that fit the direction you want to go and give credit to members of the group for coming up with these ideas, include as many "others" as possible. This will encourage group ownership of the idea. Such an approach works better than just telling people how you want to solve a problem.

Distant acquaintances who don't appear to have any connection to you can be valuable. In a study of "weak ties" among people, Stanford University's Mark Granovetter discovered that among those who landed jobs through personal contacts, only 16.7% found those positions through colleagues whom they saw at least twice a week; 55.6% found positions through acquaintances whom they saw at least once a year. A healthy 27.8%, however, found work through distant acquaintances—that is, people whom they saw less than once a year, such as an old college friends, former workmates, or members of professional associations. The study concluded that more contacts will come to you through those individuals whom you see less than once a year than from others you see twice or more a week. This difference arises because close friends share the same networks as you do, whereas acquaintances are more likely to introduce you to new contacts. It's also an important reason to use the Involve Everyone pattern. If you just stick to those persons whom you are close to and see all the time, you will reach only the same ol', same ol'. If you want your idea to take off, you've got to go beyond your comfort zone. Diverse input should be a part of your initiative to help you address skeptics; see different points of view, benefits, and costs; and help you learn about the idea and your organization.

Just Do It

A letter in the "In My Humble Opinion" column of Fast Company *magazine expressed frustration about a company filled with people who refused to try anything new. The writer claimed that she knew exactly how to save the company, but no one above her would let her do it. Seth Godin, Change Agent, responded:*

> What you're looking for is an insurance policy that will protect you against retribution if your plan goes awry. What you're waiting for is someone way up the ladder to tell you that you can launch a product or institute a cost-savings plan. You want their approval to free you from risk. That's not going to happen.
>
> Just do it. If you wait for approval, it means that you want someone to cover your backside if you fail. People higher up on the corporate ladder are well aware of the risk that comes with trusting you. If you screw up after receiving their approval, then they'll be the ones who get into hot water, not you.[98]

To prepare to spread the word about the new idea, use it in your own work to discover its benefits and limitations.

You are an evangelist-wanna-be, motivated to adopt a new idea. You are interested in spreading the word to others in the organization, but you don't have enough understanding of what the new idea can offer. When you talk about the possibilities, people ask questions that you can't answer.

You don't have any experience with the innovation yourself, just good ideas that might work. You believe that the innovation can help the organization, but you're not sure.

People will be wary if you have only a good idea and no experience to back it up. They are likely to ask questions you can't answer. Sometimes it's better to labor in secret until demonstrable success is in hand.

If you wait until you're comfortable, if you wait until you know what you're doing, you will have wasted precious time. Many of us who could be doing something do nothing because we think we don't know enough. But when we aren't willing to explore a new idea, we miss the opportunity to learn.

Do your research. Lack of experience is easy for opponents to attack, while positive experience is more difficult to refute. Your increased understanding of the innovation's limitations helps you avoid over-selling and provides insight into approaches that might be more workable.

Therefore:

Gather firsthand information on the benefits and limitations of the innovation by integrating it into your current work.

Learn as you go. Record the strengths and pitfalls you encounter along the way. If possible, quantify the benefits (although this can be difficult). Gather enough information so that you can show others how the innovation will be useful for them.

Be realistic about what you can and cannot do. Make sure that your work with the innovation does not distract from your official duties. Rather, it should relate to and improve the quality or speed of your official work; otherwise, your story will not be credible.

Before you begin, you might want to check around for others in the organization who are also working with the new idea. It is more effective, and will avoid jealous feelings, to "just do it" together rather than in separate projects.

If you find a few innovators who are also interested in exploring the new idea, ask for help. But keep this group small in number. Make sure they are willing to take it slow, set realistic goals, and follow your lead.

While you are experimenting with the innovation in your own work, search for every bit of information to help you. Read articles, look at websites, and talk with anyone you can find outside the organization who has experience using the innovation. This will provide external validation.

To spread the word about your findings, present a hometown story. Help your colleagues understand that the innovation is not beyond their grasp by using the Personal Touch pattern. Take a low-key approach when you report your experiences. Don't be overly optimistic or insistent that the new approach is a silver bullet. You may want to simply demonstrate it to a few people and tell them how you benefited from it. When you have enough information, try to convince the organization to trial run the innovation.

= = = = = = = = =

This pattern generates the knowledge you need to take on the role of evangelist. You will increase your understanding of the innovation and, in turn, be more prepared to talk intelligently about it and address other people's questions.

At the same time, recognize that you are using this pattern because you know so little. As a consequence, others are likely to see you struggle, which can turn them off to the new idea. Don't discount your struggles, but make sure others see an overall positive attitude in you.

One organization had a software application project that was stalled for a long time. Everyone mentioned it but no one was able to get it moving. Because the project was technically "adjacent" to what Daniel's team was working on, they decided to just do it. The team built a limited version of the application and called it a "test program." It allowed the team to try their preferred design, a low-risk exercise that would speak for itself if it turned out to be viable. When they started receiving some positive feedback for their efforts, they felt some hope that their work would eventually be recognized as the "first version" of the larger application.

Frances hoped to encourage her fellow team members to write their software documentation in pattern format. So she started writing her own documentation in this form. The effort allowed her to better understand the difficulties and the advantages so that she could explain these things to her team. The team members started becoming accustomed to seeing her documentation written in the new format and eventually it didn't even seem like an usual way of writing—it just began to make sense.

INSIGHTS

We have noticed that we tend to use the patterns Just Do It and Test the Waters interchangeably. Since keeping a collection of patterns as succinct as possible over time is a goal for pattern authors, we have decided to remove Test the Waters and subsume it under Just Do It.

Just Enough

Most of us have had the kind of teacher who knows so much about a certain topic that he feels compelled to tell his students all about it as fast as he can. He doesn't seem to notice the blank stares—he just keeps talking and his students just keep staring.

To ease learners into the more difficult concepts of a new idea, give a brief introduction and then make more information available when they are ready.

You are an evangelist or dedicated champion working to spread the word about a new idea in your organization.

Difficult, complex concepts can overwhelm novices.

All new ideas involve a learning curve. Some of the new things people will have to face are complex and cannot be understood in a short time. Although learners should understand the challenging concepts at some point so they can use the innovation effectively, giving a thorough explanation of such concepts while you are covering the basics can be confusing. Doing so may cause learners to think the innovation is too complicated. It may discourage busy people from taking the time to learn more.

A slow but sure introduction to a new idea can be compared to Christopher Alexander's Gradual Stiffening pattern. He recommends that, when creating a complex building structure, one should "build a building in such a way that it starts out loose and flimsy while final adaptations in plan are made, and then gets stiffened gradually during the process of construction, so that each additional act of construction makes the structure sounder."[99]

Each new concept that is taught to learners should allow their comprehension to become sounder. If you introduce too much of a good thing too fast, you may overwhelm your learners and, at the same time, reduce your flexibility and increase your costs.

Therefore:

When introducing the new idea, concentrate on the fundamentals and give learners a brief description of the more difficult concepts. Provide more information when they are ready.

If you are doing a presentation to introduce the new idea, include more advanced concepts in a slide or two. If you are having an informal discussion, give learners the information they can comfortably handle and let them know that there is more to learn. Provide enough information to start interested individuals on an investigation of their own.

When giving a presentation to high-level management, give the conclusions first. Paint the big picture and explain the details only if you're asked. Stress the gains rather than the losses. Emphasize the wins without stretching the truth or ignoring the risks.

Even though you shouldn't overwhelm learners with too many details, you want to offer the encouragement and resources they need to consider more when they have experience. Provide URLs or a list of references. Make yourself available to answer questions. Use the Personal Touch pattern to show how the innovation can be useful in their jobs.

After learners have had time to understand the basics, find opportunities for a more in-depth discussion. This will allow them to develop confidence about what they've learned, which is likely to spark their interest in learning more.

= = = = = = = = = =

This pattern initiates a slow but sure understanding of difficult topics. This approach also keeps change leaders from hyping the innovation as a perfect and complete solution from the beginning.

Of course, what works for some people will not necessarily work for others. At one extreme, some people will not comprehend the basics and may worry that there are even more difficult concepts to come. At the other extreme, some people will want to know more and may feel that you don't think they're smart enough to handle the advanced concepts. Keep lines of communication open with everyone so they are comfortable asking questions to get the amount of information they desire.

When Janet introduces patterns during her tutorials, the difficult concepts such as QWAN and generativity are mentioned as important but are not covered in detail. Instead, attendees are pointed to Christopher Alexander's book, The Timeless Way of Building, *if they wish to read more. Janet always reminds students that she is available to answer questions when they are ready.*

When moving from CMM (Capability Maturity Model) Level 1 to Levels 2 and 3, the process introductions were synched with the development cycle. Rather than try to give the team all the process changes at the beginning, "just enough" of the process changes were introduced to get through the next stage.

INSIGHTS

This pattern is broader than just how we address questions from an interested colleague. The Goldilocks Effect—not too much, not too little, but just right—applies not just to talking about change but also to deciding what to do next. The excitement and enthusiasm we have for our ideas should be tempered with restraint and listening. In many cases, we over-sell to the point of diminishing returns. One way to tell whether you've provided too much information is to notice that your listeners have stopped asking clarifying questions. More is not always better. Look for social cues that you've reached the tipping point.

Local Sponsor

One day I asked a bank manager what he did to make his branch such a successful one. "Well," he replied, "I believe my primary job is to support my employees by finding resources and taking care of all the roadblocks that prevent them from doing their jobs well."

Ask for help from first-line management. When your boss supports the tasks you are doing to introduce the new idea, you can be even more effective.

◆◆◆

You are an evangelist trying to introduce a new idea into your organization.

You need attention and resources for the new idea.

Management support legitimizes things in the workplace. It's hard to get some people involved in a new idea unless they think management is behind it.

Sponsorship is important. There must be a manager who believes that the change needs to happen, who understands the decisions that need to be made, and who has the power to allocate the resources that will be needed during the transition. Site leadership can be critical. Experience suggests that an innovation will have broad impact in those settings where local management takes responsibility for it.

We have seen no examples where significant progress has been made without first-line management and many examples where sincerely committed corporate angels alone have failed to generate any significant momentum. Managers have significant business responsibility and bottom-line focus. They head organizational units that are large enough to be meaningful microcosms of the larger organization, yet they have enough autonomy to undertake meaningful change independent of the larger organization.

Therefore:

Find a first-line manager to support your new idea—ideally, your boss.

Use the Tailor Made pattern to help managers understand how the new idea can help the organization. Offer to organize a guru review. Personally invite managers to attend events such as a brown bag or hometown story. If a big jolt visit is planned, offer the opportunity for a royal audience. Address any concerns with use of the Whisper in the General's Ear pattern. Stay in touch—keep interested managers informed on a periodic basis.

Keep any manager's part in the change initiative one of support. Similar to Jim Coplien's Patron Role pattern, the manager should be encouraged to help find resources and remove barriers that hinder progress.

If you can enlist the backing of your boss, begin to think how you can ask for help to become a dedicated champion. A first-line manager may be your best hope for capturing the attention of a corporate angel.

Sponsorship should not come from just one person. Try to build support among all the managers who have the power to influence project adoption of the innovation.

= = = = = = = = =

This pattern establishes first-line managerial support for your work in introducing a new idea. With this, you can get resources for the change initiative and capture the interest of those who look to management for guidance. You may even be able to become a dedicated champion.

The wrong kind of sponsor, however, can cause you to lose focus and direction. When you bring in managers, you run the risk that they will push things in a direction that is different from yours. An overpowering one can even steal your ideas and take the credit. A manager who is overzealous can give the damaging impression that the new idea is being mandated. Look for respected sponsors who will help, not hurt, your good intentions.

Alex had three managers who were the backbone of all the activity surrounding the new idea at his company. Yes, he did the legwork. Yes, he wrote the articles. Yes, he devoted his time. But it was the encouragement, the unflagging support of these managers and their belief in him, that made it happen.

In Amanda's organization, the change initiative would not have started without the support of her manager. He gave her the budget line to support her time and fund the activities surrounding her efforts. Without these things, Amanda would not have been able to get things off the ground as quickly as she did.

Location, Location, Location

In his book on project retrospectives, Norm Kerth has observed that onsite locations "may be seen by participants as cheap and therefore unimportant, the site is 'the same old place,' the [event] is easily interrupted, and participants may not prepare as well since they can duck out to look for whatever materials they need at the last minute."[100]

To avoid interruptions that disrupt the flow of an event, try to hold significant events offsite.

◆◆◆

You are planning a half- or whole-day seminar or other event.

When you hold an event onsite at the organization, attendees can be easily distracted with their nearby work obligations.

As any real estate agent will tell you, the three most important qualities of any property are location, location, location. The same can be said of special events in your company.

It is natural to assume that company events will be held onsite. This is normally seen as a good use of resources, and it presents attendees with a comfortable and familiar environment. However, an event that is a half-day or longer inevitably leads to breaks, and people will wander off to look at their email or may be grabbed by their managers or co-workers to just look at "a small problem." People always seem to spend longer than planned, and "a small problem" is rarely that—so people are late, distracted, or even pulled out of the event for a few hours or the duration of the event.

Such disruptions reduce the impact of the event and, as a result, people tend to believe they must get back to some task that suddenly seems more important (to someone else, if not the attendee in question). Even without actual disruption, there is often the feeling that "real work" is just a knock-on-the-door away.

Training costs money, so don't squander your investment. That means paying attention to things that may seem trivial but that actually make a big difference. Location is one of these. You could say that the worst place for workplace training is at work!

Therefore:

Hold significant events of a half-day or longer offsite but nearby.

The best place to conduct training is often in your company's own offsite facility. If this is not available, try a nearby hotel, training center, or retreat facility. The alternative location should not be inconvenient. People still have children to pick up from school, car pools to organize, and so on. A nearby location means that the usual beginning- and end-of-day rituals can continue and that if there is an interruption during the day, it is not a big effort to get back to the office.

Make sure the event is a beneficial one. It will probably take extra effort for people to come to the offsite location, so this puts added responsibility on you to make it worthwhile. A unique, comfortable location can't overcome a bad agenda.

Remind attendees to turn off mobile phones and pagers. Nothing brings back the daily work pressure more urgently, even if you're offsite.

= = = = = = = = =

This pattern creates a better environment for an event. It allows participants to be more focused because they are insulated from the worries of work minutiae, just as the sources of work minutiae are insulated from them. A new context often makes the event more special, creating a freer environment, less constrained by the expectations back at the office. It allows the opportunity for constructive discussion about the event during the breaks and for more personal contact and bonding. The sense of a company outing makes the event more fun. Some people are more open because the perception is that "this isn't work."

Inevitably, offsite venues will cost more than onsite ones. But if you're going to do it, do it right. Nevertheless, despite your best efforts, some people will not be able to get their minds off what needs to be done back at the office. Assure them that the genuinely high-priority interrupts will get through. Minor queries and problems will resolve themselves or wait, as will email. Try a variation of the "I'm Too Busy" exercise, as suggested by Norm Kerth, to help people understand that the things they want to do back at the office are not as important as what will transpire during the event.

My company is located in Campinas in Brazil. A partnering organization is located in Curitiba. Meetings were held in one city or the other, which provided an offsite experience for the visiting group. The onsite group suffered all the disadvantages mentioned in this pattern, while the offsite group gained all the benefits. The two organizations decided to have future meetings in a third city, to allow both groups to go offsite.

Kevlin ran a workshop onsite for a company just outside Oslo. Over the three days of the workshop people disappeared and reappeared mysteriously, but it was the interruption and call of work rather than alien abductions that were to blame. Whether it was the lure of email or "just a quick word" from a colleague or boss, it led to an unsettled atmosphere. The next time the workshop was run, the company rented a room offsite less than a five-minute walk away. In spite of the physical proximity, there was just enough separation to reduce interruptions. It turns out that almost everything that was normally "urgent" could wait until the end of the day or after the workshop. The atmosphere was relaxed and less transient, and all the delegates were more focused.

INSIGHTS

This pattern works well with event patterns such as Big Jolt and Brown Bag, because where you do something affects the outcome as well as what you do. But the solution involves more than just the location—for example, it also includes the facilities there. Ensure that people will be able to enjoy it with adequate seating and tables, proper lighting, and a comfortable temperature.

The pattern suggests ideas for the location, but as the global economy has hit a downturn, it may no longer be as realistic. Even so, an offsite space like a restaurant or pub at lunchtime or a party after work could work just as well for shorter conversations. Here are some ideas for simple ways to implement this pattern:

The East Bay chapter has a refreshment break in the middle of its monthly meetings. Members assign snack-bringers using alphabetical order. Once a year, at their January meeting, which they call 12th night, they meet on a Sunday afternoon instead of Friday night, and have a potluck. Last year I coached at that session and the potluck was not very enjoyable. There were no tables, and it was hard to eat and drink and talk. This year they set up tables, and I had a great time! I think others enjoyed it more, too. It seemed that people stayed around longer than last year. Maybe Do Food *is even better with* Do Food in Comfort?

At the Agile Vancouver conference, they changed the seating from classroom style to round tables because participants had no way to attend the talks with a cup of coffee and a snack while they attempted to balance their notes and other things. Everyone commented that it worked well!

Mentor

We held a three-day pilot patterns training. Everyone in the class thought there was too much material. One suggestion in the evaluations was the need for some help in the actual use of the patterns. So we expanded the three days to a full week. Monday had all-day training, while Tuesday through Friday had both a half-day of training and a half-day of mentoring. During the half-days of mentoring, we provided consulting on real projects. The new schedule made a tremendous difference in the effectiveness of the training.

When a project team wants to get started with the new idea, have someone around who understands it and can help the team.

You are a dedicated champion trying to introduce a new idea into your organization. A project team is interested in the innovation but some or all of the team members are unfamiliar with it.

People want to use the new idea on their project but don't know how to begin.

If team members are willing to introduce the new idea into their project, they can study it on their own to some extent. However, they probably need help to apply it effectively. The team is likely to make more progress if it has access to an expert who can guide them through their problems. Mentors can prevent small mistakes from growing into huge delays.

Beginners need to understand what experts do. Apprenticeship learning is ideal because it gives beginners access to an expert's "cognitive library." This is better than any help system or documentation.

Therefore:

Find an outside or internal consultant or trainer to provide mentoring and feedback while project members are getting started with the innovation.

Encourage the mentor to use a hands-on approach, work side-by-side with the team members, and let them know that he has struggled with the same problems. This will help open learners' minds to the innovation. The mentor should use the Just Enough pattern to introduce complicated topics and use the Personal Touch pattern to help each team member understand how the innovation can be useful.

Carefully check the credentials of a potential mentor. Don't simply trust what anyone claims to be able to do. Ideally, the mentor should have experience in using the innovation and should know something about the team's problem domain. In addition, look for a mentor whose personality will mesh with the team culture, although it may be impossible to find one person who everyone will like and relate to. If the mentor alienates some team members and turns them off from using the innovation, you may need to bring in mentors with different personality types for these people.

Make certain you are clear about what the mentor should do. Clearly state why you are hiring him and define the deliverables. Ask the mentor to help outline specific goals for the educational experience the team members will have.

Don't allow a team to become dependent on the mentor. Otherwise, they may not want to let him go or will call on him for every little thing. Ask the mentor when and how he plans to leave his role. The best mentors strive to work themselves out of a job. You may need to set a time when the mentor will be available and then, at some point, encourage team members to move forward on their own.

The organization may wish to use a mentor to train an entire team to prepare for a project, as described in Don Olson's pattern Train Hard, Fight Easy. The benefit lies in the shared experience of training together, which not only enables the team to communicate effectively about the innovation but also serves as a team-building exercise.

= = = = = = = = =

This pattern produces a better understanding of the innovation while people are starting to use it. Users will have an easier time because they will have an experienced person to get them over the hurdles. This helps to create a good impression of the innovation and increases the likelihood that people will be willing to continue to use it.

A mentor is not always easy to find. The number of experts is usually small compared with the number of projects, especially in the early days of an innovation's appearance. Look for mentors among the innovators and help teams grow their own expertise so that this mentoring activity continues with internal support.

Pattern guru Jim Coplien says, "The use of pattern mentors in an organization can speed the acceptance of patterns and can help provide a balance between encouraging good design practices and discouraging overly high expectations of designs based on patterns. Initially mentors can help developers recognize the patterns that they already use in their application domain and show how they could be reused in subsequent projects. Mentors should also ensure that the wrong patterns are not applied to a problem (i.e., people tend to reuse things that they know and the same temptation will apply to patterns, regardless of whether the pattern actually fits the problem)."[101]

Cathryn worked for a large defense subcontractor back in the early 1980s. The company was learning Ada and object-based design from a small consulting group. The owner of the consulting firm had hired people who used very different approaches. Cathryn thought it was just a curiosity at the time, but now she sees that this consultant-owner was very wise. He knew that different people learn differently and recognized that what would work with one person might not work with another. His team included Gary the Nice (everyone liked Gary, but as she looks back on it, Cathryn thinks if he had been the only mentor he wouldn't have been as effective; as it was, he balanced out the others), Ed the Barbarian (Ed was the owner and knew a lot but he could be a little over-the-top for some), Johan the Master (he also knew a lot but he was more subtle and more laid back, a "slow reveal"), and Brad (just Brad, a plain-spoken, good guy to work with). This way, everyone could find someone with whom they felt comfortable, and the mix provided the best way to learn the new approaches. Each mentor brought his own take on the material to the table.

INSIGHTS

The original version of this pattern focused on finding an expert helper to help you and your team develop expertise in the new idea. Research shows that the key to success in mentoring lies in the relationship, the support, the use of the Personal Touch pattern by the mentor. The expert should build a working relationship with novices and encourage people to experiment rather than simply showing them or telling them about it.[102]

You also need a mentor who can provide ongoing support and guidance for you, to help you to continue learning as much as you can about your change efforts, your organization, your new idea, and of course, yourself.

Next Steps

At the end of a training class, one of the attendees stopped by and said, "I enjoyed the class today. That's one of the perks of working here. We have the chance to learn the latest and greatest, but the problem is, I go back to my project and I don't know what to do next. Any ideas?" I realized then that I was saturating students with knowledge but not helping them to apply it.

Take time near the end of an event about the new idea to identify what participants can do next.

You are giving a presentation or having a meeting to explain a new idea.

A presentation in a training class or another event can leave attendees uncertain about what to do with what they have learned.

Hearing or learning about a new idea is different from applying it. Training classes are useful for sharing a variety of information in a short, intensive time. However, the experience can leave participants exhausted, overwhelmed, and unsure whether they can apply what they learned to their real work. A successful event can stimulate attendees to do more. Build on this excitement before the attendees leave the room.

Even when people are motivated with a clear vision of the desired future, if they don't know what to do next, little or no progress will be made.

Therefore:

Take time near the end of a presentation to brainstorm and discuss how the participants can apply the new information.

Lead the participants in creating a loose plan. Topics for discussion include the following questions: How can participants use the information? Where can it be put to use in the organization? How can participants learn more? What can be done to spread the word? Should we begin a mailing list or website? Start a study group? Invite a big jolt speaker?

If you're an outsider and have had experience in introducing the idea into other organizations, you may be tempted to tell the attendees what they should do next. Try to avoid this, because the participants know their needs better than you do and should create and own their own plan. Make suggestions only when appropriate; however, to maintain credibility, have some recommendations if you are asked to contribute.

Create a list of ideas and action items. Prioritize them. Decide what can be done now and what can wait until later. Add some time frames. Ask for help. Encourage those who attended the event to be responsible for each action item. Email the list to everyone as a reminder. Hand out a token to help people remember the new idea that was discussed during the session.

Charles Weir and James Noble's Brainstorming pattern contains some ideas for leading a brainstorming session.

= = = = = = = = =

This pattern creates an opportunity for people to expand their knowledge of the innovation and get involved in introducing it into their organization. It leaves attendees at a presentation or meeting with more than just a good idea; that is, they are left with things to do to begin applying the innovation.

The risk is that the brainstorming may be so enthusiastic that people become overwhelmed with all the things that need to be done. Help them to keep the action items realistic and centered on what the people in the organization can truly do. Encourage them to take things in baby steps.

Janice and Kim end their training courses with a discussion of how the attendees can apply what they learned. Attendees brainstorm a rough plan for sharing their knowledge with co-workers and for introducing the new ideas into their organization.

Norm Kerth, author of Project Retrospectives, *has observed that team members will get so excited about what is uncovered during a project retrospective session that they will be anxious to lead improvements in their organization. His "Make It a Mission" exercise at the end of the retrospective teaches participants how they can create and follow a mission that will actively deliver a message of change.*

INSIGHTS

In addition to defining follow-on actions at the end of a meeting, it's important to name a go-to person for each task. As Craig Freshley of *Good Group Decisions* advises:

> *"Before adjourning a meeting, make sure that a name is attached to every action item. Encourage people to take the lead. If you believe something is important, consider taking the lead yourself. Don't assign the lead to someone not present without their permission. If an item arises that no one is willing to take on, let it drop. This is a clear sign that there is not enough energy among the group to implement the thing even though it "seems like a good idea."*

Every conversation with a potential supporter can also conclude with suggested next steps—a brief reminder of who is doing what, by when, and with whom. This ensures you don't miss anything and shows how well you were listening. It applies in a face-to-face meeting as well as a phone conversation. For example, say, "As soon as I hang up, I'll <take this action> and that will get things started. Then I'll talk to <someone> as we discussed and have everything ready for Thursday."

Persistent PR

As the faculty advisor of the student management association, I tried to encourage management students to regularly check the association's web page for new opportunities and upcoming events. Nothing seemed to work until one of the officers made a simple sign with the web page address and posted it in the computer lab where many of the students work and hang out between classes. The number of hits to the site increased 10-fold!

Keep the new idea visible by placing reminders throughout the organization.

◆◆◆

You are an evangelist or dedicated champion trying to introduce a new idea into your organization.

Unless people are reminded, they may forget about the new idea.

People like to be in the know, but many don't have the time to periodically read articles or information on the web. Yet, they'll notice and are likely to discuss things that are posted in places they see often. E. M. Rogers has shown that keeping a new idea visible throughout an organization has a positive impact on the rate at which people adopt it. A gathering place, where a group can come together and talk among themselves, is one means for communicating a new idea and showing progress.

215

Therefore:

Post information about the new idea around your organization—wherever people are likely to see it and discuss it.

Display information so it will be noticed and not forgotten. Materials placed in high traffic areas may be easy for people to see but also easy to forget as they move on. Malcolm Gladwell, author of *The Tipping Point*, suggests that you make your message "stick" by using bright colors, an usual graphic, or a memorable quote. Provide ways for the viewers to interact in the space by asking for feedback or posing a question that will stimulate discussion. Ask for help. Include announcements about upcoming events. Update the information regularly; otherwise, people will get used to it and not notice it any more.

As Paul Taylor explains in the Team Space pattern, consider putting information in a physical space for casual, unplanned interaction. Christopher Alexander's pattern Work Community also describes a way of encouraging the formation of small clusters in the workplace. Author Alistair Cockburn, in *Agile Software Development*, describes an "Information Radiator," a display of information in a place where passersby can see it. The passersby don't need to ask questions; the information simply hits them as they go by. Cockburn suggests that the information change over time because it will make it worthwhile to look at the display frequently.

Be creative in finding the space. Look for the bulletin board that just seems to accumulate junk flyers and make it more appealing. Also, you can simply post a sign near your office that says, "Ask me about <new idea>."

= = = = = = = = = =

This pattern establishes a place where people can see and discuss the latest information about the new idea. It will stay in the space and in the mind of the organization. People who see the space may become intrigued enough to become involved in the change initiative.

Unfortunately, despite your best efforts to make the message noticeable, people can become oblivious to the space if they see it all the time. Try to make it something that people look forward to seeing or consider moving it to a new location once in a while.

Joe Bergin has applied this pattern to a larger space. He is one of the educators who formed the Pedagogical Patterns Project (http://www.pedagogicalpatterns.org/). The team is working on documenting successful teaching practices in the form of patterns.

To encourage contributions, Joe has created buttons with witty sayings about the project. Team members and other supporters wear these buttons and provoke interest at conferences and other gatherings.

Ralph and Julie read about something they thought was a big problem in their department—one author called it "SpecGen." They made signs with the letters "SG" in a red circle-slash and the slogan, "Thank you for not speculating." The signs were a big hit. Nearly every cubicle had one posted by the end of the day.

INSIGHTS

This pattern used to be named In Your Space, but we decided that Persistent PR is a better name.

We often make the mistake of thinking that one technique, such as a good PowerPoint presentation or a company-wide email message, will catch everyone's eye. In reality, a variety of techniques are needed to appeal to different kinds of listeners. Because people are busy, send multiple reminders, with a variety of promotional techniques, at regular and strategic times. Don't use just one method, such as regular emails—after a while people will tune it out. Experiment with colorful attention-getting artwork in your notices.

Lasse Koskela provides the following example that the best approach involves more than a one-time hit.

In my experience, people need to see a topic arise several times at different places to "catch fire." It's good that your co-worker looked at your book. Next time he sees an article about it, he might think, "Hmm, sounds like I've heard that before." Then he sees the topic on a conference poster—"Hmm sounds familiar." The next time he sees your book, he is likely to say: "That really seems to be a hot topic. Can you tell me more about it?"[103]

Personal Touch

A manager was struggling with one of his staff. He had tried his standard approaches for bringing him on board and failed. He asked me how he should handle the problem. Should he fire the recalcitrant employee? After all, his usual techniques had not worked. I asked the manager to show me his key ring. I selected a key and queried, "What does this open?"

"The door to my car."

"Will it also unlock your wife's car?"

"No, of course not."

"Well, it's a perfectly good key. We know it works. Why don't you just junk her car and get another one that will open with this key?"

People are different, so we can't expect everyone to fit with the way we see things. Instead, find out what will unlock each person's resistance to the new idea.[104]

To convince people of the value in a new idea, show how it can be personally useful and valuable to them.

You are giving a presentation or having a meeting to explain your new idea. You are an evangelist or dedicated champion who is introducing a new idea into an organization.

Presentations and training will arouse curiosity and some interest in the new idea, but you must do more—the old habits of most individuals will not die without effort.

We tend to focus on the change we want to see in a team, a department, or an organization, when in reality, change happens one individual at a time. Changing a paradigm in an organization means convincing the individuals in the organization. People take change personally. They want to understand how the new idea can personally benefit them.

As David Baum reminds us, your employees do not work for you, the department, the organization, the board of directors, or even the company's clients. They work for themselves. Consequently, in a time of organizational change, what matters most is the individual benefit each employee sees for his own life. It's not that humans are inherently selfish, but rather that all change is essentially local.

One of the biggest mistakes change agents make is to just talk about the technical benefits. People need to first see a personal need for an innovation before they will listen to a discussion of its benefits. Successful change agents will determine what individuals need and ensure that the innovation addresses those needs.

Therefore:

Talk with individuals about the ways in which the new idea can be personally useful and valuable to them.

Take time to learn a person's needs before you talk to him. Consider "eavesdropping" on problem discussions to discover how the innovation can solve an immediate problem. Ask questions and do a lot of listening. Practice "active listening" by acknowledging, restating, and summarizing ideas and discussion points.

Explain how the new idea will help with a work-related problem and how it is an improvement over what is already in place. You may want to concentrate on the ways it can help meet deadlines, because this is usually more convincing than showing how it may improve the quality of work. Keep in mind that your goal is not to change people, but rather to help them become more of who they already are.

Take advantage of the fact that people who learn about a promising innovation and see even small successes will seek additional information. When you see that someone is interested, find a comfortable, informal environment for discussion. Use the Just Enough pattern to introduce that individual to the concepts.

Don't wear yourself out by trying to talk with everyone. Recognize that you do not have the power or the personality to convince everyone. When someone doesn't want to listen to you, try to find a bridge builder.

= = = = = = = = =

This pattern builds a relationship with individuals, enabling them to discuss their personal needs that the innovation might address. People who hear about something that is personally useful to them are more likely to move past curiosity and become more interested and enthusiastic.

Some individuals may see you as their personal guide to the innovation and run to you with every problem. This can take time away from your primary responsibilities. Use persistent PR to communicate general solutions and uses for the innovation.

At one site in a global Fortune 500 *company, the new technology group worked hard to become a part of each development team. They attended team meetings and listened for developers' pain and tried to understand team dynamics. This helped them formulate a strategy that they could use when negotiating changes later. They looked for opportunities to add value and provide impromptu explanations of the new technology.*

Budget cutting and layoffs often create an organization full of overworked, busy people. This is true in Jerry's organization. So when he wanted to introduce a new idea, his colleagues responded with questions about the amount of work the idea would save them and create for them. Because everyone's job is different, Jerry had to respond with different answers for each person.

INSIGHTS

The focus of this pattern is still the same—answering the question "What's in it for me?" (WIIFM)—but it may be broader than we originally thought. As Dale Emery suggests, what some people might really be asking is, "What's in it *from* me?"; your response should show them how they can make a valuable contribution to the change effort. Others won't care one way or the other about the details—they will care only about their own problems. These people are focusing on getting their own work done and, therefore, want to know if your idea promises to help do that.

Adam Grant says the answer to the WIIFM question is not just self-interest, but also involves benefits to others. The definition of utility includes "whatever you value." Research shows that different cultures value different things. Individual Americans react differently to an appeal for the "greater good." Those with European backgrounds are not moved by this appeal, while Asian Americans often are. All Americans react favorably to the appeal to independence, freedom, and liberty.[105]

Think of all the reasons why the other person wants to continue as he always has, then address those issues in a reasoned argument. You might also want to ask each person to specify "that one thing" he wants to keep during the change initiative. For example, when a new manager began to make changes in one department, she first asked individuals for that one thing they hoped would not change. Even though she couldn't promise to grant everyone's wishes, she was able to understand the hot buttons that were important to each of her employees.

Piggyback

I, on the one hand, was convinced that red meat was bad. No doubt about it, my family was going to eat tofu. They, on the other hand, were preparing for battle: "No way! That tofu stuff is slimy and yucky!" I could see the ordinary arguments about healthy eating were doomed. Then I found a recipe for tofu cheesecake. My friend Susan was the first to experiment. A group from our co-op had lunch one afternoon and, you know what, it was great!

I slyly presented it the next weekend and the family lapped it up. "Hey! This is great cheesecake! Is it a new recipe?"

I debated—yes, no, yes, no. Finally, I decided. "Yup, it's a new recipe. If you like it, I can do a chocolate version next time!"

"Yeah, chocolate! Thanks, Mom!"

When faced with several obstacles in your strategy to introduce something new, look for a way to piggyback on a practice in your organization.

You are an evangelist or dedicated champion. There are some practices in place in your organization that relate to the new idea.

Several procedures or hurdles are required for the introduction of your new idea but you're looking for an easier way.

We're all being asked to do more with less these days. Consequently, when you have a new idea, it can be hard to find the time and energy to do all the things you know will help get the idea accepted by the organization.

All organizations have policies and procedures that are important for creating order and decreasing misunderstanding. It's often necessary to follow some of these procedures to some degree to create a place for a new idea. This can take a lot of time and become frustrating because the idea can get caught in inertia.

But organizations also have established practices that, over time, have become well accepted and could be used to help bring in the new idea. If you can market a new idea as an add-on to one of these practices, you are likely to bypass some of the rules and procedures it would take to introduce the idea as something completely new and different.

After all, in many cases the new idea is just another way to help people do their current work. Promoting it as an entirely new initiative can generate a lot of hoopla and apprehension. It is likely to be introduced in a much calmer manner and meet with less resistance when it is viewed as an extension or small improvement to an established approach.

Therefore:

Piggyback the new idea on a well-accepted practice in the organization.

Introduce the new idea as an improvement rather than as an entirely new initiative. Leverage the environment, resources, and opportunities.

Ask for help from others who might be able to develop ways to take advantage of what's already in place. Enlist the support of those who know the current solution.

When looking for opportunities to talk about your idea, take advantage of already-planned events in the organization. Try to get on the agenda of a team meeting or on the program of an internal conference. Make a brief announcement when it is appropriate in any gathering.

= = = = = = = = =

Using this pattern gets the new idea going in the organization with a minimal amount of red tape. By associating the change with something that is well established, you show that the new idea is not some hair-brained scheme. It can also ease some of the negative effects that concern the people who are fearful of the new idea.

Of course, your effort to help people see the new idea as an add-on might also cause them to think it isn't really anything special. This can limit the resources made available for continuing and building it. Stay in touch with your supporters even after the idea has been established.

Members of a university department wanted to introduce a new program—an MFA in software design, using fine arts teaching methods for software design. Creating a degree program is a complicated committee approval process, so they started with a certificate program, which required only department approval. After a year of success with the certificate program, the program became an alternative for an MS in computer science—a change that once again required only department approval. By that time, the plan for a master of software engineering (MSE) degree program was under way. The supporters had enough success to propose the two-year MFA-style program as an alternative to the second year of the MSE degree work. Finally, they proposed that the two-year MFA-style program stand on its own, perhaps as a master of software arts or master of software engineering (design).

Anne-Marie had been talking about the new idea in the organization, but it didn't seem to be sparking a great amount of interest. She needed to give a presentation. Her boss suggested getting on the agenda for the monthly Tech Talk series. All Anne-Marie had to do was sign up; the people responsible for the Tech Talk series did all the publicity and other work. That presentation turned out to be her first big break. It was well attended and allowed her to identify innovators and a guru who were interested enough to help her spread the word about the new idea.

INSIGHTS

This pattern originally recommended taking advantage of existing capabilities, like a monthly Tech Forum, but now we see that it includes building on anything that will make the innovation easier to accept—for example, aligning with another project that has a budget or influence. Instead of merely looking at the pain points, look around at what's working and build on that.

The pattern also applies to language and vocabulary. If you can introduce your new idea using existing terminology, by saying that the new approach is just a small tweak on the old, then listeners are more likely to be open to what you have to say. For example, early evangelists for Agile software development methodology often claimed that unless you were doing "these 10 things," then you weren't doing <some brand of the methodology>. Others, however, found that this all-or-nothing approach is not how you convince people to try something new. Instead, consider aligning your idea with what's already working well in the organization. This will allow your initiative to fly "under the radar" and be less threatening to the status quo.

Often we immediately adopt the buzzwords of the new technology and start using them in our conversations to influence others. Instead of impressing our listeners, this tactic often frightens them and makes them feel incompetent. If we use terms they are familiar with and minimize any differences, we encourage others to see the benefits. If the discussion is presented in an experimental way, as a trial run, most listeners are likely to be more receptive.

The temptation for many teams who are trying something new is to look different. The excitement over the innovation often leads us to want to call attention to ourselves. Do your best to resist this prospect, and instead consciously try to be less threatening to others who are watching. Draw in others by emphasizing similarities, not differences.

In applying this pattern, you are attempting to make the unfamiliar appear familiar. We are attracted to things that resemble what we like. This is true for food, music, art—indeed, every aspect of our life. If the new idea can appear to be like something we already know, at least at the beginning, initial resistance can be reduced.[106] Sometimes just allowing people to use their own words can help them become more comfortable with the change.

Plant the Seeds

When I give a presentation, I always have a stack of publications on the topic, both for reference during the talk and for perusing at breaks and after the presentation. People like looking at them. One participant said, "Some of my happiest times have been spent with books."

To spark interest, carry materials (seeds) and display (plant) them when the opportunity arises.

◆◆◆

You are an evangelist or dedicated champion working to introduce a new idea into your organization. You have some printed materials about the idea.

You want to spark some interest in the new idea.

People like to keep up on the latest buzzwords and will be drawn to sources of information, especially if those sources are easily accessible. When they are in the early stages of making a decision about a new idea, they are persuaded by mass-media materials, such as articles and books.

The rule of reciprocity holds across cultures. We feel an obligation to repay others when they have given us a gift. Charities rely on reciprocity to help them raise funds. For years, the Disabled American Veterans organization, using only a well-crafted fundraising letter, reported an 18% response rate to its appeals, but when it started enclosing a small gift with those mailings, the response rate doubled to 35%. The gift, which consisted of personalized address labels, was modest, but it wasn't the item the donors received that made the difference. Instead, it was the fact that they had received anything at all. The articles and books you bring to a meeting may not seem like much, but those who take a copy of an article or borrow a book will be positively influenced toward you and your idea.

Therefore:

Carry materials about the new idea to events where people gather. Put them in places where people are likely to pick them up and look at them.

When you give a presentation or attend a meeting, provide sources of external validation, such as books, journal articles, and online articles. Make copies of online materials rather than simply providing the URL, thereby making it more likely people will see the information you think is important. If you want to point out some interesting things on the web, make the URLs available electronically to save the recipient the trouble of typing them. Prominently display anything that has your name as author, or acknowledged contributor, to increase your credibility.

If possible, don't just place the materials on a table and walk away. Make yourself available to answer questions. This will also help ensure that valuable things, like your books, don't disappear!

If you are scheduled to give a presentation during the event, refer to the materials to spark even more interest. The books or articles will attract attention and get conversation going during breaks.

When people ask to take or borrow the materials, stop by your office later, or send an email asking for more information, use the Personal Touch and Just Enough patterns to show how the new idea may be useful to them. Don't be discouraged if most people simply stack any handouts you provide in their office and never look at them. People like to pick up free material, but only some will read those documents and become interested in the new idea. But don't underestimate the power of this pattern. Although the "seeds" usually spark interest in only a few people, they may be key individuals, such as connectors, early adopters, or a guru on your side, who can help you spread the word to others.

= = = = = = = = =

This pattern creates awareness of a new idea and sparks some interest in it. People will be drawn to the materials, pick them up, and ask about them.

Carrying a lot of books or articles can be a problem on a plane. Even in a car, you might have to make several trips to the parking lot or get help unloading material. If books are displayed, you run the risk that someone could borrow one and not return it. Make sure your name clearly appears on all your valuable materials.

Alan takes patterns books to every object technology or Unified Modeling Language (UML) training course he delivers. The books always generate a lot of interest. In fact, he's learned to bring them out only on the last day, or he risks losing the attention of the participants for the topic at hand. Most often, if consultancy follows, it's on patterns, not object technology or UML.

Karl reports good experiences when he brings drafts of unpublished books to training sessions. It shows his audience that the topic is still evolving and interesting and ensures that he is a source of information about what's going on, so the trainees get the latest information.

INSIGHTS

This pattern was originally about displaying books and articles at events for a new idea. In those early days, books were important. For example, when trying to convince people of the value in patterns, evangelists often shared Christopher Alexander's publications or the Gang-of-Four book.[107] Now, print material has become less interesting to most people, so the Plant the Seeds pattern seems to be interpreted by many as a "Johnny Appleseed" approach to spreading the word about the innovation.[108] We've updated our abstract (in the Appendix) to reflect this broader approach.

The Right Time

It's good to request the last or second-to-last interview slot of the day, since these are the time slots that are the most memorable for the interviewer. If you want to be remembered, make your appointment as late in the day as possible.

Consider the timing when you schedule events or when you ask others for help.

♦♦♦

You are an evangelist or dedicated champion trying to introduce a new idea into an organization.

When people face deadlines and have too much to do, they tend to focus on things that move them toward completing necessary tasks and making the deadlines.

People are busy. However, there are less busy times.

When you're really excited about a new idea, you want to tell everyone immediately. But you should temper your enthusiasm with the realization that by springing your news at an inconvenient time, you risk irritating members of your target audience and losing converts to your cause.

Timing is also crucial when approaching someone to ask for help. If people are busy, they could react as if you're trying to add one more thing to their busy schedules. But if your request comes when they're less busy, they are likely to be more responsive.

Therefore:

Be aware of those times when people are likely to be the busiest. Schedule events and requests for help outside those times.

Some suggestions for less busy times: immediately after a project has been delivered, at the beginning of a new year, or possibly during the summer. The best timing will vary from organization to organization, group to group, and person to person. What is good for one will not be good for another. Avoid planning events when almost everyone is too busy to attend.

If you're able, personally ask as many individuals as you can about their time preferences for an upcoming event. This will make them feel that you would really like them to be present.

Don't worry about finding the perfect time. You can spend a lot of effort trying to find the best time when there really isn't one. One approach is to schedule the event more than once. Choose different days or times so more people can attend.

Announce dates as early as possible and use persistent PR. Busy people need lead time and reminders. Personally remind individuals when you have the opportunity.

Elicit feedback. Ask attendees at any event what could have been done to improve the event—and this includes timing. You might learn that some people, for example, would like an early morning event, while others prefer a noontime brown bag or a late afternoon meeting at the end of the day.

You don't have to consider the timing in planning every event. For example, study groups are usually held on a regular basis and it is expected that people will come when they can. Big jolt presentations have to be held at the convenience of the speaker.

Be sensitive of timing during meetings or conversations. "When the student is ready, the teacher appears" is a big part of this pattern. Keep your ears open for a problem that the new idea can help to address. The receptiveness of your group will increase considerably at a time when they have an immediate application.

= = = = = = = = = =

This pattern creates more appropriate timing for introducing the new idea. If you can find a good time, you are likely to increase participation.

Despite your best efforts, some people will inevitably claim to be too busy to do or attend anything that doesn't directly relate to their immediate job. Use the Personal Touch pattern to reach them. Encourage them to hear a one-time big jolt speaker.

Ian tried to be aware of the needs of many different people while he waited for the opportunity to help someone with a problem. It doesn't help a team to talk about testing patterns during design or to talk about configuration management patterns during analysis. When the solution fits the needs, the timing is right and people will be ready to listen.

Nilesh held the first workshop about a new idea during the start of a semester. The second one was held at the end of the semester, just after grades were due. Both events were well attended. Attendees were excited about continuing the workshops. But when the third event was scheduled during the fourth week of the semester, just as the workload was heating up, it had to be cancelled due to lack of positive responses.

INSIGHTS

We recognized that there are good times to introduce new ideas and other times that are not as good because of constraints such as looming deadlines or tightened budgets. We've learned that this pattern is also a way to look at organizations and ask if there is ever a "right time." Tom DeMarco, in his book *Slack*,[109] talks about the need for organizational breathing space to allow the organization to grow. If there is *no* slack time, then the organization can't learn. It takes an investment in time and energy to adopt innovations. In addition to using the Know Yourself pattern, be sure you know your organization, too. Reflect on the organization initially and throughout the change effort to determine if it has the requisite slack to take on something new.

Royal Audience

The first time my company invited a big-name speaker, I tried to make sure the day was full of activities. I wanted as many people as possible to take advantage of the opportunity. Then he said, "I'll be here the night before; if anyone is interested, we could do dinner." Aha! Dinner! Lunch! Good times for interaction! I learned from this experience to always invite people to meals with any famous visitor because the relaxed atmosphere can be more fun and even more interesting than the visitor's formal presentation.

Arrange for management and members of the organization to spend time with a big jolt visitor.

You are an evangelist or dedicated champion. A big jolt visitor has a few spare hours during the day or during the evening before and/or after the day of the visit.

You want to get the most out of a visit from a famous person.

It's better if a visit from a well-known individual is more than just a presentation to a large group. Famous people are usually charismatic and can give your cause a boost. If management and other influential people in the organization will take time for a short, one-on-one meeting with the big jolt visitor, this can lead to more interest and support for the new idea.

Therefore:

Use spare hours or lunchtime during the day or evenings, before and/or after the featured presentation, to make the visitor available for teams, individuals, or managers.

Arrange lunch, dinner, or time for informal discussion with the speaker during the day. Personally invite people to attend, especially those who have helped with the change effort. The visitor may also be willing to take some one-on-one time with managers who still need to be convinced of the value in the new idea. This can lead to support from a local sponsor or corporate angel. It is also a good way to stay in touch.

If you can, try to schedule several audiences, enough opportunities so that no one minds not being invited to all of them. For example, dinner may need to be a small group, but lunch in the cafeteria could be open to everyone. You might schedule "consulting time" when the visitor could meet with teams to discuss particular problems.

Don't wear out the visitor. Make certain he agrees to do more than a presentation. Give him a chance to turn down any opportunities that he wishes. Sometimes we assume that someone who comes in for a presentation will want to spend lunch and dinner with us, but we should be sensitive to the fact that everyone needs time to relax away from others. Remember to offer sincere appreciation for any extra time he spends with the organization.

Don't expect everyone to accept the invitation to meet with the speaker. It is important that you offer them the opportunity. For those who can't come, it may be enough for them to know that they were invited.

= = = = = = = = =

This pattern creates an opportunity for people to meet with a big jolt speaker. Participants will enjoy the time spent getting to know a famous person. The experience can be a reward for those who have helped with the effort, and it can be a public relations opportunity for management who have not yet bought into your new idea.

But be careful that this plan doesn't backfire. If you need to keep the audience small, people can be upset at not being invited. If you always involve everyone as much as you can and are a fair person, however, then people will accept that they weren't invited to a particular occasion but will be included in the next one or will be involved in some other way.

Dorothy sent invitations to everyone to join famous visitors for lunch or an open discussion forum. Free consulting time was also announced on the forum. Even if people couldn't attend, they always felt that the opportunity was open to them.

Deloy always invited everyone to meet with well-known visitors for lunch or a coffee break after the presentations. Because the meetings were held in the cafeteria, there was room for everyone at the presentation to attend. Even those who couldn't talk one-on-one with the visitor still enjoyed listening to him chat with others in an informal setting.

Shoulder to Cry On

When I was trying to introduce a new idea into the organization, I would often make mistakes and become discouraged. Then I would see one of my favorite movie lines displayed on my office bulletin board: "One of the best things you have going for yourself is your willingness to humiliate yourself" (Simon to Melvin in the movie As Good as It Gets). That was just like me, and because of this, I was willing to continue trying to introduce the new idea despite the embarrassing mistakes. Instead of giving up, I'd usually find a shoulder to cry on—someone who would help me recognize that things weren't as bad as I thought they were.

To avoid becoming too discouraged when the going gets tough, find opportunities to talk with others who are also struggling to introduce a new idea.

You are an evangelist or dedicated champion working to introduce a new idea into your organization.

When you're struggling to introduce a new idea, it's easy to become discouraged.

Misery loves company, but if it's the right kind of company, commiserating can lead to rejuvenation. Getting together with others who share the same or similar problems can lead to surprising solutions. The group dynamic helps everyone become more creative in tackling tough situations. Research has shown that for certain issues, group support can be very helpful. Even if you are enthusiastic about the new idea, you will need and deserve a boost now and then. You'll want to feel like you're not the only one dealing with an issue. This realization by itself is useful.

Those who are first to adopt an innovation are often frustrated when they can't understand complicated material. A common solution is to form a user group. Together they can solve problems that individuals in isolation can't.

Therefore:

Get together regularly with others who are also working to introduce the new idea or are interested in the process.

Meet informally for lunch, dinner, or coffee. Try to find a place away from home or the office. Look for a "third place"—a local, public establishment that is a friendly, neutral spot where people gather together to relax and talk and take a break from everyday life.

If funding permits, attend a conference where you can learn more about the innovation and meet with others to talk about your mutual struggles.

There should be give-and-take among the participants. Give everyone a chance to "cry" and to "provide a shoulder to cry on." Remember to offer sincere appreciation for any support.

When you can't find a group of people, consider the Cardboard Consultant pattern written by Charles Weir and James Noble. It recommends that when you can't find a solution to your problem, you explain it, in detail, out loud to someone or something. This will help you understand your basic assumptions, the chain of logic that led to your being stuck, and your conclusions. Weir and Noble claim this works even with your dog as the audience.

= = = = = = = = = =

This pattern creates opportunities for you to discuss the challenges and successes you are having with your change effort. A community begins to form wherever people gather with a shared purpose and start talking among themselves. This community provides a confidence boost when you're discouraged and represents a source of helpful suggestions and strategies. It is also a good way to meet innovators and connectors in your larger community.

But if you are not careful, a meeting can degenerate into a whining session. This kind of experience will simply make people drown in the negative and feel sorry for themselves. While some complaining is appropriate, focus on solutions to the problems that people raise. Once people have the chance to unload, you can use the larger intelligence to move forward.

When the Houston Independent School District made a major commitment to purchasing technology for the classrooms, teachers found that they had to confront the technology alone, using ideas from scattered sources with only modest results. The Electronic Community of Teachers was created to help teachers across the district learn from one another about computing in the classroom. This virtual community of practice allows teachers who find themselves isolated in their classrooms to build relationships with other teachers as they share experiences and document their best practices.

In the Greenville, South Carolina, area, business people gather monthly at the Wall Street Capitol Breakfast Club America meeting. During a recent event, the guest speaker, Rich DeVos, the co-founder of Amway Corporation, reminded them, "You are never alone. There are people all around you at this meeting to help and support you."

INSIGHTS

In our original description of this pattern, we mentioned that only the evangelist may need a shoulder, but we all need sympathy when the going gets tough. By definition, all change involves loss. Be prepared to provide a shoulder to cry on for others in your organization who are struggling with loss as a result of the new idea.

In economics and decision theory, loss aversion refers to our tendency to strongly prefer avoiding losses to acquiring gains. This explains why individuals fight long and hard when confronting a loss and why evangelists and other supporters of a change must provide understanding, compassion, and recognition of their loss.

Sincere Appreciation

A friend of mine was laid off from a large company where he had worked for nearly 30 years. I saw him after his last day and he said that the worst thing about the experience was that no one, not even his boss, had come by to say they would miss him or that they appreciated his work. I thought about my last day when I was laid off. I recall a constant stream of people coming by to share a brief story—how something I had done or said had influenced their lives for the better and how I had made a difference for them and the company. I don't remember sadness on that day but an overwhelming gladness at having had the chance to work in that company with those people—and all they did was just say "Thanks!"

To show your appreciation, say "thanks" in the most sincere way you can to everyone who helps you.

You are an evangelist or a dedicated champion. Others are helping you introduce your new idea into the organization.

People feel unappreciated when they work hard and no one notices or cares.

It's easy to take for granted the work that people do—after all, they're getting paid for it! Nevertheless, people are happier and feel their contribution is appreciated with a simple acknowledgment and encouragement. Even when you don't have resources to reward supporters with anything tangible, an expression of your gratitude costs nothing and means so much to the receiver.

A recent survey of 1400 chief financial officers showed that a simple "thank you" can go a long way in motivating employees. When asked what, other than monetary reward, is the most effective means of motivating employees, 38% chose frequent recognition of accomplishments as the best way to encourage staff members.

In today's fast-paced business world, there often isn't enough time or resources to acknowledge these efforts in large ways. There may not be enough money to buy gifts for everyone or time in busy schedules to celebrate accomplishments with a meal.

Usually, everyone on a team performs a heroic act during any project. We seem to have lost the ability to give someone a "high five" or say "great job," so heroes often remain unappreciated. Yet, when many different company presidents and CEOs were asked the question, "What do you know now that you wish you'd been told 25 years ago?" their advice was to occasionally stop for a few moments and think about the people to whom you owe thanks, and then take the time to express your gratitude to them.[110]

Therefore:

Find everyone who has helped you and say "thanks" in the most sincere way you can.

Even an informal recognition will make an impression—a private discussion, a phone call, or even an email message. Spending a small amount of money can generate a huge return—a card, a morning pastry, a piece of fruit, or a small gift. These tokens show that you took extra effort and time to think about what the receiver might like. When you can, give supporters something they will value. It does not have to be anything expensive; recipients just have to attach value to it and associate it with their efforts in the change initiative. An invitation to a royal audience is another way to acknowledge people whose work made a difference.

Take a few minutes to write a thank-you note. Nancy Austin, author of the management classic *A Passion for Excellence*, reminds us that a personal note is a quick, responsive, cheap, and surprisingly effective way to win friends and influence people. It is "shoestring marketing. . . . People remember thank-you notes (and the people who write them) because good ones are so rare."

When appropriate, acknowledge achievements publicly. Recognize special effort and the people who helped achieve even small successes.

Don't thank only the individuals who have lent a hand. Also consider the people who attended an event you organized, such as a brown bag or hometown story. Let them know how much you appreciate their time. A follow-up gesture of thanks will go a long way to help people remember what you had to say.

Tailor the thanks to each individual. Let people know they are appreciated by interacting with them frequently. Be generous with the acknowledgment and always make people feel important. Even if a considerable amount of time has passed, don't let this stop you from telling people you are still thankful for what they have done.

= = = = = = = = =

This pattern builds stronger relationships with people who have contributed to the initiative. A sincere expression of gratitude is likely to make such an impression on people that it will be easier to ask for help and receive their assistance again in the future. The spirit that it creates is incredible. More importantly, it will remind you that you didn't do it all alone. Saying "thank you" will keep you humble and be a real boon for those who have made a difference in your efforts.

But once you start thanking people, you run the risk of offending others who feel they were left out or did not receive the same level of appreciation as another person did. Try to reward contributors equally. Thank everyone who helps you, not just the people who take on the high-profile tasks. Continually apologize in case you forget a contribution to anticipate a sin of omission.

The inspiration for this pattern came from a co-worker who expressed extreme frustration because her manager did not say thanks after a long, difficult project was completed. Although she didn't mind working the long hours, she was very upset that her manager didn't show appreciation with even a simple "thank you" to the team.

Adam was a team leader at a large satellite telecommunications company. As each phase of the project was completed, he wrote personal, printed hardcopy letters to the supervisors of everyone who contributed (they were all contractors), expressing his appreciation for their effort. The trickle-down benefit was amazing. The contractors were surprised and delighted to be treated well and even complimented, so the barriers between the company and the contractors came down, at least in this area. Such expressions have a big payoff over the long term.

INSIGHTS

We have decided that Sincere Appreciation is a better name for this pattern. It's really not Just Say Thanks (the former name of this pattern), which for many of us means a quick word without much behind it. Rather, the value lies in taking the time to be sincere, to use the person's name and describe what the person has done. You want the recipient to feel that you truly appreciate the contribution.

We realize that companies can be short of cash for other forms of recognition, but simply giving sincere appreciation is not only cheap but also very effective.

We originally thought this pattern provided benefits to the recipient of the thanks, but now we recognize there are considerable benefits to the giver of the thanks as well. Research suggests that grateful souls are happier and, as a result, have healthier lives and more success in their careers. Studies show that grateful people have more energy and optimism, are less bothered by life's hassles, are more resilient in the face of stress, and suffer less depression than the rest of us. Those who practice gratitude are also more compassionate, more likely to help others, less materialistic, and more satisfied with life. It seems like such a simple fix for many of the ills of the world.[111]

Researchers at Japan's National Institute for Physiological Sciences found that praise activated similar areas of the brain that light up in response to a financial windfall. A recent survey by Maritz Research Inc., a St. Louis–based employee-consulting firm, indicates that showing appreciation pays off. In this survey, 81% of employees who had never received a "thank you" from the boss said they were likely to leave their current job. By contrast, among employees who received "frequent" workplace recognition, only 25% said they were likely to leave. Research by Adam Grant and Francesca Gino has shown that saying "thank you" not only results in reciprocal generosity—where the thanked person is more likely to help the thanker—but also stimulates pro-social behavior in general. In other words, giving thanks increases the likelihood that your employee will not only help you, but also help someone else. Praise family, friends, and colleagues whenever you can. Compliments can be as rewarding to their brains as cold, hard cash![112]

Mark Goulston, in his book, *Real Influence*,[113] describes a Power Thank You:

1. Appreciate something specific that was above the call of duty. "Joe, thanks for working over that three-day weekend to make our presentation deck perfect."
2. Acknowledge the effort or personal sacrifice in doing the above. "I realize how important your family is to you, and that working on this cost you the time you'd planned to spend with your daughters. Yet you did it without griping or complaining. Your dedication motivated everyone else on the team to make the presentation excellent."
3. Describe the business impact. "Because of your effort, our customer was really happy with our meeting and I think they're going to sign that contract."

Telling someone to his face is effective, but when you say these things to someone else (either within earshot or with the idea that it will get back to the person you want to influence), the compliments can be much more powerful, as illustrated in this story:

Dr. Smith recently gave a talk about the efficacy of a drug. Jane, the sales rep for that drug, was really impressed with the talk. She went up to Dr. Smith and told him in detail what she liked about the talk (not just "Oh, it was great"). Dr. Smith thanked her for the feedback. A short time later, one of Dr. Smith's colleagues came up to Jane and she again mentioned, in detail, what she really liked about Dr. Smith's talk. Dr. Smith overheard the conversation. Later that week, when Jane called on Dr. Smith, he said that he appreciated her comments after his talk, but that it really meant more when he overheard her making the detailed comments to his colleague. It wasn't that he didn't believe Jane when she said the same things to him, but somehow the comments really hit home when he heard her telling someone else.

What's really surprising about this pattern is how well it works. It seems trite and overblown, but we're heard from many users with stories like the following:

I would like to share a hometown story. In one of the companies I worked, there was an "internal service desk." There was a huge amount of frustration about this function, probably because the personnel didn't have time enough to solve the number of problems reported. Most work was done for the person screaming loudest or with the most managers noted on the CC list about the reported issue. It was normal to have weeks of waiting time and a really poor service where most of the time no one told you when they finally did resolve the issue. Then suddenly, for reasons I don't know about, I got a response about my issue in a reasonably short time after sent it: They told me they worked on it, and a hour or so later I got the message that my issue was solved.

I was sincerely appreciating this fast handling and rich communication around the issue, and I did send a mail to thank them, and I did put on their boss as a CC. Magic, absolute magic! From now on, when I send in a request, I get a quick answer and help to solve my problems. Every time I send them a "thank you" for the help and the quick handling, even if they just did what they are supposed to do. This went so long that it ended up with my colleagues in my department asking me for help every time they needed help from the internal service desk. "Why do you always get help?" "Please, Michael, can you please send a mail to service desk so I can get help with my issue" I now have the insight on why the story ended up this way.

Once again, thank you for giving me this insight.

Best Regards,
Michael Nilsson

Finally, there is the problem of receiving thanks. Often we denigrate the effort of the giver of thanks by saying, "Oh, it was nothing," which makes the giver feel small. Some suggestions:

+ Treat recognition as a gift—which it is—from the giver.
+ Be aware of how you respond when people recognize you. Learn to just say, "Thank you."
+ If you catch yourself diverting thanks, you can always go back and tell the giver that you are working on trying to get better at accepting thanks and then say, "Thank you for taking the time and for what you said earlier."

You can help others develop their ability to accept appreciation by saying in a friendly way, "No need to be embarrassed. I just wanted to tell you that I appreciated your effort."

Small Successes

As David Baum, author of Lightning in a Bottle, *recommends, "If you talk about what you want rather than what you don't want, your subconscious can rarely tell the difference. Focus on the positive and you will move toward it with deliberate speed."*[114]

To avoid becoming overwhelmed by the challenges and all the things you have to do when you're involved in an organizational change effort, celebrate even small successes.

◆◆◆

You are an evangelist. You've applied some patterns from this language, and some worked—but others didn't.

Every organizational change effort has its ups and downs. It's a difficult process.

We are often so caught up in our destination that we forget to appreciate the journey. After successfully completing a task, we may not acknowledge our achievement or may even underestimate what we have done. Our memory can be so focused on the struggle it took to get the job done that we don't take the time to appreciate what we have accomplished. We often concentrate on everything that still needs to be done instead of the small successes that have come our way. Usually we're too busy. Our "to do" list is infinite, so when we finish any task, we're already thinking about the next one. We can become discouraged and burned out.

All too often, our focus is on that "big win"—some dramatic event that defines success. We care more about some magic silver bullet than about the continuous improvements that will eventually lead to our desired goal. As a result, most jobs provide few opportunities to be recognized as a winner. Celebrations are usually reserved for the big events, and only a few are singled out.

Author and software guru Luke Hohmann urges us to remember that "achieving any goal should be an opportunity for enjoying the fruits of your labor. You've earned it! More importantly, achieving one goal gives you the confidence to do it again, producing a positive feedback loop of goal-setting and goal-achieving success!"[115]

Large-scale change can be a long, formidable undertaking, so create short-term wins. A number of early victories, even if they are small, will increase self-confidence and instill the belief that bigger successes are possible. This belief builds a psychological momentum that sustains the effort needed for large-scale, long-term change.

Therefore:

As you carry on in baby steps, take the time to recognize and celebrate successes, especially the small ones.

These events don't have to be big celebrations. You can buy a cake for everyone to share or just give a "high five" all around. Involve everyone who has helped to achieve the small success. Even when you can't include others, it is still important to give yourself a pat on the back.

Success can come in many forms. Look for it. For example, at the end of the week, ask yourself what you and your team have learned or done differently. This simple question can go a long way in promoting continual, but focused, change.

Focus on the gains rather than the losses. Even when you don't get all the things you wanted, you can still celebrate the things you *didn't* get that you didn't want!

Take time for reflection and view each success as an opportunity to work toward larger undertakings. Your present success, no matter how small, is something to be proud of because it allows you to do bigger and even more successful things. Build on what you have accomplished.

Use persistent PR to inform others about the progress. The smell of success will attract others.

= = = = = = = = =

This pattern creates the realization that each small success puts you one step closer to the goal. Even though work remains to be done, recognizing and celebrating small accomplishments encourages a focus on the positive. It makes you feel productive and energized to do even more.

Sometimes, your success may turn off people who are jealous and resentful of what you are trying to do. Others may see the celebration as a sign that the effort is at an end. Stay in touch with your supporters and nonsupporters alike to ensure that everyone is on the same page. Help them understand that the small successes are cornerstones for tackling the bigger problems and their support is still needed to reach the final goals.

Since 1961, Peace Corps volunteers have embarked on ambitious projects but are often overpowered by feelings of frustration. Successful change agents persist despite setbacks and celebrate even small successes. A small success is worth a lot because it empowers the volunteer and the community members to try another new project. After a small victory, a volunteer could make more suggestions because the locals will no longer think that the outsider is quite so crazy. Some volunteers finish their stint with Peace Corps thinking they didn't accomplish much. Taking time to recognize the small successes is the key.

John was leading the development of a new center in his organization. There was a lot of work to be done. The task could have become overwhelming if not for the "action items" that the team created during each weekly meeting. At the following meeting, team members looked forward to going over that list and would often cheer "All right!" when one of the larger items was finally completed or all of the smaller items on the list could be removed.

Smell of Success

It is both invisible and intangible, yet it invokes such powerful human reactions that people are swayed to affection or revulsion because of it. It is that most subtle and subjective of senses—the sense of smell.

When your efforts result in some visible positive result, people will come out of the woodwork to talk to you. Treat this opportunity as a teaching moment.

You are an evangelist or dedicated champion trying to introduce a new idea. You've had at least limited success.

When you start to have some success, newcomers will ask you about the innovation.

Some people, especially members of the early majority and the skeptics, are drawn to a new idea when there is visible success. Unlike the innovators, who love the excitement of being part of the latest and greatest trend, must others wait until the early bugs are worked out and some evidence indicates that a new idea is useful. This evidence can be provided by the successes others are having. When people who have not yet adopted a new idea smell success, they are likely to become interested enough to ask you about it.

Therefore:

When people comment on the success they see with the innovation, treat their inquiry as a teaching moment.

Use the Just Enough pattern to spark some interest and the Personal Touch pattern to match the innovation to the inquirer's needs. If you think it is appropriate, ask for help—identify a small task and ask the inquirer to complete it. This is the "Yes, that's a difficult problem—would you volunteer to tackle it?" ploy!

Manage the expectations of people who smell success and then look forward to the introduction of a silver bullet. Give them a realistic view of what has been accomplished and what still needs to be done.

Learn what you can from these inquiries. Even as you experience success and become convinced of the value in the new idea, remain open and listen to comments from everyone.

= = = = = = = = =

This pattern creates the opportunity for you to use your success to create more successes. It draws people to the new idea, giving you the opportunity to answer their questions and encourage them to become active supporters.

But a smell of success can also draw people who have been negatively impacted by the new idea. If they are looking for a way to neutralize that effect, listen to their story and use the Fear Less pattern to find a win-win solution.

After a project was completed on schedule and received high acclaim from the users, someone from another team dropped by to talk about some issues that concerned her in our project's technology. She seemed interested in knowing how our techniques, which were quite different from the "standard" practices, allowed us to be productive and successful—despite our having an inexperienced team. It was the perfect opportunity to enlighten her about our new approaches.

My work with patterns attracted the interest of someone who was well known and well respected in the patterns community. When he offered to come to my organization to give a presentation, people were impressed. As a result, inquiries about patterns increased. I made sure I addressed each one, often by suggesting that we take a coffee break or have lunch to discuss their questions.

Stay in Touch

Everyone is busy and overworked. Yet I've discovered that if I don't take a moment to stop by my co-workers' offices to have a chat now and then and occasionally spend lunchtime with them, I lose touch with the most important part of my organization— the people.

Once you've enlisted the support of key persons, don't forget about them and make sure they don't forget about you.

You are an evangelist or dedicated champion working to introduce a new idea into an organization. You've captured the interest of a handful of key persons.

Your key supporters have too many things to think about and can forget about the new idea.

Support for any new idea depends on the continuing awareness of that idea on the part of management and other key people, but their support can lapse. Because there's always something important going on and critical decisions to be made, your message will be lost if you don't call attention to it.

Finding proactive ways to keep the information flowing is essential. You do not want your key supporters to feel embarrassed or frustrated because they lack information about the change initiative. Any effort to keep a communication link will pay off handsomely in the end.

Just because people decide to adopt an innovation, that decision doesn't mean they can't change their minds. They're always seeking reinforcement for their decisions. They always have new questions. If they don't get answers, they may revert to their old ways.

Therefore:

Stay in touch with your key supporters.

Make an effort to talk regularly with people such as early adopters, local sponsors, the guru on your side, and the corporate angel. You're busy as well, so put the "stay in touch" reminder on your calendar. The contact can be a short meeting, lunch, or coffee break, or just an informal stop by an office. Present information in a helpful manner. Keep messages timely and interesting. Use the External Validation pattern to make your supporters aware of what is happening outside the organization. If a big jolt visitor is of special interest to your supporters, offer them a royal audience with that individual.

On the one hand, you should strive to build relationships with key supporters so you can casually but continually make them aware of progress in small ways. On the other hand, you don't want to make a pest of yourself. Be sensitive to individual tolerances for new information. Don't overwhelm anyone, or people may become annoyed when they see you coming. It can be hard to determine the happy medium for information, so you may want to ask how often each person would like to receive a formal report, and at the same time provide informal reports when you get a good opportunity.

Talk to management even when you don't need anything. Some people make the mistake of reporting to management only when they need support. As a result, managers will think that any time you come to talk, you must want something.

If you need a more formal approach for staying close, submit a regular status report that contains a concise record of your activities. Record your accomplishments, even small successes, so people know you are making progress. Also note your concerns so that your manager, or your local sponsor, has the information he needs to help you.

= = = = = = = = =

This pattern establishes more solid connections with key supporters. Over time, it turns support into an expanding community of relationships.

But staying in touch takes work. A personal interaction is best, but persistent PR can help. If it is difficult to reach some upper-level managers, ask connectors or your local sponsor to help.

It was easy for Amy. The company brought in 8′ × 8′ cubicles and the vice president was nearby. Well, perhaps he had two cubicles, one with a little conference table, and his secretary's cubicle was also part of his area, but he was still just around the corner from Amy's team. When she walked in each morning, the vice president was often there. If he looked up, she could sometimes catch his eye and say, "Good morning!" If he asked, and usually he did, she could tell him about the latest activity surrounding the introduction of the innovation. She wouldn't let him forget about it!

Bradley was the chair of a large international conference. His committee consisted of 12 people located in various countries. In between the meetings, Bradley made random calls to each individual just to ask how things were going. One day he connected to a frantic committee member on the other end of the phone. She was amazed at the timing of his phone call because she had just discovered a major error in her duties. He calmed her and then explained what he could do to "fix" things. They both appreciated the value of staying in touch that day.

INSIGHTS

We have learned how important this pattern is. Keeping an idea visible and alive must be a continuous effort throughout the change initiative. We agree with Diana Larsen who asserts, "*When implementing a change, there's no such thing as too much communication.*" Never rest on your laurels and assume that your supporters are still with you.

Study Group

Joshua Kerievsky, well-known Agile software development coach, writes about learning: "While attendees of a lecture may seek information, attendees of a study group seek transformation; they want to make what they study not only something they understand, but something they may use in their everyday lives or work. The study group thus acts as a bridge, helping people move from passive to active learning."[116]

Form a small group of colleagues who are interested in exploring or continuing to learn about a specific topic.

You and others in the organization would like to learn more about a new idea. There are some resources on the topic, such as books or other written materials.

There may be little or no money for formal training on the specific topic.

Software guru Gerald Weinberg describes the lecture method as "getting material from the teacher's notes into the student's notes without passing through the brain of either one." The intense training experience can be compared to drinking from a fire hose. It isn't the best learning environment, especially for adults, who want to think about useful information and contemplate how it could be applied to their daily work.

When you read a book by yourself, what you get out of it is limited by your own perspective and experience. When you read a book in a group setting, you can take advantage of a variety of backgrounds and expertise. More formal independent study has its own difficulties. The learner relies on a technical interface, videotapes, or broadcast classes but little social interaction. As a result, the learner goes through material in isolation with no chance for discussion or timely questions.

Research shows that simply explaining or lecturing to a group does little to change the members' way of thinking. By comparison, discussion groups, role-playing, and visualization techniques are powerful persuaders. In one study, two groups were introduced to a new approach. One group was given a presentation on the advantages of the approach. The other was led through a discussion and a group decision-making process. There was little or no change in behavior resulting from the training presentation, while the number of people adopting the new approach varied from more than 60% to 100% in the group that had used facilitated decision making.

Institutional learning depends on developing the ability to "flock"—moving people around and fostering an effective mechanism of social transmission. Teams of disparate people must undergo some kind of training experience where they are expected to both teach and learn.

Therefore:

Form a group of no more than eight colleagues who are interested in exploring and studying an interesting topic.

Cover a chapter in a book or a well-defined topic at each regularly scheduled meeting. Make sure that participants understand that they must be prepared. Assign one participant to act as the facilitator who guides everyone through the material. Rotate the facilitation role to spread this responsibility throughout the group.

If resources are available, ask your company to buy the material you will study, such as books or copies of articles. Consider meeting over lunch if this is the time when most people are free. Have a brown bag if no resources are available for food.

Linda has co-authored an article about one company's success with study groups. It was published in the *Bell Labs Technical Journal* and can be downloaded from her website, http://www.lindarising.org. Joshua Kerievsky has another useful source of information for this effective learning activity;

see *Knowledge Hydrant: A Pattern Language for Study Groups* at http://www
.industriallogic.com/papers/khdraft.pdf.

= = = = = = = = = =

This pattern provides an opportunity for individuals to explore an interesting topic at a reasonable pace. The group members get a genuine educational
experience and focus on topics they have chosen. The Study Group pattern
allows timely, convenient scheduling and a sense of ownership of the learning
path. The result is maximum learning with minimal money invested. Even
when companies buy lunch for eight participants and individual copies of a
book, the cost per learner for a 12-week study group is less than $200. Other,
more formal training costs are likely to run from $800 to $2000 per learner.

However, the discovery process in study groups isn't appropriate for all
types of learning. Technical topics, such as a programming language, may
need an expert to be present when learners get stuck on problems. In addition, this type of exploration may not work for everyone, especially those
individuals who are not energized by interaction with others or are "sponges"
rather than contributors. Study groups are just one way of learning; they
should be considered as a part of the total teaching and learning strategy in an
organization.

*A few years ago, Todd recognized a real gap in the company's knowledge of XML.
Because the company is a systems integrator, this could have been a fatal hole. There
weren't any homegrown experts, so employees formed a study group to make themselves
knowledgeable about the subject. They turned what they learned in the study groups into
a course that they originally described as "The Myopic Leading the Blind." They now
have key work done with XML as well as a broad curriculum of XML classes that they
teach internally and one that they are teaching externally.*

*A four-year university and a nearby community college wanted to incorporate more
"service learning" in their institutions, but they needed to understand how to make these
types of experiences more meaningful for students. Faculty from each institution banded
together to form a study group with 12 members. The university purchased books on the
topic, and members partnered into teams of two to lead a biweekly group discussion on
one of the sections. The participants learned techniques for making service learning successful as a pedagogical technique in their classes, and they are preparing to spread the
word to other faculty.*

Sustained Momentum

We can think of introducing ideas as analogous to planting a sapling: Without water, sun, and a source of nourishment, the young tree will die. It will need attention to keep it alive and growing. Sometimes we forget how important this ongoing support is—for all living things.

Take a proactive approach to the ongoing work of sustaining the interest in the new idea in your organization.

◆◆◆

You are a dedicated champion. You have made some progress introducing the new idea into your organization.

The many other things that need to be done will tempt you to put the task of introducing the new idea on the back burner for a while. Doing so can cause you and other people to lose interest in it.

It takes work to maintain interest. Even though it may be easy to start the change effort with a lot of enthusiasm, the never-ending list of things to do can make you feel tired of the investment it takes to introduce the new idea. But without continuing, proactive efforts, any new idea can wither and die on the vine. If you don't reinforce the benefits of your new idea, you run the risk that excitement and interest will fade, especially when everyone gets busy with other things. You can't become complacent. You may have told your story countless times, but you have to keep on giving your sales pitch and providing support. This effort never really ends, because there are always new people to bring in and new management to sell.

When success is evident in the change initiative, it becomes all too easy to just rest on your laurels and not do anything for a while. But even when the new idea has been accepted and is being used, people still require periodic confirmation that their decision to adopt it was a good one or they may discontinue their use. They need continuous invitations to become involved and continuous reassurances that they will get their wins.

During any change initiative, you must keep yourself inspired. Newton's Third Law was never so true: An object at rest tends to stay at rest until acted upon by external forces. You need to keep the new idea in a state of motion that is difficult to stop, because momentum is hard to regain once you lose it.

Therefore:

Take a proactive approach in the organization to the ongoing work of sustaining the interest in the new idea. Take some small action each day, no matter how insignificant it might seem, to move you closer to your goal.

The following are some suggestions for ongoing activities that will keep the information flowing:

- Keep your message center alive and interesting.
- Use the Personal Touch pattern and talk about the new idea every chance you get.
- Plan frequent events, such as a brown bag or hometown story.
- Bring in a big jolt speaker to stir up more curiosity and interest.
- Start a study group to keep people learning.
- Piggyback on already scheduled events.
- Be aware of outside happenings and call them to the attention of the organization.
- Attend conferences to learn new things and network with others. Share this information with others using the External Validation and Stay in Touch patterns.

- Keep your knowledge up-to-date. Your continuous learning is an important part of this effort. Read and make information available—plant the seeds.
- Take time for reflection to learn what is working well and what should be done differently.
- Offer sincere appreciation so that people feel their continuing support is appreciated.

Keep the momentum going even when you encounter a setback. Those people who get "back on the horse" and do something constructive will probably make it, whereas those who have trouble weathering the storms are likely to fail. Find a shoulder to cry on for help in handling your difficult problems.

= = = = = = = = =

This pattern builds a sustained change initiative. It keeps the idea alive in you and in others, and helps to reinforce individuals' decisions to adopt it. When the change effort is a living and growing entity, members of the organization will see the new idea as active and evolving, even when they are too busy to take advantage of everything that is offered.

In reality, maintaining a steady momentum on any one project goes against the grain. Our natural tendency is to work in cycles. After completing a big task, we like to do something else for a while. Unfortunately, the longer we wait, the harder it is to return to the project because we lose some of our passion for it. In the long run, we usually find that periodic bursts are more stressful and less effective than simply doing something—even something small—on a regular basis.

It never occurred to Carl that introducing patterns is like growing a garden. You can't just throw the seeds in the ground and say, "That's that!" No, you have to water, feed, and weed the tender plants. Carl discovered this after he had given a few brown bag presentations. As more people came by to ask about one design pattern or another, he realized that he was now the official encourager of pattern use—and that once the mantle had been placed on his shoulders, it was up to him to make sure he thought about it all the time. After a while, it became second nature. He would say, "I 'do' patterns!"

Poet David Whyte writes, "I decided on two things: firstly I was going to do at least one thing every day toward my future life as a poet. I calculated that no matter how small a step I took each day, over a year that would come to a grand total of 365 actions toward the life I wanted. One thing a day adds up to a great deal over time. One thing a day is a powerful multiplier. Sometimes that one thing was writing poetry itself or memorizing lines of a newly read poem that caught my eye, or just writing a letter to an organization to say I was available for readings or talks. Sometimes it was a phone call to someone in a position of influence, letting them know what I could do. Sometimes it was preparing the ground in my mind before the conversation. Soon I felt as if I was being prepared by the conversations themselves. Over the ensuing weeks it was beginning to add up. I began to overhear a background buzz in the ethers that added to my dedication."[117]

INSIGHTS

This pattern was originally included in the "Keep It Going" chapter, but now we realize that successful change leaders will sustain the change initiative's momentum from the beginning. This includes growing and learning, with baby steps, as you and your team move through the journey of change.

The beginning of any journey usually includes a level of excitement and anticipation that generates energy and enthusiasm. Unfortunately, many projects lose steam as the novelty wears off and boredom becomes your enemy. During the times of monotony, a "finish strong" mentality can help to keep momentum going. Instead of using obstacles as reasons to quit, let them be your incentive to work even harder.[118]

The real lesson in sustained momentum is that the job is never done. You have to keep at it. Never assume that you've got it made and that you can ease up or quit.

Tailor Made

I was having trouble convincing Tom, a fellow manager, of the usefulness of my new idea until I mentioned that it could be used as a tool in the organization's knowledge management efforts. This was something Tom could understand, and it was enough to convince him that the new idea could be of value in our organization.

To convince people in an organization of the value they can gain from the new idea, tailor your message to the needs of the organization.

You are a dedicated champion using a personal touch to show how your new idea can be personally useful.

Individuals can be intrigued by interesting ideas, but to have impact on an organization, the idea has to be more than just interesting.

An innovation is good not because it is cool or trendy, but because it is *useful*. The value a new idea can provide to an organization is not always apparent because results do not appear overnight. Yet, when management and early adopters consider a new idea, they want to see the benefits to the organization.

Decision makers are more willing and able to adopt innovations that offer clear advantages, do not drastically interfere with existing practices, and are easy to understand. They want to see how a new idea can fit into and improve what the organization already does. When it comes to new ideas, packaging matters. Even the best ideas will have no impact if they are not sold in a way that gets through people's filters. A commonly heard piece of advice is "Don't sell the technology; sell the business solution."

Therefore:

Tailor your message about the innovation to the needs of the organization.

Study the processes and goals to identify a need or a problem that the innovation can solve. You must first help people realize that what they have now is not working before you can convince them that your idea is worth considering. Then, rather than presenting the general benefits of the new idea, explain the specific advantages it can offer. Use buzzwords and information from specific projects in the organization that people will relate to. Persuade them from their point of view. Focus on what people are trying to do and show how the innovation can create change for the better.

Frame your new idea in a way that speaks to the manager who will be funding the initiative. Listen carefully when you meet with him and then include his needs in your proposal. Describe the steps you can take to solve the problems he has discussed with you.

Don't hype the innovation as a perfect solution. No matter how beneficial it may be, implementation is usually riddled with glitches.

Be clear about the motivations for the change. While these can appear obvious to you, this understanding may not be shared by everyone.

If there is an organization similar to yours that is having success with the innovation, use the External Validation pattern. Management likes to hear about what other companies are doing, especially from the same business domain, a partner, or even a competitor.

Make no mistake about it: This is a sales job, and you will need to give a different sales pitch to different groups. But make certain that each pitch contains the same basic facts and philosophy.

= = = = = = = = =

This pattern produces an understanding of how the innovation can help the organization. It helps to spark confidence in the decision makers that the innovation is not simply a good idea but rather is something to provide a way to improve its current practices.

It takes a special effort to use this pattern. Instead of relying on a canned presentation, you have to do some research. You must take the time to examine the needs of the organization so that you can match the new idea to these needs.

Sybil works for a large organization and sent us this advice: "Particularly in today's market when everybody is tightening belts, the things that will sell to upper managers are those that can be executed fairly quickly and will lead to faster time to market, reduction of cost, or a proven practice that leads quickly to higher quality. I frame any new idea as an outcome that speaks to the manager who will be funding the effort. I listen a lot the first couple of times I meet with him and then include the needs that I have heard in the proposal that I make. Then I describe the steps that we can take that will lead to solving the problems that have been articulated."

Nationally syndicated business columnist Dale Dauten writes, "I remember reading that the one reason people say 'no' to a salesperson is the fear of making a mistake. This changed the way I sold my ideas to the company. I realized that while I was going on about the wonderful things we might accomplish, executives were sitting there thinking only one thing: What can go wrong? I've learned to explain how we can minimize risk, especially the risk of management looking bad."[119]

INSIGHTS

We originally thought that helping listeners understand the benefits of the innovation to the organization would help supporters see the benefits in your idea, but we have learned that the Tailor Made pattern is really targeted for management. The average worker probably doesn't care about how the innovation fits with and can benefit the organization. The Personal Touch pattern works better for non-management individuals because they are more likely to focus on "What's in it for me?" and "How will it affect me?"

When you use this pattern, remember to speak in the language that management understands. Keep it simple. Don't become infatuated with the technology; rather, understand its business value. Frame it in terms of costs and benefits.

When you're thinking about an innovative approach, it rarely works to keep managers in the dark. Start with a good executive summary. Describe your goal in two minutes or less, with an elevator pitch that says why it's good for your organization and what you need from them to make it happen.

Test the Waters

David Baum, in his book Lightning in a Bottle, *notes, "The change process for most people is to slowly dip their toes into the water and ease into the shallow end, splashing a little water around and complaining about how cold it is."*[120]

When a new opportunity presents itself, see if there is any interest by using some of the patterns in this language and then evaluating the result.

You are excited about a new idea and you would like to be an evangelist for it in your organization.

When you learn about something new, you wonder if the organization is ready for it.

It isn't always obvious where to start when introducing a new idea into an organization. You don't want to put much effort into introducing it if there really isn't any interest. There's a natural tendency for an enthusiastic change agent to try to make an impact much too quickly. Yet, you need to get your bearings. A "listen and learn" approach shows that you are willing to consider the opinions of others as you explain your new ideas.

You can't fix everything at once, so the trick is to find the minimum number of leverage points to create a dramatic impact. Once you find the hot buttons, you can get things going.

Therefore:

Choose a pattern or two from this collection, use them, and then evaluate the result.

Begin with a few things that don't take much effort:

+ Use the Personal Touch pattern during a coffee break to informally talk with one of your colleagues, who might be an innovator or become a guru on your side.
+ Use the Just Do It pattern and then give a simple demonstration or tell a hometown story to a few colleagues.
+ Schedule a brown bag event to present the idea to the rest of your team.
+ Piggyback on a regularly scheduled event.
+ Plant the seeds around your organization.

These initial steps can help you decide what to do next. Evaluate what went well and what didn't. Use the Time for Reflection pattern to determine if now is the right time for the new idea in your organization. If you encounter resistance, you might need to modify how you are presenting the proposed change. If you see some spark of interest, try some other patterns that will take more effort, such as Big Jolt or Study Group.

Don't just use this pattern when you begin to introduce an innovation. Experiment along the way and every time you see a new opportunity.

= = = = = = = = =

This pattern builds a foundation upon which you can use other patterns. It is the first step in trying to become an evangelist. It helps you to see if you should proceed and, if so, what you should do next.

Be prepared for possible disappointment. Sometimes an idea is too new or radical to win ready acceptance from an organization, or it may run counter to other constraints, such as a preference for a vendor or product. Rather than pushing harder, it might be better to wait a bit until the organization can support the change. Save your energy for when you can get payback. The time you took to investigate and learn about the innovation will still work to your own personal advantage.

When Peace Corps volunteers arrive at their destination, they are brimming with energy and enthusiasm. But volunteers must fight the impulse to hit the ground running because a slow crawl works much better. Volunteers are advised, "During your first two weeks onsite, don't start calling meetings and making pronouncements. Spend time observing your village and listening to people talk about their lives. Slowly, you will identify some natural places where you can intervene and share some ideas. To earn trust, you must demonstrate a presence and show that you're genuinely interested in learning as well as teaching."[121]

In their best-selling book, Built to Last, *Jim Collins and Jerry Porras noted, "3M did not select innovations based strictly on market size. With mottos like 'Make a little, sell a little' and 'Take small steps,' 3M understood that big things often evolve from little things; but since you can't tell ahead of time which little things will turn into big things, you have to try lots of little things, keep the ones that work, and discard the ones that don't."*[122]

INSIGHTS

We have noticed that we tend to use the patterns Just Do It and Test the Waters interchangeably. Because keeping a collection of patterns as succinct as possible over time is a goal for pattern authors, we have decided to remove Test the Waters and subsume it under Just Do It.

Time for Reflection

How noble and good everyone could be if, every evening before falling asleep, they were to recall to their minds the events of the whole day and consider exactly what has been good and bad. Then, without realizing it, you try to improve yourself at the start of each new day; of course, you achieve quite a lot in the course of time. Anyone can do this, it costs nothing and is certainly very helpful.[123]

—*Anne Frank at age 15*

To learn from the past, take time at regular intervals to evaluate what is working well and what should be done differently.

You are an evangelist or dedicated champion using the Just Do It pattern to try to introduce a new idea into your organization.

We make the same assumptions and the same mistakes based on those assumptions over and over again.

It is much easier to keep doing what we've always done than it is to stop and think about whether it is the best thing to do. In our attempts to use every moment to full advantage, we rush to do this, to do that. Keeping this

265

continual pace makes it difficult to step back and reflect, to take a broader view. It can be uncomfortable to do this because we may discover that what we are doing is no longer working. Yet, Betty Sue Flowers, author of *The Power of Myth*, explains that most of us create the future by extrapolating from the past.

In the movie *Dances with Wolves*, a tribe of Native Americans takes time to examine the success of a buffalo hunt by telling and retelling the story of the hunt around a campfire. This is an important ritual because it provides lessons for all the hunts to come. It is the way wisdom is passed on. A retrospective works in much the same way. Its purpose is to review a recent project and understand what worked well and what can be done differently next time.

In 1988, Joseph M. Juran wrote about deriving lessons learned from retrospective analysis and named this process after philosopher George Santayana, who once observed, "Those who cannot remember the past are condemned to repeat it." Many large organizations engage in some form of the Santayana review and call it a retrospective, postmortem, postpartum, or project review. The idea is simple: Examine what happened on the last project and learn from it.

Even failed projects can identify valuable accomplishments of which a team can be proud. At the same time, even in the most successful project, things can be improved. To create learning organizations, we must make it a practice to discuss what went on in our projects. Similarly, to learn as an individual, we must take the time to reflect. President Abraham Lincoln stated that we may learn more from what has *not* been done right than from what has been done right. But learning doesn't happen unless we allow time for it.

Therefore:

Pause in any activity to reflect on what is working well and what should be done differently.

Take time out at regular intervals. Reflection is more likely to occur if it is made part of the process rather than something that happens only when you have extra time on your hands. Build reflection time into the process as you apply the Baby Steps pattern and evaluate the necessary adjustments in your strategy. When you celebrate small successes, talk with others about what is going well and what should be done differently. Even when things aren't going as well, you don't need to feel bad about making mistakes as long as you take the trouble to learn from them. Often, you learn more by being wrong for the right reasons than you do by being right for the wrong reasons.

To reflect as a group, run a project retrospective—that is, a series of fun and highly effective activities that help a team review the past so that the members can become more productive in the future. Use the Location, Location, Location pattern if possible. For more information on leading a retrospective, see Norm Kerth's excellent book *Project Retrospectives*.

= = = = = = = = =

This pattern helps you understand what happened in the past and what can be improved in the future. You'll see things that hadn't occurred to you. You can plan your next step, note the things that are going well, and think about how you can improve. You can even document your successful practices so that they can be shared with others.

Of course, you have to carve out time to reflect, and this isn't easy in our fast-paced world. Yet, it can be argued that failing to think about the past and plan your next step can cause you to lose even more time in the long run because of the mistakes you may be making over and over again.

"Every day, I have to make difficult decisions, and I base them primarily on what has happened in the past," says Nathan Myhrvold, Chief Technology Officer of Microsoft Corporation. "History can lead you to see important abstractions, and it also offers great lessons. . . . If you want to make good decisions about what's to come, look behind you."

Blockbuster Inc. wanted to increase the amount of time its employees spent with customers by decreasing some of their administrative duties. Company personnel made observations and brainstormed suggestions from the people doing the work. Their reflection created some improvement. For example, employees changed their reshelving process by putting videos/DVDs on a cart so that customers taking movies off the cart would reduce the effort of putting them back. As a result of some process changes, employees went from spending 36% of their time with customers to 50% and climbing. They learned that a company can conceive of new ideas for improvement when they stand back and reflect on what they already do.

INSIGHTS

Cognitive scientists tell us that we can't know, just by reflecting, how we are doing.[124] We need trusted advisors (coaches or mentors) who can give us feedback, because we can't really see ourselves objectively. Self-reflection is important, but it provides only part of the story. To be effective, this pattern must include feedback from sources outside yourself.

There's a lot of talk about "learning organizations," but most of us need retrospectives to make that happen. Include retrospectives at all levels—not just for development, but also for executives. Encourage everyone in the room to listen and learn.

When a change leader blames something "external," he probably has no, or little, control over it. In reflection exercises, identify what you can control—only then can you truly make progress.

Our good friend, Jutta Eckstein, has completed work for a master's degree with interesting results. She has been using retrospectives to support organizational change.[125]

Mary Lynn tells this story about a project she was involved in:

After one retrospective, we discussed something that didn't go well, but then realized this experience could help us improve in the next iteration. One of the guys on the team called it a "successful failure." I wonder if a failure that is not followed by reflection and a plan to improve is an "unsuccessful failure."

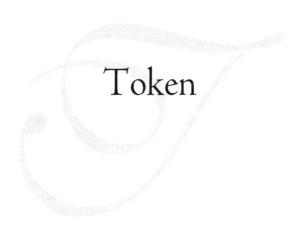

Token

I collect name badges from the conferences I attend and hang them on the walls of my cubicle. They remind me of the conferences I have attended, the many friends I have met, and the things I have learned.

To keep a new idea alive in a person's memory, hand out tokens that can be identified with the topic being introduced.

You are a dedicated champion trying to get people interested in a new idea. You have limited resources.

People may be enthusiastic about a topic when they first hear about it, but the enthusiasm quickly wanes as they forget tomorrow what excited them today.

Our brains can hold only so much: Today's information will be quickly replaced by tomorrow's information. Individuals need reminders. A physical object associated with a particular topic can nudge their memories. It can help people reconnect with a new idea even after their thoughts have moved on to something else or with an event long after it has taken place.

Sociologists have observed that in all cultures, the receipt of even a small gift obligates the receiver, even if the gift was not highly valued. Free samples are given away in supermarkets and by salespeople in a variety of settings because the value of the return has been shown to be more than the cost.

Therefore:

Hand out small tokens that will remind people of the new idea.

Examples of tokens include magnets, buttons, coasters, cups, pencils, or a set of bound notes, a "quick reference" printed on special paper, or copies of articles. Be creative in finding or constructing items that will form a link with the event. The monetary value need not be high.

Don't get carried away and distribute too many tokens—it reduces the effect. There is no need to be disappointed if some people dispose of them; not everyone will appreciate them. Those who don't "get" the topic will be less inclined to keep them around. We know what it's like to have another thing around that just takes up space. Most will get cleaned out over time, and that's OK.

= = = = = = = = = =

This pattern creates a reminder of the new idea. People who identify with the topic will keep their token, often prominently displayed, as a memento. Initially, this identifies the group of people to each other, helping to create a critical mass and establish a group identity. Over time, the token serves as a reminder to the individual to revisit the topic.

Sometimes, it might be difficult to convince your organization to fund tokens. In this case, think about spending some of your own money. It doesn't have to take a lot of cash, but your colleagues and your management will be impressed that you believe in the new idea enough to support it.

At our poster session at a conference, we gave "Good Job!" stickers for participants' badges if they drew a picture of any pattern we had displayed on our poster. The sticker was just a token but it got their attention. Many who said they couldn't draw were convinced by the ridiculously small sticker, even though it meant they had to read every pattern, looking for one that spoke to them.

Craig Tidal, President and CEO of Net Solve Inc., teaches customer interaction to new employees, from receptionists to senior managers. He rewards correct answers with a crisp $2 bill. "It's just a token, but if somebody puts one in their wallet, it will remind them of the event," he says of the gimmick.

INSIGHTS

Originally, this pattern was about small concrete objects: mugs, buttons, T-shirts, books. Now we realize that it's about giving something meaningful to someone, and often that gift can be intangible.

Christopher Avery talks about "efficient gifts"—favors that cost you little or nothing, yet provide great value to the receiver. These are often treasured more than traditional exchanges. Efficient gifts include giving a heads-up on an opportunity or threat, proofreading a document, or making an important introduction. Give these often and don't keep score or turn gifts into exchanges by demanding or offering immediate reciprocity—owing one and being owed one are often great positions to hold in partnerships. Invite recipients of your efficient gifts to pay it forward or pass it on.

Small, unexpected rewards can have disproportionate effects on employees' satisfaction with a change initiative. Gordon M. Bethune, while turning around Continental Airlines, sent an unexpected $30 check to every employee when Continental made it to the top five for on-time airlines. John McFarlane, former CEO of ANZ Bank, sent a bottle of champagne to every employee for Christmas with a card thanking them for their work on the company's "Perform, Grow, and Break-out" change program. Most change managers would refer to these as token gestures and argue that their impact is limited. Employees on the receiving end beg to differ: They consistently report back that the rewards have a disproportionately positive impact on change motivation that lasts for months, if not years.[126]

Trial Run

To me, a bicycle was balloon tires and baskets. You rode it to your friend's house or maybe to school. I loved my bicycle—a blue three-speed from Wards. When I met Karl, he had more than one bicycle and he raced. He wore funny clothes and a helmet. When I found out how much the equipment cost, I was horrified. I bought my bike for about $100 and I thought that was a lot of money. "Just try it," he coaxed. "You can see for yourself what a racing bike is like. Even if you ride in jeans, you can tell the difference." I wasn't convinced, but I thought I would be nice and, what the heck, it was just a ride around the block. I hopped on. The seat needed some adjustment. The handlebar was down and it seemed a little strange, but then I began to pedal. The bike took off. It almost had a life of its own. It seemed to be pedaling for me. "Wow!" I shouted! "This thing really goes!" I was hooked after that run!

When the organization is not willing to commit to the new idea, suggest that it experiment with the change for a short period and study the results.

You are an evangelist. You're getting worn out as you attempt to address the concerns people have about the new idea because it doesn't look like the questions and objections are going to end anytime soon.

There are people in the organization who are expressing an endless stream of objections to the new idea. It would be a daunting, or even impossible, task to try to ease everyone's worries before the new idea is adopted.

Fear is often what keeps us talking and questioning but stops us from doing anything. However, even though people may be fearful of change, they usually love to experiment. Change means risk. An experiment is something you can undo and walk away from when you are all the wiser.

Ideas that can be tested on an installment plan are generally adopted more rapidly than those that are not. If people are offered a trial period, they will have the opportunity to experiment with the innovation under their own conditions. This is likely to ease their uncertainties and give meaning to something that was previously seen as merely an abstract idea.

It's more effective to let people convince themselves through sight and touch than to try to convince them with words and logic. "For test purposes" is a convenient label for temporarily transferring "unacceptable" ideas into an "acceptable" category, until such time that the idea can gain the persuasive power to become part of the established way of doing things.

Therefore:

Suggest that the organization, or a segment of the organization, try the new idea for a limited period as an experiment.

Be specific about the time and what will be done during this period. Suggest how you and the organization will evaluate the success of the new idea at the end of this period. People must feel that there is limited risk and no obligation to go on after the trial period.

Make certain people understand that their concerns will not be discounted during the trial period; keep a record of all points of view. Use the Fear Less and Champion Skeptic patterns for people who are not willing to temporarily put their skepticism aside during the experiment.

Adopt the attitude that any failure during this trial run is not a mistake, but rather a lesson. If you take time for reflection, you will find that growth is a process of experimentation—a series of trials, errors, and occasional victories. Things that don't work out as you had hoped are as much a part of the process as the things that do work.

If you see some small successes, spread the word with a hometown story. Start a study group to explore the future possibilities.

Don't expect to get everyone on board after this limited experiment. A trial run is just one way to just do it. It is likely to be most effective for reaching innovators and early adopters, but even the die-hard skeptics may appreciate a new idea if you can show that it will make their jobs easier.

= = = = = = = = =

This approach builds validation for the new idea as it moves through the test period. The trial will help potential users understand how the innovation can fit into their organization. This puts you in a better position to capture the attention of a local sponsor and to justify continuing work with the new idea. If it is truly a good idea, it will sell itself. If it's not, it remains a "test" and fades away.

This trial period can place a lot of extra work on your shoulders. People will probably see you as the leader of the experiment, even though you are still learning about the innovation yourself. Prepare for this task by first taking the time to just do it before you suggest a trial run in the organization.

Ellen devised a new process for assigning individuals to committees. Because it was quite different from what was already in place, it was met with controversy. Ellen patiently addressed as many concerns as she could, but when the proposal came to the decision makers for approval, the questions continued during the meeting for almost 30 minutes. Finally, one of the few supporters said, "Look, what we have isn't working now. We need something better. This document is what we're proposing . . . if you don't like it, propose something else, but for heaven's sake, propose something because our present system needs to be improved." After a few moments of silence, Ellen suggested that the organization just try the new process, evaluate it, and make any needed modifications after it had been in place for a year. She also promised to take an active role in carrying out the details. The document passed with an 8 to 3 vote in favor of the new process.

The Office of the Vice Chancellor was overworked. The university had grown and, as a result, the number of issues and problems was increasing at a rate that could no longer be handled by the office with any efficiency. So the vice chancellor proposed adding three associates to the office. The faculty responded with fear because they were not accustomed to dealing with an additional level of administrators. The vice chancellor arranged a few forums in which he explained the serious problems that existed in the office. He responded to many questions but, at the final forum, he realized that there was still a great amount of trepidation. So he asked the faculty to accept the new structure for a few years and assured them that he would readjust it if it didn't work well. The faculty finally agreed. Throughout the following months, when someone would voice his apprehension about the new structure, someone else would usually remind him that it wasn't a permanent arrangement.

Whisper in the General's Ear

I noticed that a particular manager was always absent from my presentations about the new idea. He had good excuses, but I think he was avoiding the subject. His staff never came to any of my training classes. I stopped by his office and said, "I know you're too busy to come to my presentations. I understand that, but I'm willing to get together one-on-one, at any time, to answer any questions you have."

He was caught. He fumbled with his calendar. "Hmm, not much time. I do have an open slot but it's at 7:00 a.m. next Friday. That's probably too early for you" (he was hoping).

I jotted down the date and said, "Great! Thanks for your time." I stopped by the day before our meeting and said, "See you tomorrow!" On Friday, we spent a good half-hour talking, and he seemed relieved that my idea wasn't just some new technology thing but really did apply to his area. He never became an enthusiastic supporter, but he never spoke up against it and his people started coming to my training classes.

Managers are sometimes hard to convince in a group setting, so meet privately to address any concerns.

◆◆◆

You are a dedicated champion working to get management support for your new idea. There are troublesome managers who have not been convinced by any presentations you have made.

Managers who are against your new idea have the power to block your progress.

Many managers aren't that interested in technical details. In a group situation their attention span is much less than it is in a one-on-one setting. Managers are overwhelmed by new ideas and are reluctant to head blindly down new paths without some justification. You can't publicly push a manager in a new direction, but in private you can gently show the benefits of a new way of doing business that will reflect well on those who are successful with the new approach. Many managers need a little extra time to think about a new idea before they're willing to support it publicly.

Because accountability is always centralized and flows to the top of organizations, executives feel an increasing need to know what is going on, while recognizing that it is harder to get reliable information. That need for information and control drives them to develop elaborate information systems alongside the control systems and to feel increasingly alone in their position atop the hierarchy.

Some high-level executives are "productive narcissists" and are extremely sensitive to criticism or slights. They cannot tolerate dissent. In fact, they can be extremely abrasive with employees who doubt them—with subordinates who are tough enough to fight back. Some are so defensive that they make a virtue of the fact that they don't listen. As one CEO bluntly put it, "I didn't get here by listening to people!"

Therefore:

Set up a short one-on-one meeting with a manager to address any concerns with the innovation and the effort to introduce it.

Say exactly what you know and what you can do to help. Don't exaggerate what your new idea can do. Nothing can hurt your cause more than overselling something. Play the evangelist role—let your natural enthusiasm show. Encourage the manager to ask questions to understand technical details. This may be embarrassing for him to do in front of others, because it's human nature to want to save face in front of a group.

Make sure the information is tailor made appropriately for the management audience. Be ready to address the costs and benefits of your idea but don't overwhelm the manager with data. Tell him just enough—that is, educate, but don't talk down or overburden him with too many technical details. When first hearing of a new idea, managers usually want to know what the big picture is and how it will impact them.

Give the manager ideas, but consider letting him take the credit for them. Find out what he thinks before presenting your views. If you believe he is wrong, show how a different approach would be in his best interest. Take his views seriously. Analyze them, don't brush them aside—they often reveal sharp intuitions. Disagree only when you can demonstrate how he will benefit from a different point of view.

Always empathize with the manager's feelings, but don't expect any empathy back. Understand that behind any display of infallibility, there hides a deep vulnerability. Praise his achievements and reinforce his best impulses, but don't be shamelessly sympathetic. An intelligent narcissist can see through flatterers and prefers independent people who truly appreciate him. Show that you will protect his image, inside and outside the company.

Persuade, don't alienate. Stay calm. Back off when he starts to glaze over or push back. Great salespeople will tell you the way to influence others is to understand their needs and communicate on their level, not on yours. The idea is that in the process of talking to him, the manager will have an "aha" moment: He's come to this realization on his own, and he'll own the idea and feel comfortable about asking for help with the next steps.

If you are persistent and patient but still have not succeeded in scheduling a meeting with the manager, there is one other tactic you can use in extreme cases. The next time you see the manager heading from his office to the cafeteria, walk along and causally mention some arresting piece of news. Keep a two-minute "elevator pitch" in your head at all times. A good salesperson must take advantage of unscheduled opportunities as well as rehearsed and organized ones.

Remember that your goal is to build trust with the manager. This will take time. The manager who needs this kind of special attention may be insecure or may have been burned by false promises. It will take patience and great strength of character on your part to face these obstacles.

Once you have the manager's support, stay in touch so he won't forget about you.

= = = = = = = = =

This pattern builds management support for the new idea. It maintains the manager's dignity while giving you the chance to get your story heard and achieve your objectives.

Your private meetings with a manager can look like back-room dealing to outsiders. Be open and straightforward with others. Let them know you have talked with the manager, but don't break any confidences by revealing details of the discussion, especially if they might show the manager in a bad light.

David Pottruck, the number-two executive for Charles Schwab Corporation, frequently clashed with his boss, Larry Stupski, at top-management meetings. Pottruck made two big mistakes: He failed to recruit others to his cause, and he disagreed in an unpleasant way. Then Pottruck met with his boss and proposed a solution. He would never publicly argue with him again. He might disagree, but he would do so only in private. By questioning his boss only behind closed doors, he got his ideas into the room and kept the power struggle out of it.

Anna had a boss who was hard to convince in a group meeting (darn near impossible!). The boss would move forward on an issue during a meeting only if he had all the information and all his doubts removed beforehand. Anna learned that when an upcoming meeting would deal with an issue that was important, she should meet with her boss before the meeting and address his questions and concerns one-on-one.

INSIGHTS

This pattern can be applied at any level of an organization. It's not just for executives. The "general" is anyone who has some degree of influence and is afraid to show ignorance in front of others for fear of losing face. It's your job to encourage the "general" to ask questions and make comments, secure in the knowledge that you will not reveal any of the conversation.

This story shows the value in this pattern:

An evangelist struggled to introduce Agile software development into an organization. He thought he could gather all the executives in a room and explain what Agile was all about and answer all their questions. Instead, he wound up with a lot of alpha male (and female) displays but no requests for information. After he learned about this pattern, he said succinctly, "It's not a good idea to try to have discussions with executives in groups!"

External Pattern References

Throughout this part we have referenced patterns outside our pattern language. This is good for several reasons. It shows that we didn't write our patterns in a vacuum; we were aware of others' contributions and pointed to their work. It also means that we didn't struggle to capture good ideas that have already been documented. Finally, it points out that patterns are grown by a community. We need to show connections to that community by showing how our work relates to the contributions of other pattern writers. Here's a little information on the external patterns and where you can read more about them.

Brainstorming. Get the team members together for a brainstorming session. http://www.charlesweir.com/Publications.html

Cardboard Consultant. Explain the problem out loud to someone or something. http://www.charlesweir.com/Publications.html

Communal Eating. Give every institution and social group a place where people can eat together. C.A. Alexander et al., *A Pattern Language* (Oxford, UK: Oxford University Press, 1977).

Diverse Groups. Include different kinds of members in a team to create requirements. J. O. Coplien and N. B. Harrison, *Organizational Patterns of Agile Software Development* (Upper Saddle River, NJ: Prentice-Hall, 2004).

Get a Guru. Managers should establish a trusting relationship with a guru and defer to him on technical matters. D. S. Olson and C. L. Stimmel, *The Manager Pool* (Boston: Addison-Wesley, 2002).

Gradual Stiffening. A flimsy structure can gradually be made sturdier by building on prior work. C.A. Alexander et al., *A Pattern Language* (Oxford, UK: Oxford University Press, 1977).

Holistic Diversity. Create teams from members with multiple specialties. J. O. Coplien and N. B. Harrison, *Organizational Patterns of Agile Software Development* (Upper Saddle River, NJ: Prentice-Hall, 2004).

Introvert–Extrovert. Teach yourself to play a role so that observers believe you are extroverted, bold, and outgoing. Teach yourself to recognize the situations in which this role is appropriate and to gather your resources and play the role. http://csis.pace.edu/~bergin /patterns/introvertExtrovert.html

No Surprises. Adjust schedule or feature commitments without losing the confidence of groups that depend on your components by announcing changes early and negotiating solutions. D. M. Dikel, D. Kane, and J. R. Wilson, *Software Architecture: Organizational Principles and Patterns* (Upper Saddle River, NJ: Prentice-Hall, 2001).

Patron Role. Give the project access to a visible, high-level manager who champions the cause of the project. J. O. Coplien and N. B. Harrison, *Organizational Patterns of Agile Software Development* (Upper Saddle River, NJ: Prentice-Hall, 2004).

Piecemeal Growth. Incrementally address forces that encourage change and growth and allow opportunities for growth to be exploited locally as they occur. B. Foote and J. Yoder, "Big Ball of Mud," in *Pattern Languages of Program Design 4*, ed. N. Harrison, B. Foote, and H. Rohnert (Boston: Addison-Wesley, 2000), 668.

Shameless Ignoramus. Managers should give up the attempt to know it all and become a shameless ignoramus when it comes to technical matters. D. S. Olson and C. L. Stimmel, *The Manager Pool* (Boston: Addison-Wesley, 2002).

Team Space. To maximize people's productive time at work, allow team members to own their space for everything from decision making to social events. P. Taylor, "Capable, Productive, and Satisfied: Some Organizational Patterns for Protecting Productive People," in *Pattern Languages of Program Design 4*, ed. N. Harrison, B. Foote, and H. Rohnert (Boston: Addison-Wesley, 2000), 627.

Train Hard, Fight Easy. To establish a team mentality and shared skills, train the team together in the innovation. D. S. Olson and C. L. Stimmel, *The Manager Pool* (Boston: Addison-Wesley, 2002).

Work Community. To create a feeling of community in the workplace, build small clusters of workplaces that have their own common area. C.A. Alexander et al., *A Pattern Language* (Oxford, UK: Oxford University Press, 1977).

Quick Guide to the Patterns

This appendix provides a quick guide to all of the patterns in both our first and second collections.

The Patterns

Name	Summary
Accentuate the Positive	To influence others during the change initiative and inspire them to believe the change can happen, motivate them with a sense of hope rather than fear.
Ask for Help*	Since the task of introducing a new idea into an organization is a big job, look for people and resources to help your efforts and encourage involvement.
Baby Steps* (formerly Step by Step)	Take one small step at a time toward your goal.

*Denotes summaries that may have changed since *Fearless Change* was published. The updated summaries are shown in this table.

Name	Summary
Big Jolt*	To provide visibility for the change effort, hold a high-profile event to showcase the new idea.
Bridge Builder*	Ask those who have accepted the new idea to talk with those who have not.
Brown Bag*	Use the time when people normally eat together as a convenient and relaxed setting for hearing about the new idea.
Champion Skeptic*	Ask for help from opinion leaders who are skeptical of your new idea, and use their comments to improve your effort, even if you don't change their minds.
Concrete Action Plan	To make progress toward your goal, state precisely what you will do as you take the next baby step.
Connector	To help you spread the word about the innovation, ask for help from people who have connections with many others in the organization.
Corporate Angel	To help align the innovation with the goals of the organization, get support from a high-level executive.
Corridor Politics*	Informally work on decision makers and key influencers before an important vote, to ensure they understand the consequences of the decision.
Dedicated Champion	To increase your effectiveness in introducing your new idea, make a case for having the work become part of your job description.
Do Food*	To influence attendees, bring special food to a meeting.
e-Forum (now part of Persistent PR)	Set up an electronic bulletin board, distribution list, listserve, or writeable website for those who want to hear more.

Name	Summary
Early Adopter	Win the support of the people who can be opinion leaders for the new idea.
Early Majority*	To increase support, show that many people are starting to use the innovation.
Easier Path	To encourage adoption of a new idea, experiment with removing obstacles that might be standing in the way.
Elevator Pitch	Have a couple of sentences on hand to introduce others to your new idea.
Emotional Connection	Connecting with the feelings of your audience is usually more effective in persuading them than just presenting facts.
Evangelist	To begin to introduce the new idea into your organization, do everything you can to share your passion for it.
Evolving Vision	While taking baby steps through a change process, periodically set aside time for reflection to reevaluate your vision.
External Validation*	To increase the credibility of the new idea, bring in information from sources outside the organization.
Fear Less*	Turn resistance to the new idea to your advantage by respectfully listening to and learning from skeptics' point of view.
Future Commitment	To make it more likely that you will get help in the change initiative, ask others to do something you will need much later and wait for them to commit.
Go-To Person	Identify key people who can help with critical issues in your change initiative.

*Denotes summaries that may have changed since *Fearless Change* was published. The updated summaries are shown in this table.

Name	Summary
Group Identity*	Give the change effort an identity but encourage wide participation to involve everyone.
Guru on Your Side*	Enlist the support of influential people who are esteemed by members of the organization at all levels.
Guru Review*	Gather a group of trusted advisors and other interested colleagues to evaluate the new idea for managers and other developers.
Hometown Story*	To help people see the usefulness of the new idea, encourage those who have had success with it to share their stories in an informal setting.
Imagine That	To kick-start the change initiative, engage others in an exercise to imagine future possibilities.
Innovator	When you begin the change initiative, ask for help from colleagues who like new ideas.
Involve Everyone*	For a new idea to be successful across an organization, everyone should have an opportunity to make his or her own unique contribution.
Just Do It*	Don't wait for the perfect moment when you have the resources and knowledge you think you need; instead, take the first baby step and start learning.
Just Enough*	To ease people into the new idea, avoid over-selling and overwhelming them by providing an appropriate amount of information that they can understand and use at that particular time.

Name	Summary
Know Yourself	Before you begin, and throughout the long journey required to lead a change initiative, consider whether you still have a real and abiding passion and the talents and abilities to make it happen.
Local Sponsor*	Ask for help from first-line management; when your boss supports the tasks you are doing to introduce the new idea, you can be more effective.
Location, Location, Location*	When holding an event that focuses on the new idea, consider the comfort and enjoyment of the participants so the surroundings do not interfere with their ability to listen and participate.
Low-Hanging Fruit	To show progress in the change initiative, complete a quick and easy, low-risk task with wide impact and then publicize the results.
Mentor*	When a project team wants to get started with the new idea, have someone around who understands it and can help the team.
Myth Buster	Identify misconceptions surrounding the change initiative and address them in a timely and forthright manner.
Next Steps*	Take time near the end of an event or conversation to identify which actions participants can do next.
Persistent PR* (formerly In Your Space)	To keep the new idea in front of everyone, consistently promote it in a variety of ways.
Personal Touch	To convince people of the value in a new idea, show how it can be *personally* useful and valuable to them.

*Denotes summaries that may have changed since *Fearless Change* was published. The updated summaries are shown in this table.

Name	Summary
Pick Your Battles	Before you expend your energy in conflict, ask yourself whether you believe the issue is really important and if you have the resources to carry your fight through to the end.
Piggyback*	To help the new idea be less threatening, build on existing practices and use current language.
Plant the Seeds*	Take every opportunity you can, no matter how small, to spark an interest in the idea.
The Right Time*	Consider the timing of competing obligations when you schedule events or when you ask for help.
Royal Audience*	Arrange for management and members of the organization to spend time with a special visitor.
Shoulder to Cry On*	To avoid becoming too discouraged when the going gets tough, find opportunities for everyone to have supportive listeners.
Sincere Appreciation* (formerly Just Say Thanks)	To help people feel appreciated, express your gratitude in the most sincere way you can to everyone who makes a contribution.
Small Successes*	To avoid becoming discouraged by obstacles and slow progress, celebrate even a small success.
Smell of Success*	When your efforts produce a visible positive result, treat this opportunity as a teaching moment.
Stay in Touch*	Once you've sparked some interest in people, don't forget about them, and make sure they don't forget about you.
Study Group*	Form a small group of colleagues who are interested in exploring or continuing to learn about your new idea.

Name	Summary
Sustained Momentum*	Be proactive in keeping your change initiative going.
Tailor Made*	To convince management and executives in the organization, point out the costs and benefits of your new idea.
Test the Waters (now part of Just Do It)	When a new opportunity presents itself, see if there is any interest by using some of the patterns in this language and then evaluating the result.
Time for Reflection*	To learn from the past, at regular intervals, evaluate what is working well and what should be done differently. Self-reflection requires outside feedback.
Token*	To keep a new idea alive in a person's memory, give tokens, especially valuable intangibles that can be identified with the topic being introduced.
Town Hall Meeting	As early as possible and throughout the initiative, schedule an event to share updates about the new idea, solicit feedback, build support, uncover new ideas, and bring in newcomers.
Trial Run*	When the organization is reluctant to commit to the new idea, suggest an experiment for a short period and learn from its results.
Wake-up Call	To encourage people to pay attention to your idea, point out the issue that you believe has created a pressing need for change.
Whisper in the General's Ear*	Because managers and others at any level of authority are usually hard to convince in a group setting, meet privately to address any concerns.

*Denotes summaries that may have changed since *Fearless Change* was published. The updated summaries are shown in this table.

Notes

PART ONE

Chapter 1

1. http://www.learnical.com/playing-fearless-change-patterns-lego/
2. Preston Smith, *Flexible Development* (San Francisco: Jossey-Bass, 2007).
3. Christopher Alexander, *The Timeless Way of Building* (New York: Oxford University Press, 1979).
4. Dan Straker, *Changing Minds* (Crowthorne, UK: Cromwell Press Group, 2010).
5. David Kolb, *Experiential Learning Experience as a Source of Learning and Development* (Englewood Cliffs, NJ: Prentice Hall, 1984).
6. Dale Carnegie, *How to Win Friends and Influence People* (New York: Simon and Schuster, 1964).
7. Christopher Alexander, *A Pattern Language* (New York: Oxford University Press, 1977).
8. Charles Duhigg, *The Power of Habit* (Random House, 2014), 10.
9. James E. Zull, *The Art of Changing the Brain* (Sterling, VA: Stylus Publishing, 2002), 191.
10. http://fearlessjourney.info/
11. Mary Lynn Manns and Linda Rising, "Additional Patterns for Fearless Change," in *PLoP '08: Proceedings of the 15th Conference on Pattern Languages of Programs* (New York: ACM, October 2008).
12. Mary Lynn Manns and Linda Rising, "Additional Patterns for Fearless Change II," in *PLoP '09: Proceedings of the 16th Conference on Pattern Languages of Programs* (New York: ACM, August 2009).
13. Mary Lynn Manns and Linda Rising, "Additional Patterns for Fearless Change III," in *PLoP '10: Proceedings of the 17th Conference on Pattern Languages of Programs* (New York: ACM, October 2010).

Chapter 2

1. Timothy Wilson, *Strangers to Ourselves* (Cambridge, MA: Belknap Press, 2004).
2. "Good Group Tip: My Part," http://www.CraigFreshley.com.
3. Philip Gary.
4. Karl Weick, "Small Wins: Redefining the Scale of Social Problems," *American Psychologist* (January 1984): 40–49.
5. Peter M. Gollwitzer and Paschal Sheeran, "Implementation Intentions and Goal Achievement: A Meta-analysis of Effects and Processes," *Advances in Experimental Social Psychology* 38 (2006): 69–119.
6. Stephen Spiller and Amy Dalton, "Too Much of a Good Thing," *Journal of Consumer Research* 39, no. 3 (October 2012): 600–614.
7. Forbes.com, Entrepreneurs, "Healthcare Costs: Low-Hanging Fruit," April 4, 2014.

Chapter 3

1. https://soundcloud.com/techwell/want-to-gain-peoples-attention
2. Anthony K. Tjan, "The Power of Restraint: Always Leave Them Wanting More," http://blogs.hbr.org/2013/10/the-power-of-restraint-always-leave-them-wanting-more/?utm_source=feedburner&utm_medium=feed&utm_campaign=Feed%3A+harvardbusiness+%28HBR.org%29&cm_ite=DailyAlert-101613+%281%29&cm_lm=sp%3Alinda%40lindarising.org&cm_ven=Spop-Email

Chapter 4

1. Formerly the Persistent PR pattern.
2. Daniel Goleman, "The Must-Have Leadership Skill," *HBR Blog Network*, October 14, 2011, http://blogs.hbr.org/2011/10/the-must-have-leadership-skill/
3. Formerly the Just Say Thanks pattern.

Chapter 5

1. Jeffrey Pfeffer, "Win at Workplace Conflict," *HBR Blog Network*, May 29, 2014.
2. Cordelia Fine, *A Mind of Its Own* (New York: W.W. Norton & Company, 2008).
3. Richard Thaler and Cass Sunstein, *Nudge* (New York: Penguin Books, 2009).

PART TWO

1. Formerly the Step by Step pattern.
2. Formerly the In Your Space pattern.

PART THREE

1. Allen Carr, *The Easy Way to Stop Smoking* (New York: Clarity Marketing USA LLC, 2004).
2. Noah J. Goldstein, Steve J. Martin, and Robert B. Cialdini, *Yes: 50 Scientifically Proven Ways to Be Persuasive* (New York: Free Press, 2008), 42.

3. Neena Newberry, "How to Keep Your Good Ideas from Being Shot Down," *McCombs Today*, December 2, 2010. http://www.today.mccombs.utexas.edu/2010/12/how-to-keep-your-good-idea-from-being-shot-down

4. Alan Deutschman, *Change or Die* (New York: HarperCollins, 2007), 39.

5. Dan Pink, *Drive* (New York: Riverhead Hardcover, 2009).

6. Albert Bandura, *Social Foundations of Thought and Action: A Social Cognitive Theory* (Englewood Cliffs, NJ: Prentice Hall, 1986).

7. Virginia Satir et al., *The Satir Model* (Palo Alto, CA: Science and Behavior Books, 1991).

8. David Collinson, "Prozac Leadership and the Limits of Positive Thinking," *Leadership* 8, no. 2 (May 2012).

9. Alan Deutschman, "Change or Die," *Fast Company* (May 2005). http://www.fastcompany.com/magazine/94/open_change-or-die.html?page=0%2C0

10. Matthew Feinberg and Robb Willer, "Apocalypse Soon? Dire Messages Reduce Belief in Global Warming by Contradicting Just-World Beliefs," *Psychological Science* 22, no. 1 (January 2011): 34–38.

11. Paul Tough, *How Children Succeed* (New York: Mariner Books, 2012), 92.

12. http://www.psych.nyu.edu/gollwitzer/

13. Charles Duhigg, *The Power of Habit* (New York: Random House, 2012), 6.

14. Dennis Sparks, "From Hunger Aid to School Reform," *Journal of Staff Development* (2004) Vol 25, Issue 1: 46.

15. http://www.inudgeyou.com/

16. Hayagreeva Rao and Robert Sutton, "The Ergonomics of Innovation," *McKinsey Quarterly* (September 17, 2008): 98.

17. http://en.wikipedia.org/wiki/Kurt_Lewin

18. Robert Cialdini, *Influence: The Psychology of Persuasion* (Boston, MA: Allyn and Bacon, 2008).

19. Johanna Rothman, *Which Obstacle Should You Tackle Today?* (2010). http://www.jrothman.com/2010/01/which-obstacle-should-you-tackle-today/

20. Daniel H. Pink, *To Sell Is Human* (New York: Riverhead Trade, 2013).

21. Robert B. Cialdini, *Yes: 50 Scientifically Proven Ways to Be Persuasive* (New York: Simon & Schuster, 2008).

22. Robert I. Sutton and Huggy Rao, *Scaling up Excellence: Getting to More without Settling for Less* (New York: Crown Business, 2014).

23. James Carville and Paul Begala, *Buck up, Suck up . . . and Come Back When You Foul up* (New York: Simon and Schuster, 2003).

24. John P. Kotter and Dan S. Cohen, *The Heart of Change* (Cambridge, MA: Harvard Business Review Press, 2012).

25. http://publicquotes.com/quote/13466/if-you-can-t-write-your-idea-on-the-back-of-my-calling-card-you-don-t-have-a-clear-idea.html

26. Daniel H. Pink, *To Sell Is Human* (New York: Riverhead Trade, 2013).

27. Peter J. Denning and Nicholas Dew, "The Myth of the Elevator Pitch," *Communications of the ACM* 55 (June 2012): 6.

28. Craig Harrison, "Build New Relationships: Your 16-Second Success." http://www. expressionsofexcellence.com/ARTICLES/elevate_ISOs.htm

29. Norelli Law. http://www.norellilaw.com/ronald-c-reece-phd.php

30. Al Kuebler, "What My Clients Taught Me," *Computer World* (August 2008). http://www.computerworld.com/action/article.do?command=viewArticleBasic&articleId=9112546

31. Antoine Bechara and Antonio R. Damasio, "The Somatic Marker Hypothesis: A Neural Theory of Economic Decision," *Games and Economic Behavior* 52 (2005): 336–372.

32. Steven W. Anderson et al., "Impairment of Social and Moral Behavior Related to Early Damage in Human Prefrontal Cortex," *Nature Neuroscience* 2, no. 11 (1999): 1032–1037.

33. Daniel Kahneman, *Thinking Fast and Slow* (New York: Farrar, Straus and Giroux, 2013).

34. Gardiner Morse, "Decisions and Desire," *Harvard Business Review* (January 2006): 42, 44–51.

35. Maynard Brusman, "Leadership Secrets for Emotional Persuasion." http://ezinearticles.com/?Leadership-Secrets-For-Emotional-Persuasion—The-Brain-Science-of-Persuasive-Powers&id=1379252

36. Barry L. Duncan, Scott D. Miller, Bruce E. Wampold, and Mark A. Hubble, eds. *The Heart and Soul of Change: Delivering What Works in Therapy* (2nd ed.) (Washington, DC: American Psychological Association, 2010).

37. John P. Kotter and Dan S. Cohen, *The Heart of Change* (Cambridge, MA: Harvard Business Review Press, 2012).

38. Stephen Denning, *The Leader's Guide to Storytelling* (San Francisco: Jossey-Bass, 2011).

39. Kare Anderson, "Stanford's Smashed Melons Experiment: Scaling Capacity to Sway and Grow," *Forbes Leadership* (December 29, 2013). http://www.forbes.com/sites/kareanderson/2013/12/29/stanfords-smashed-melons-experiment-scaling-capacity-to-sway-and-grow/

40. Martin E.P. Seligman, *What You Can Change and What You Can't: The Complete Guide to Successful Self-Improvement* (New York: Knopf, 1993).

41. *Leadership Talks Archive* (February 27, 2004). http://www.leadershipforchange.org/talks/

42. Robert B. Cialdini, *Yes: 50 Scientifically Proven Ways to Be Persuasive* (New York: Simon & Schuster, 2008).

43. Dan Gilbert, *Stumbling on Happiness* (New York: Vintage Books, 2006).

44. Heidi Grant Halvorson, *Succeed: How We Can Reach Our Goals* (New York: Penguin Book, 2012).

45. Jeffrey Gandz, "Go To People: What Every Organization Should Have," *Ivey Business Journal* (2007). http://www.iveybusinessjournal.com/article.asp?intArticle_ID=675

46. Craig Freshley, *Good Group Decisions* (Cohousing Books, 2010). http://www.craigfreshley.com

47. Eknath Easwaran, *Conquest of Mind* (Tomales, CA: Nilgiri Press, 2010).

48. Richard N. Bolles, *What Color Is Your Parachute?* (Berkeley, CA: Ten Speed Press, first published in 1970; updated annually). The Library of Congress lists this book as one of "25 Books That Have Shaped Readers' Lives."

49. Michael Watkins, *The First 90 Days* (Cambridge, MA: Harvard Business Press, 2003).

50. Nancy Kline, *Time to Think* (London: Ward Lock Wellington House, 1999).

51. James Pennebaker, *Opening up* (New York: Guilford Press, 1990).

52. Timothy D. Wilson, *Strangers to Ourselves* (Cambridge, MA: Belknap Press, 2002).

53. Cordelia Fine, *A Mind of Its Own* (New York: W. W. Norton and Company, 2006).

54. Stephen R. Covey, *The 7 Habits of Highly Effective People* (New York: Simon & Schuster, 1989), 66–67.

55. James Carville and Paul Begala, *Buck up, Suck up . . . and Come Back When You Foul up* (New York: Simon & Schuster, 2003).

56. Interview with Jane Goodall, *Harvard Business Review* (April 2010): 124.

57. John Kotter, *Leading Change* (Cambridge, MA: Harvard Business School Press, 1996).

58. Karl E. Weick and Richard L. Daft, "Toward a Model of Organizations as Interpretation Systems," *Academy of Management Review* 9, no. 2 (1984): 284–295.

59. Art Kleiner, "The Dueling Myths of Business," *Strategy+Business* (February 26, 2013). http://www.strategy-business.com/article/00151?pg=0

60. Kristin Szakos and Joe Szakos, *We Make Change: Community Organizers Talk about What They Do—and Why* (Nashville, TN: Vanderbilt University Press, 2007).

61. Edward de Bono, *Six Thinking Hats* (Boston, MA: Back Bay Books, 1999).

62. Jean Tabaka, *Collaboration Explained: Facilitation Skills for Software Project Leaders* (Boston, MA: Addison-Wesley, 2006).

63. "In Summer of Angry Voters, Whither The Town Hall?" *NPR All Things Considered* (August 25, 2011).

64. David A. Garvin and Michael A. Roberts, "Change through Persuasion," *Harvard Business Review* (February 2005): 104–112.

65. Bob Doppelt, *The Power of Sustainable Thinking* (London: Routledge, 2008), 70.

66. David Collinson, "Prozac Leadership and the Limits of Positive Thinking," *Leadership* 8, no. 2 (May 2012).

67. John P. Kotter and Dan S. Cohen, *The Heart of Change* (Cambridge, MA: Harvard Business Review Press, 2012), 3.

68. Bob Sutton, "Work Matters." http://bobsutton.typepad.com/my_weblog/2012/02/my-main-focus-for-2011-scaling-good-behavior.html

69. Thomas L. Friedman, *The World is Flat* (New York: Farrar, Straus and Giroux, 2005).

70. David A. Garvin and Michael A. Roberts, "Change through Persuasion," *Harvard Business Review* (February 2005): 104–112.

71. Hayagreeva Rao and Robert Sutton, "The Ergonomics of Innovation," *McKinsey Quarterly* (September 17, 2008).

72. A. Lamott, *Bird by Bird: Some Instructions on Writing and Life* (New York: Anchor Books, 1995).

73. D. Whyte, *The Heart Aroused: Poetry and the Preservation of the Soul in Corporate America* (New York: Currency Doubleday, 1994).

74. P. Senge et al., *The Dance of Change: The Challenges to Sustaining Momentum in Learning Organizations* (New York: Doubleday, 1999).

75. Robert Cialdini, *Influence: Science and Practice* (Boston: Pearson, 2008).

76. Seth Godin, blog post, January 6, 2014. http://www.sethgodin.com

77. Mario Livio, *Brilliant Blunders* (New York: Simon & Schuster, 2013).

78. Chip Heath and Dan Heath, *Switch: How to Change Things When Change Is Hard* (New York: Crown Business, 2010).

79. Neal Pierce and Curtis Johnson, *Boundary Crossers: Community Leadership for a Global Age* (College Park, MD: Academy of Leadership, 1998), 70.

80. Tom DeMarco, *Slack* (New York: Crown Business, 2002).

81. Edward de Bono, *Six Thinking Hats* (Boston, MA: Back Bay Books, 1999).

82. Dayleyagile. http://www.dayleyagile.com/2009/05/losing-my-champion-skeptic/

83. Kenneth G. Brown, *Influence: Mastering Life's Most Powerful Skill* (Great Courses).

84. C. A. Alexander et al., *A Pattern Language* (Oxford, UK: Oxford University Press, 1977).

85. Brian Wansink, *Mindless Eating* (New York: Bantam Dell, 2006), 97.

86. Formerly the In Your Space pattern.

87. G. A. Moore, *Crossing the Chasm* (New York: HarperCollins, 1999).

88. B. Waugh and M. S. Forrest, *Soul in the Computer* (Makawao, HI: Inner Ocean, 2001).

89. B. Waugh and M. S. Forrest, *Soul in the Computer* (Makawao, HI: Inner Ocean, 2001).

90. Roger Fisher, William Ury, and Bruce Patton, *Getting to Yes* (New York: Simon & Schuster, 1987), 17–55.

91. Seth Godin, daily email, December 4, 2013. http://www.sethgodin.com

92. Dale Emery, "Rewriting the Story of Resistance." http://www.ayeconference.com/rewriting-the-story-of-resistance/

93. Henri Tajfel, "Experiments in Intergroup Discrimination," *Scientific American* (1970): 96–102.

94. Janelle Weaver, "Get out the Vote," *Scientific American Mind* (January/February 2012): 22.

95. Leo Widrich, "What Listening to a Story Does to Our Brains," bufferapp.com (November 29, 2012). https://blog.bufferapp.com/science-of-storytelling-why-telling-a-story-is-the-most-powerful-way-to-activate-our-brains

96. Everett M. Rogers, *Diffusion of Innovations*, 5th ed. (New York: Free Press, 2003).

97. M. J. Wheatley, *Leadership and the New Science: Discovering Order in a Chaotic World*, 2nd ed. (Oakland, CA: Berrett-Koehler, 1999).

98. S. Godin, "In My Humble Opinion," *Fast Company* (November 2001): 80.

99. C. A. Alexander et al., *A Pattern Language* (Oxford, UK: Oxford University Press, 1977).

100. N. Kerth, *Project Retrospectives: A Handbook for Team Reviews* (New York: Dorset House, 2001).

101. B. Anderson, "Toward an Architecture Handbook," *OOPSLA Addendum to the Proceedings* (Washington, DC: ACM Press, January 1994).

102. Atul Gawande, "Slow Ideas," *The New Yorker* (July 29, 2013). http://www.newyorker.com/reporting/2013/07/29/130729fa_fact_gawande?currentPage=all

103. Lasse Koskela, posted on JavaRanch. http://www.javaranch.com

104. W. S. Brown, *13 Fatal Errors Managers Make and How You Can Avoid Them* (New York: Berkley Books, 1985).

105. Adam Grant, *Give and Take* (New York: Viking Adult, 2013).

106. Robert B. Cialdini, *Influence: Science and Practice* (Boston: Allyn & Bacon, 2008).

107. Erich Gamma et al., *Design Patterns: Elements of Reusable Object-Oriented Software* (Reading, MA: Addison-Wesley, 1995).

108. John Chapman (1774–1845), often called Johnny Appleseed, was an American pioneer nurseryman who introduced apple trees to large parts of the Midwestern United States by spreading apple seeds randomly everywhere he went.

109. Tom DeMarco, *Slack* (New York: Crown Business, 2002).

110. R. Edler, *If I Knew Then What I Know Now: CEOs and Other Smart Executives Share Wisdom They Wish They'd Been Told 25 Years Ago* (New York: G. P. Putnam's Sons, 1995).

111. "Gratitude Healthy: 10 Reasons Why Being Thankful Is Good for You." http://www.huffingtonpost.com/2012/11/22/gratitude-healthy-benefits_n_2147182.html

112. Adam M. Grant and Francesca Gino, "A Little Thanks Goes a Long Way: Explaining Why Gratitude Expressions Motivate Prosocial Behavior," *Journal of Personality and Social Psychology* 98, no. 6 (2010): 946–955.

113. AMACOM, 2013.

114. D. Baum, *Lightning in a Bottle: Proven Lessons for Leading Change* (Ft. Lauderdale, FL: Dearborn, 2000).

115. L. Hohmann, *Journey of the Software Professional* (Upper Saddle River, NJ: Prentice-Hall, 1997).

116. J. Kerievsky, "A Learning Guide to Design Patterns." http://www.industriallogic.com/papers/learning.html.

117. D. Whyte, *The Heart Aroused: Poetry and the Preservation of the Soul in Corporate America* (New York: Currency Doubleday, 1994).

118. Jason Selk, *Executive Toughness* (New York: McGraw-Hill, 2012).

119. D. Dauten, *The Gifted Boss* (New York: William Morrow & Company, 1999).

120. D. Baum, *Lightning in a Bottle: Proven Lessons for Leading Change* (Ft. Lauderdale, FL: Dearborn, 2000).

121. A. Layne, "Training Manual for Change Agents," *Fast Company* (November 2000).

122. J. C. Collins and J. I. Porras, *Built to Last: Successful Habits of Visionary Companies* (New York: HarperBusiness, 1994).

123. Anne Frank, *The Diary of a Young Girl* (New York: Bantam Books, 1967).

124. Timothy Wilson, *Strangers to Ourselves* (Cambridge, MA: Belknap Press of Harvard University Press, 2004).

125. Jutta Eckstein, *Retrospectives for Enabling Organizational Change*, master's thesis for master of arts in business coaching and change management, Europäische Fernhochschule Hamburg, University of Applied Sciences in Hamburg, Germany.

126. Shelter Chieza, "Money Is Not Everything," *The Herald* (December 28, 2013). http://www.herald.co.zw/money-is-not-everything/

Index

www.ingramcontent.com/pod-product-compliance
Lightning Source LLC
Chambersburg PA
CBHW080153060326
40689CB00018B/3957